D0065600

Carte Blanche
for Chaos

Lillian R. Boehme

CARTE BLANCHE

FOR CHAOS

ARLINGTON HOUSE
New Rochelle, New York

To the City of New York, the whole of which will, perhaps, one day be worthy of the American Dream; the dream of an America which had once been, and may yet be: the America whose true spirit is symbolized by that triumph of purposeful thought—the magnificent rock-crystal sculpture of blazing lights and skyward-thrusting towers erected by man on the shores of the Hudson;

and

to Walter K. Boehme.

Table of Contents

Acknowledgements

Years of inveterate reading have led me to the conclusion that the "acknowledgements" customary in non-fiction books are the place where the author thanks (1) the foundation that supported him while he was writing his tome; (2) all the librarians in all the libraries which he haunted in the course of composition; (3) his or her children, if any, for keeping quiet while genius burned; (4) his wife, if the author be male, for keeping said children quiet; (4-a) her husband, if the author be female, for subsisting on TV dinners and breathing dust during the travail of creation; (5) his publisher, for taking a chance on him; (6) his editor, for catching his lapses, grammatical and otherwise; (7) his typist; (8) any and all friends who read the manuscript and gave—or did not give—advice.

Such acknowledgements are, I suspect, rarely read, except by foundation staffs, librarians, wives, husbands, children, typists, et al., and their assorted relatives, friends, and (on occasion) enemies.

No foundation supported me. Nor do I have much use for the endless catalogue-style acknowledgements of the conventional variety. As a sop to such proprieties, however, I hereby acknowledge the help of Nathaniel, the Boehme cat, who never once reminded me that the publisher's deadline was ten, nine, eight, seven, six . . . days off; and who, when I was temporarily written dry or mentally forming phrases, never once interrupted either my catatony or my creativity by talking.

I do, however, want to express my gratitude and appreciation to those who, some of them unknowingly, played a vital part in bringing this, my first book, into being:

To Robert G. Shettler, Ph.D., and Virginia S. Hendrickson, of Woodbury (New Jersey) High School; and to Ralph B. Allen, Ph.D., formerly of the Department of English, Rutgers University, my thanks for having helped to instill in me a love for the reading and the writing of the English language; and for helping me to acquire the technical tools for what, although I did not then quite realize it, would one day be my chosen work.

To the authors of some of the works of philosophy and political economy which are listed at the end of this book, my deep appreciation for their thinking and their writing, which have illuminated, challenged, and stimulated my own.

To Anne Wortham, my thanks for sifting from the reams of print which crossed her desk, and sending to me, material which would, in all likelihood, have been unavailable to me or might have gone unnoticed, but for her unerring eye and slashing clipping shears.

To Eugene Guccione, my appreciation for his enthusiasm, for source material, and for exciting conversation.

Greatest of all, however, has been the contribution of Walter K. Boehme, publisher of *The Libertarian*. His merciless wielding of the editorial pencil; his relentless insistence on comprehensiveness and clarity; his appreciation—and his deprecation; his invaluable assistance as sounding-board, idea-igniter, intellectual catalyst, and occasional debunker, are an intrinsic part of this book, and have been of greater value to the creation of *Carte Blanche for Chaos* than its author can possibly express.

LILLIAN R. BOEHME

Carte Blanche
for Chaos

CHAPTER I

The Past as Prologue

During the "long, hot summers" of the late nineteen-sixties, virtually in the shadow of towering buildings soaring skyward in triumphant affirmation of the greatness possible to man, the barbarism of the Dark Ages came back to life in the streets of the United States. Those streets became the phantasmagoric scene of nightmare made real, as sirens wailed, and bricks and clubs struck human flesh and bone. Mobs roamed the streets, while shattered fragments of shop windows littered the pavements, the shards of glass glinting orange with reflected flame. Gutted buildings crumbled to earth, as blocks of stores and homes were reduced to gaping wastelands of rubble.

As the shadowy images of pillage flashed across their television screens; as the cry of a dozen tortured cities rent the air; as thousands of clamoring headlines reflected the black of charred embers, the people of the United States begged for reasons—and for remedies. Bewildered and outraged, they beheld, in stunned disbelief, the triumph of naked savagery on the streets of their once-civilized nation. And they asked, "*Why?*"

They asked it of themselves. They asked it of each other.

And they asked it of the leaders of their government—the men sworn to protect the innocent; to uphold the law.

"*WHY?*" people asked, and clamored for reasons.

But it is not reason with which the leaders of our day are accustomed to dealing. The Age of Reason, those leaders tell us, is past.

They are right. We live in the Age of the Rioter.

The Report of the National Advisory Commission on Civil Disorders (the *Kerner Report*) was the response of the government of the United States to the anguished "why?" of citizens aghast at plunder in the streets. It was a response. It was not an answer. But no one seemed to notice—least of all the press.

While church choirs intoned litanies composed of the *Report*'s phrases; while the hierarchy of the Girl Scouts issued press releases declaring their fealty to the *Report*'s decrees; newspapers and newsmagazines, like carnival mirrors endlessly reflecting and re-reflecting each other's distortions, repeated the *Report*'s recommendations and its warnings of more pillage to come. And, always and everywhere, the ubiquitous, unctuous voices of television commentators droned on, hailing the *Report* as revelation.

The *Kerner Report* was published March 1, 1968.

In the early days of April, street mobs added a postscript—and a prelude—of their own. The *Kerner Report*, for all its official language, had been a multi-billion-dollar blackmail note to the productive of the nation: a demand that billions of dollars of tribute be proffered quickly—or else. The mobs added, "We mean it." And the officials of a nation heeded.

On Thursday, the fourth day of April, the "non-violent" prophet of the mobs was murdered, under circumstances never fully explained. The admirers of Martin Luther King took to the streets to express their grief; officials ordered policemen to hold their fire—as the Kerner Commission had advised. In the nation's capital alone, when the orgy of destruction was done, the stores and savings of a thousand shopkeepers had been reduced to ashes; the homes of hundreds, consumed by flames or damaged beyond repair. The toll of plunder and arson exceeded any yet amassed; the statistics of destruction in human terms were written in the faces of the victims. There was the lined face of Mrs. Claudia Howard, a gray-haired cleaning woman whose home was destroyed. "I just stood there and saw everything burn down," she said. "I didn't get out nothing, not one thing. I was full of tears and so upset." There was the face of Mrs. Ethel Dickens, whose beauty shop and home of 30 years were totally destroyed. "I never saw anything to equal that," she said. "I just stood there, knowing all I had was going down." And there was Abraham Zevin, standing amidst the ruins of the hardware store his 79-year-old father had founded 50 years before and tried to defend. "I suppose I shouldn't say this," he told a reporter, "but it was very hard to stop crying on Saturday."

As the mobs made their point, a policeman cried, "I think we could have stopped this, if they hadn't put us under wraps so." But, he said despairingly, "we just had to stand there."

And, in the limpid April twilight, the dome of the nation's Capitol was photographed with the smoke of burning buildings behind it, and motionless soldiers before.

A year later, the rubble from the riots lay as rubble still; random weeds pushed up through charred brick and splintered timbers, the only sign of life in a spread of blackened death.

Of the thousands arrested in Washington alone, a mere handful went to jail. They had not, said an official, been in trouble before; they "probably will not be again, unless aroused by another riot. It is natural for the courts to be somewhat lenient with such people." The Kerner Commission had thought so, too.

Endless months after the *Report* was issued, its name and its credos were relentlessly repeated among the journalistic cleverisms of *Time* and *Newsweek.* On radio and television "talk shows" hosts and guests vied with one another to profess *their* commitment to the Kerner proposals and their impatience with the inadequacy of "the nation's" response. "Ghetto special" followed "ghetto special" as the nation's networks, anxious to show the "compassion and coverage" the Commission had demanded of them, showed the likes of Daniel Moynihan picking their way through filth-strewn backyards and bewailing the "squalor," while neglecting to ask by whom the filth had been flung. Cameramen

zoomed in on rats and overflowing garbage pails; solicitous reporters interviewed welfare "clients" and commiserated with them
over the inadequacy of welfare checks.

On one such special, the screen briefly revealed an elderly Negro lady, clean and neat, surveying, from her porch, the wreckage
of her part of Detroit. "These kids don't want to work," she said,
referring to the rioters. "They just hang around. Why don't they
stop them before we lose everything we've got?" The camera
quickly swooped past her; it was not her "minority opinion" to
which the Commission demanded "commitment"; it was best not
to linger too long.

In Washington, the old leaders passed from the scene. New
faces and new slogans headed the parade—but the procession and
its destination had not changed. In Detroit, in Watts, in cities
across the nation, barren lots stretched in weedy desolation where
buildings once had stood—and the exuberant profusion of bright
store displays disappeared behind bricked-up windows and iron
doors erected by those shopkeepers who dared remain in the
"ghettos."

"Long, hot summers" became the expected and the usual, a fact
of nature like hail storms and hurricanes, and, like natural disasters, were "reinsured" against with tax monies, as the Kerner
Commission had suggested. The press, castigated for "sensational-
ism" and "overemphasis on damage" by the Commission, took
care to play down the "disorders" in the months which followed
the *Report.* But the first eight months of 1968 saw the number of
"disorders" triple the total for all of 1967; there were injuries in
the thousands, hundreds more than in all the previous year; property damage in the April riots alone was the worst yet sustained.
Progress, however, had been made—"only" 69 had died.

Debates on the probable length and hotness of the coming summer became a standard spring feature of newspapers and newsmagazines, as the question became, not *whether* "disorders"
would take place, but *what kind* of "disorders" there would be.
Universities erupted and bombs exploded to punctuate the "demands" of non-qualified non-students recruited from the "ghettos" as the Commission had suggested; random brick-throwing
gave way to planned ambushes in California and in Cleveland,
where three police officers were lured to their deaths; meanwhile,
ex-convicts were recruited and hired with federal aid funds to

provide "community liaison" with rioters in the cities—as the Commission had also proposed.

Savagery in the streets changed its forms, but not its aims or its premises; rational men previously unconscious of race found themselves apprehensive when groups of Negro youths approached; television sets spat the hatred and venom of "black separatists"; and the people of the nation were told that the accelerating destruction, the increase in racist-based tensions and hatreds, were the result of the people's default on the debt which the *Report* had claimed "the nation" owed its destroyers. "The fuse is growing short," threatened the Urban Coalition on March 1, 1969. On that date, the anniversary of the *Report*'s publication, the Coalition and Urban America, Inc. issued *One Year Later*, a summing up of "the nation's response" to the *Kerner Report.* The book was billed as the first of an annual series.

Meanwhile, at the behest of the *Kerner Report*, and with the enthusiastic concurrence of the *Report*'s echo-chambers in politics and press, *more* acres of *more* cities were scheduled for "renewal" demolition. Planners scheduled the reshuffling and uprooting of millions to make "Model Cities" of the planners' dreams, oblivious to the implications of the fact that the worst of the riots had taken place in cities where acres upon acres had already been urban-renewed into wasteland, and the homes of thousands destroyed. More thousands of families, their homes declared "substandard," were slated for "relocation" ahead of the wrecking ball and the federal bulldozers—"relocation" to where, no one knew and few cared.

And a new Administration, whose head had deprecated the *Report* until elected, quietly instituted first one and then another of the *Kerner Report*'s proposals, thus affirming its dedication to the Commission's proposition that blackmail pays.

The *Kerner Report* was published over two years ago. Two million copies have been sold. Many of the *Report*'s proposals have become part of the law of the land, with more such laws yet to come.

To some, the *Report* may seem ancient history, long dead and buried beneath the refuse of a hundred crises since. But the *Report* is not dead, nor has it been buried. It lives on, affecting the life of every citizen in the nation; it will, unless challenged and refuted, continue to do so for years. Legislation spawned or extended at the

Report's behest is being enacted and enforced daily, extending the insidious, steely fingers of governmental force into every life and every livelihood in the nation:

—into the life of the "ghetto" child, or even infant, whose mother is paid government hush-money to "observe the techniques" of the social worker who dandles the child on her knees, reading him rhymes and teaching him "social awareness."

—into the lives of the widows of policemen stomped by mobs, and the lives of citizens fearful of their safety because their elected protectors—including the Vice Chairman of the Kerner Commission—make public speeches on the sanctity of human life: the lives of looters, not the lives of policemen.

—into the lives of businessmen and residents left unprotected victims of plunder and arson as a mayor panders to racists and rioters by withdrawing first white policemen, than all policemen, at the behest of "liaison agents" who promise that the rioters will "police themselves."

—into the life of a teenager spat upon and stoned by a Negro, because he is white—and of the Negroes he stones in turn, because they are black.

—into the lives of law-abiding store customers bullied and intimidated by "welfare rights" ruffians whose organizational credo comes straight from the pages of the *Kerner Report*, and who announce, by sit-in and sit-down and plain terrorism, that they have a "right" to welfare, and department store credit, too.

—into the lives of all who must pay the cost of fulfilling the "right" claimed by "welfare mothers" who took over government offices demanding money allowances for furniture. "Don't give me food," said their sign, "and expect me to eat it off the floor." Such "welfare mothers," said Robert Finch of HEW, "are an important constituency" of his Department. The Kerner Commission had said it before him.

—into the life of the small child shunted from one end of the city to another to establish the "desirable proportions" of black, to white, to "affluent," to "deprived," to "poor," to "non-poor" students, proportions determined by some bureaucratic decree.

—into the life of the college applicant who cut grass and dug ditches to pay for his education; who studied and learned and passed his exams, but who found "no vacancy" at the college he chose; who was denied entrance by a university which "negotiated" with those who razed its buildings, and agreed that thenceforward *half* the students admitted—the qualified half—must meet entrance standards; the other half need merely be "black," "deprived," and unqualified to be admitted without question or payment.

—into the life of the working adult illiterate, denied access to the literacy course his taxes helped pay for, on the grounds that *he* is employed.

—into the lives of housewives told to economize to pay their taxes, while those in power announce for a "guaranteed income" of cash, food stamps, and status for everyone—except those who work, to the extent that they work well.

—into the life of a worker turned down for job training, because an employer collecting training subsidies finds him "too qualified."

And meanwhile, the people of the United States are told that they sit upon a volcano which may erupt at any moment; that their peace and safety depend upon their placating and pleasing the "deprived"; that the "ghettos" are a seething mass of hatred; that a Negro, any Negro, hates white men, any white man—and that he should.

These, and more, are the proposals and premises picked up from the gutters, echoed, and authorized, by the *Kerner Report*.

And, as violence intensifies and the "summer riot season" extends into spring and fall to become a yearlong "rite," the nation is told that the reason for the accelerating destruction; the "polarization" of black and white racists; the nihilism evident on every hand, is that the proposals of the *Kerner Report* have not been accepted or acted upon by the nation.

The chaos all around us exists, we are told, because we have not heard and not heeded what the *Kerner Report* had to say.

That is not why the chaos exists.

The chaos around us exists, not because the Kerner premises and proposals have *not* been accepted, but because they *have* been.

It is time those premises and proposals were examined.

The *Kerner Report*, in itself, would not be worth such detailed dissection. The *Report* is worth study only as a laboratory specimen of a disease which is convulsing a great nation.

The *Kerner Report* and the measures taken in its name are merely the logical end-product of a long-prevalent set of premises: a philosophy of politics and economics. It is as a distillation of that philosophy that the *Report* warrants examination, for the reason and the remedy for chaos in the streets lie in *ideas*.

A set of ideas spawned the *Kerner Report*.

A set of ideas spawned the riots.

Those ideas are the same.

CHAPTER II

The Foregone Conclusion

Shortly after taking office, Lyndon Johnson, President of the United States, declared, "We are going to try to take all of the money which we think is unnecessarily being spent and take it from the 'haves' and give it to the 'have-nots' who need it so much."[1]

It had been said before, but not so bluntly. It had been acted upon before; but never on so vast a scale. Government spending programs of unprecedented magnitude followed fast upon the President's words. Street violence of unprecedented magnitude followed also. The self-proclaimed "have-nots," it seemed, were doing some taking on their own.

Some two years later, Hubert H. Humphrey, then Vice President of the United States, sanctioned the takers' actions yet more explicitly:

"I want to say right now," he said, "that, as hot as it's been up in my part of America, and as warm as it is here, if we had a heat wave all over, I'd hate to be stuck in a tenement with rats nibbling on the kids' toes—and they do, with the garbage uncollected—and it is—with the streets filthy, no swimming pools, with little or no recreation. I'd hate to be put in those conditions, and I want to tell you that if I were in those conditions, and that should happen to have been my situation, I think you'd have had a little more trouble than you've had already, because I've got enough spark left in me to lead a mighty good revolt under those conditions."[2]

By the summer of 1967, months of intensifying destruction wrought by the so-called "have-nots" had left whole city blocks in smoking ruins. And the same President whose words had given the mobs their official sanction felt called upon to announce his appointment of an official Commission to inquire into the causes of the cataclysm. To all appearances, the irony of the situation was lost on both the President and the press.

In appointing the National Advisory Commission on Civil Disorders and adjuring them to find answers to the "why?" of stunned and frightened citizens, the President implored the Commission to eschew preconceived conclusions, to challenge fashionable dogmas, to check painstakingly all premises in order to find the underlying causes of the riots, whatever those causes might be.

"Sometimes," Johnson said upon appointing the Commission, "various Administrations have set up Commissions that were expected to put the stamp of approval on what the Administration believed."[3] He continued:

> This is not such a commission. We are looking to you, not to approve our own notions, but to guide us and guide the country through a thicket of tension [and] conflicting evidence.
> So, Mr. Chairman and Mr. Vice Chairman, let your search be free. Let it be untrammeled by what has been called the "conventional wisdom." As best you can, find the truth, the whole truth, and express it in your report.

And whom had the President appointed to lead the untrammeled quest for truth and enlightenment? As Chairman: Otto Kerner, then Democratic Governor of Illinois, who, although since somewhat in eclipse despite the *Report*'s immortalization of his name, at that time enjoyed considerable status and some renown among the more "liberal" members of his Party. As Vice Chairman: the Honorable John V. Lindsay, Mayor of the City of New York, "liberal" Republican beloved of television and press.

Among the Commission's more prominent members: Senator Fred R. Harris, Democrat and "liberal," since made head of the Democratic National Committee; Senator Edward Brooke, a nominal Republican "liberal" enough to rate a 100 cumulative voting score from the AFL-CIO Committee on Political Education (COPE); Roy Wilkins, Executive Director of the NAACP; and, as the obligatory "business leader," Charles B. Thornton of Litton Industries, "forward-looking" industrialist and Job Corps contractor.[4]

To seek the whole truth, to re-evaluate the conventional wisdom, the President had appointed a Commission dominated by members whose lives and careers had been devoted to the doctrines of that "conventional wisdom": statism, the "policy of concentrating extensive economic, political and related controls in the state"; the political philosophy of governmental interventionism and governmental "welfare programs"; statism, the political embodiment of the doctrine that the "good" of "society" transcends all rights of individual men. "Don't approve my own notions," the President had said. "Let your search be free."

The absurdity of those particular words addressed to that particular body by that particular man escaped all but a few, who wondered whether men with a lifelong commitment to statism, appointed by a man who had gained power on the strength of a similar commitment, would have the courage or the integrity to re-examine their version of the conventional wisdom of governmental interventionism even when its patent failures stared them in the face.

Man, however, has the power to think—and thus the power to change his convictions. During the months of the Commission's work there might have lingered the still, small hope that these men would, at last, see the connection between their cherished doctrines and the destruction of a nation. On March 1, 1968, that still, small hope was extinguished. The *Report of the National Advisory Commission on Civil Disorders* was released.

The content of that *Report* was precisely what the cynical—or was it the astute?—considered foreordained on the day the Commission had been named. The significance of the fact that the intensity of rioting in the nation's streets had increased, even as government controls and "welfare programs" multiplied, and that the city sustaining the most massive damage from rioting (Detroit) was also the city having the greatest multiplicity of "poverty programs," appeared to have escaped both the Commission and the President who appointed it. The untrammeled search for truth had never materialized. The Commission's "investigations" were an expensive farce, a shabby attempt to rationalize a foregone conclusion, to justify doctrines which had failed. The recommendations of the Commission were a hackneyed compendium unrelievedly statist in orientation. "We have," the Commission itself declared, "uncovered no startling truths." (p. 13) The adjective is superfluous.

The Kerner Commission had been instructed to check its premises. Instead, it regarded those premises as axioms requiring no proof; not even requiring statement; axioms assumed as the given, to be taken for granted by all. Thus, two antipodal sets of premises govern the Commission's conclusions, as they governed the Commission's investigation: the official premises, which are stated; and the unofficial, unquestioned premises, which are never stated as such, but which permeate the *Report*'s every line. It is from the latter, not the former, that the Commission's recommendations stem. It is the Commission's unquestioning acceptance of the *unstated* premises which nullifies all hope of its achieving the goals which its *stated* premises imply.

The official premises of the Commission are set forth on page 16 of the *Report:*

Two premises underlie the work of the Commission:
—That this Nation cannot abide violence and disorder if it is to ensure the safety of its people and their progress in a free society.
—That this Nation will deserve neither safety nor progress unless it can demonstrate the wisdom and the will to undertake decisive action against the root causes of racial disorder.

The unofficial, unstated, but crucial premises of the *Report* are implicit on every page.

The first premise is that "poverty" is in itself a direct, understandable, and condonable cause of destruction and theft; that "needs" and "grievances" and "dissatisfactions" regarding the state of one's home, one's schools, one's income, or one's sources of amusement constitute just claims upon the lives of others. It is by means of this first premise that the President and the Commission served—in principle—as the official sanctioners of, and apologists for, the looters.

Thus, adducing no proof, spoke psychologist Kenneth D. Clark in testimony quoted by the Commission:

> This society knows ... that if human beings are confined in ghetto compounds of our cities and are subjected to criminally inferior education, pervasive economic and job discrimination, committed to houses unfit for human habitation, subjected to unspeakable conditions of municipal services such as sanitation, that such human beings are not likely to be responsive to appeals to be lawful, to be respectful, to be concerned with property of others. (pp. 157-158)

The testimony of Dr. Clark, which ignores the existence of millions who, although living in "slums," do *not* riot; who *do* assume responsibility for their own actions; who even sweep their own sidewalks, carry out their own garbage, and trap their own rats, provides the leitmotif of the *Report*.

Thus, depicting mob violence as a normal, predictable, inevitable, and appropriate response to such "incidents" as traffic arrests, the *Report* states:

> In virtually every case a single "triggering" or "precipitating" incident can be identified as having immediately preceded ... the outbreak of the disorder. But this incident was ... by itself *substantially disproportionate to the scale of violence that followed.* (p. 68 —my emphasis)

Some violence, the Commission is saying, necessarily must follow "incidents" which annoy the mob. It is only the *scale* of such violence which should be questioned.

The second implicit premise of the *Report*—the premise supporting its recommendations—is that government's proper role in riot "prevention" and control should not, indeed *must* not, be restricted to government's police functions (protecting the lives and property of innocent citizens and apprehending and trying those who molest them).

Thus the Commission was "disturbed" to find that "despite the institution of some post-riot programs" such as government-furnished manpower training, housing, "welfare" services, and "community action" programs, "little basic change in the conditions underlying the outbreak of disorder has taken place." In several cities, the Commission complained, "the *principal* official response has been to train and equip the police with more sophisticated weapons" (my emphasis).

Taxation-financed "welfare" programs–statist interventionism–are, in the Commission's view, a proper function of government, and a necessary "response" to "disorders." This is the doctrine to which the Commission was committed from the start; the doctrine of what Frédéric Bastiat identified as "legalized plunder."

"When property is transferred without the consent of the owner," he wrote,

> and without compensation, whether by force or by fraud, from the one who possesses it to anyone who has not created it, I say that property rights have been violated; that plunder has been committed.
>
> I say that this is precisely what the law is supposed to suppress, always and everywhere. If the law itself commits the act that it is supposed to suppress, I say that this is still plunder, and, as far as society is concerned, plunder of an even graver kind. ... The prevailing illusion of our age is that it is possible to enrich all classes at the expense of one another—to make plunder universal under the pretext of organizing it. Now, legal plunder can be committed in an infinite number of ways; hence, there are an infinite number of plans for organizing it: tariffs, protection, bonuses, subsidies, incentives, the progressive income tax, free education, the right to employment, the right to profit, the right to wages, the right to relief, the right to the tools of production, interest-free credit, etc. etc.[5]

(When Frédéric Bastiat wrote those lines, more than a century ago, all the bright, shiny, new proposals to be found in the *Kerner Report* were being tried in his native France—as they had been in the Roman Empire, and with the same result.)

It is their two unstated premises—that "need" constitutes a right, and that legal plundering is a proper function of government —which hopelessly biased the Commission's "untrammeled search." Hampered by their commitment to a foregone conclusion, the Commission's investigation became a search, not for answers, but for alibis. But before examining the premises themselves, it is pertinent to substantiate the charge of bias by means of a brief scrutiny of the Commission's investigatory techniques and manner of presentation.

THE QUEST FOR RATIONALIZATION

People Talking to Themselves: The Hearings

The Kerner Commission held extensive closed hearings at which more than 130 witnesses (some with entourages) testified at length. The roster makes illuminating reading. Of those testifying before the Commission, elected officials or their aides comprised 11 percent. All were proponents of statism; none was even a nominal proponent of capitalism.

Capitalism, the official, but not actual, politico-economic system of the United States, is "an economic system in which the ownership of land and natural wealth, the production, distribution, and exchange of goods, and the operation of the system itself, are effected by private enterprise and control."[6] Capitalism is a laissez faire politico-economic system in which government is limited to its police function of *retaliatory* force, and economic affairs are totally independent of government manipulation and *initiatory* government force, i.e., "redistribution" and "controls." Today's so-called "conservatives" are frequently described as advocates of capitalism (free enterprise). In actuality, "conservatives" do not advocate capitalism. "Conservatives" generally advocate a "mixed economy" combining various proportions of freedom and controls. "Conservatives" differ with "liberals" concerning the desirable scope and specific nature of controls, the desirable cost and nature of governmental "welfare" programs, and the level of government which should impose and administer controls and "welfare." Few "conservatives" question the *principle* of either controls or "welfare" programs.

Mayor Samuel Yorty of Los Angeles and Mayor Thomas Whelan of Jersey City, both of whom testified before the Kerner Commission, have lately been termed "conservatives" by some of the press—Yorty, primarily because of his emphasis on subversive conspiracies to abet the rioters; Whelan, because of his opposition to permissive tactics toward rioters. Both men, however, accept and espouse the *principle* of governmental "welfare" and governmental interventionism. Neither is a proponent of capitalism. Both were outnumbered by "liberals" with an even more far-reaching commitment to statism.

Of the elected officials testifying before the Commission, all, then, were committed to the President's—and the Commission's—statist premises. None might be expected to contravene or even question them. From the evidence in the *Report,* none sought to.

Fully 26 percent of the witnesses were paid appointed officials of the executive branch of local, state, or national governments. (This category does *not* include officials connected with the law enforcement function of government: the judiciary, the police, or the armed forces.) Of these witnesses, representatives of federal, state, and municipal "welfare" agencies—OEO officials, HEW factotums, "relief" administrators, "community action" organizers, "human resources" experts—were well in the majority, comprising 16 percent of all witnesses heard. "War on Poverty" personnel were most heavily represented of all.

Sixteen percent of the witnesses were members of so-called civil rights organizations. These ran the gamut from "moderate" (the Commission's adjective) groups such as the NAACP and the National Urban League, to "militant" groups (also the Commission's adjective) such as CORE (Congress of Racial Equality), SNCC (Student Non-Violent [Violence-] Coordinating Committee), something called the Ad Hoc Committee of Black Militants, and US—a truly militantly militant organization which more recently made headlines out West by engaging in shoot-outs with its rival gang, the Black Panthers. Stokely Carmichael, who had publicly and repeatedly urged his followers to tear down cities block by block to gain their "demands," was provided with a microphone and given the Commission's courteous attention at taxpayers' expense.

The average observer, moreover, may be hard put to grasp the Commission's criteria for distinguishing between "moderate" and "militant" civil "rights" groups. In New Jersey, Mrs. Irene Smith, State President and a National Vice President of the "moderate" NAACP, publicly threatened that policemen entering a predominantly Negro section "will not come out the way they came in" unless a policeman incurring NAACP ire were immediately removed from the community police force. Phillip Savage, a tristate secretary of the NAACP, presented a set of student "demands" to a local school board, and, when the board refused to fire a teacher as "demanded," warned, "You had better have the police around the school in the morning."[7]

The "militant" militants dominated the "civil rights" contingent at the Commission's hearings and formed nearly 13 percent of witnesses heard.

Nearly 60 percent of those testifying, then, were persons having a direct, vested interest in the continuation and expansion of government "welfare" programs—either as recipients or as well-paid (via tax funds) dispensers of the goodies.

Who else came?

Eleven percent were university researchers, professors of the social sciences, or members of foundation staffs such as that of the Ford Foundation, with its long-standing commitment to governmental "planning." Dr. Kenneth Clark, whose testimony is quoted above and whose book, *Dark Ghetto*, will be referred to later (see Chapter V), was one such witness. Dr. Dan W. Dodson, Director of the New York University Center for Human Relations and Community Studies, and advocate of massive federally aided education projects, was another.

Five percent of those testifying were politically appointed members of official or semi-official commissions and committees such as the Civil Rights Commission.

Only 10 percent of the witnesses were connected with law enforcement—even if one includes members of attorneys generals' staffs. Stokely Carmichael and crew—the representatives of the rioters—were out in greater force than the official representatives of law and order. Moreover, the testimony of law enforcement officials quoted in the *Report* demonstrates that involvement with law enforcement is in itself no guarantee of an understanding of the connection between life and property. In regard to the question of firing on looters: "I am not," testified Major General George Gelston, commander of National Guard Forces at Cambridge, Maryland, "going to order a man killed for stealing a six-pack of beer or a television set." In this connection it is pertinent to note that J. Edgar Hoover, Director of the FBI, whose opinions regarding the protection of life and property differ markedly from the Commission's, also testified. Major Gelston is quoted in the *Report*. Director Hoover is not.

The professions and official positions of the remaining witnesses varied. One group, however, was conspicuously absent from the roll: the victims. People whose homes had gone up in flames, small shopkeepers whose stock vanished in the arms of looters, were not heard. If an Ad Hoc Committee of Riot Victims was formed, the Commission didn't hear it. In a disapproving passage concerning television coverage of the "disturbances," the Commission makes clear its position regarding attempts to give *victims* a public hearing: ". . . some interviews involved landlords or business proprietors who lost property or suffered business losses because of the disturbances and thus held strongly antagonistic views" toward the rioters. Such interviews, the Commission implied, might give viewers a false impression, and were detrimental to coverage of "underlying grievances." (See Chapter IX.)

In the untrammeled search for truth, the views of the perpetrators of violence were given courteous official attention. The "antagonistic views" of the victims of violence were deemed irrelevant to the Commission's quest.

The Surveys: Playback Equals Input

The *Kerner Report* postulates many sweeping generalities concerning the educational accomplishments, job and social "status," environments, exchequers, wanderlusts, and psyches of those who rioted—and of those who (ostensibly) did not. The generalities, manipulated into "profiles" of riots and rioters, are constantly referred to in the Commission's conclusions and recommendations. Whence were the components of the "profiles" derived?

The pages of the *Report* are stuffed with statistical data, and the Appendix boasts a veritable jungle of lush statistical growth: graphs showing "levels of violence" to prove things get worse before they get better; census data on income and education and marital status and fertility rates and the condition of paint and plumbing (which, in the name of anti-racism, are neatly categorized by race). The conclusions concerning the "attitudes" of the rioters themselves, and the employment, income, mobility, and education tabulations shaped up into the so-called profiles, however, were obtained from two Commission-sponsored surveys.

One survey, made in Detroit, drew its percentage statistics from 393 interviews. The other, made in Newark, used 233. A number of the conclusions, in fact, were drawn from tabulations of less than 50 responses. From such a paltry percentage of the thousands who participated in or observed the 1967 riots were the widely quoted "typical profiles" drawn. From such a small sampling were the Commission's conclusions reached.

How?

In the Detroit survey, the 393 respondents were classified, *on the basis of their word alone*, as "Rioters," "Counter-Rioters," and "Non-Involved." The designation "Counter-Rioter" is a curious one—but typical of Commission Newspeak. "Counter-Rioter" refers, not to persons who rioted against other rioters, as the term certainly implies, but to persons who claim to have taken "socially positive actions," which the Commission defines as "calling the fire department" or "taking to the streets to urge rioters to 'cool it.' " (Since a number of "disorders" involved cases of fire alarms being set off to lure firemen out into ambushes and brick barrages, the social positiveness of the fire-department callers might be subject to some question: see Chapter X.) In the Newark survey, "counter-rioters" were lumped with the "non-involved."

In Detroit, those unwilling to state whether or not they had participated in the rioting were omitted from the final tabulation of responses. In the Newark survey, those who refused to state whether or not they had participated were—by some inexplicably convoluted mental process—classified as "non-involved." The survey was confined to Negro males over 15 years of age "in order to enlarge the sample of those who were likely to identify themselves as rioters" (p. 330); in Newark an upper age limit of 35 was set. Approximately one third of "eligible respondents" in both cities refused to respond.

The sloppiness of the survey design casts considerable doubt upon figures such as those for employment and income and makes exact comparisons between the Detroit and Newark tabulations impossible. In Newark, *family* income was used to compile income statistics; in Detroit *individual* income was used. In one survey, students were excluded from the tabulation of unemployed; in the other they were included. In one survey, "counter-rioters" were listed separately; in the other they were included among the "non-involved," etc., etc., etc. See p. 330 *et seqq.* of the *Report*.

The questions asked in the surveys offer some truly splendid examples of the use of a priori assumptions to put words into people's mouths. These "have-you-stopped-beating-your-wife"-type gems included: "*How much* did anger with the police have to do with causing riots?" (my emphasis). Such phrasing clearly implies that "anger with police" has *something* to do with causing riots, the only question being how much. A question used in both Detroit and Newark, "Who do you think are more dependable? ( ) Negroes ( ) Whites ( ) About the same," is typical of an entire series of questions pandering to the racist assumption that such traits as "dependability" are racially determined. It is the phrasing which is crucial to this point. Such questions do not seek to determine whether or not the respondents are racists. The questions start *from a racist premise* and then attempt to determine the *direction* of the racism. Similar questions included: "Negroes who make a lot of money are just as bad as whites: ( ) Agree ( ) Disagree." This question, with its built-in assumption that "whites" are "bad," was used to determine "hostility toward middle-class Negroes." Conclusions concerning allegedly developing "race pride" and "race consciousness," attitudes the Commission considered laudable in Negroes though reprehensible in whites, were drawn from questions such as "All Negroes should study African history and language: ( ) Agree ( ) Disagree," and a question asking whether respondents preferred to describe themselves as "Black," "Negro," or "colored." "Political consciousness" of respondents was determined from their ability to identify various political figures by race; the frequency of their involvement in "Negro civil rights" discussions; and whether or not they had attended or participated in meetings of "civil rights" groups. (Since a number of what the Commission calls "civil rights" groups are ardent advocates of the "meet-our-demand-or-else" theory of "rights," it is perhaps not surprising that more rioters than so-called "non-involved" respondents were active in such groups, and thus were "politically aware" by the Commission's standards.)

The Conclusions: An Exercise in Sophistry

Even if one accepts the survey data as statistically valid and representative of the opinions of riotous and lawabiding "ghetto" residents alike, the conclusions drawn by the Commission do not necessarily follow from its data. For example, the "need to provide jobs" is a primary theme of the *Report*. Yet, according to the Commission's own studies, *70 percent of the rioters were employed.* The *Report* itself admits: "The Detroit and Newark surveys, the arrest records from four cities, and the Detroit arrest study all indicate that there are no substantial differences in unemployment between the rioters and the non-involved." (p. 75) By the time the Commission gets around to making its employment recommendations, however, the similarity in employment/unemployment percentages of rioters and "non-involved" is ignored; the focus is upon the percentage of unemployed *rioters* only—a percentage beefed up by the addition of the "underemployed."

No positive conclusions can actually be drawn from employment percentages alone. The most plausible conclusion to be drawn from the similarity of the figures for rioters and "non-involved" (assuming the statistics are correct) is that it was not lack of employment which spurred the rioters to riot. Everyone—and especially the Commission—"knows," however, that despair from lack of employment is a primary cause of riots.

Therefore, the Commission's reaction to the discrepancies between its employment statistics and its assumptions was to beat the drums for a new term—"underemployment"—to drown out uncomfortable questions. It's a handy term—the more so for having numerous definitions. In the course of its *Report* the Commission appears to be using, at one time or another or simultaneously, at least three:

1) The Department of Labor's. This definition categorizes as "underemployed": full-time workers earning less than $3,000 a year; dropouts from the labor force; and part-time workers looking for full-time jobs—the criterion for inclusion in the last category is being laid off at least one month a year. Since those qualifying for the designation are a bit hard to track down and count, the Labor Department "estimates" that the "underemployed" in the "ghettos" are two-and-one-half times as numerous as the unemployed. ("Unemployment" figures are primarily derived from records of the number of applicants for unemployment compensation and of those who register for work with government employment services. Both groups are assumed to be ready, willing and anxious to work.)

2) The Equal Employment Opportunity Commission's definition. This describes "underemployment" as "the status of men and women who perform work which does not fully utilize their education, skills, and talents," all of which the EEOC is presumably clairvoyant enough to measure. For example, a writer working as a secretary to make ends meet would, by this definition, be "underemployed."

3) The Kerner Commission's own fillip. This consists of defining "menial" jobs "at the low end of the occupational scale" which "often lack the necessary status to sustain a worker's self-respect," as "underemployment."

Combined, these categorizations enable the Commission, in effect, to list as "underemployed" anyone with a job which (1) pays him less than he or the Commission thinks he ought to get, and/or (2) consists of doing something he'd rather not be doing, because no one has hired him to do what he wants to do. Such artful combinations enable the Commission's conclusions to follow from its statistics, which follow from its conclusions.

Similarly, everyone—the Commission members particularly—"knows" that poverty is a primary cause of "disorders." Hasn't everyone, on the Commission and off, been saying so for years? Now, according to the "profile" tabulations, 32 per cent of the self-confessed rioters in Detroit—*nearly two thirds of whom were under 25*—were receiving *individual*, not family, incomes of between $5,000 and $10,000 a year. Some had incomes of $15,000 a year. The Commission, however, was positive that the crushing effects of poverty had been instrumental in causing the riots—and when they asked the rioters whether they didn't agree, the rioters agreed. The Commission's thesis couldn't be wrong; all that was required was a re-evaluation of "poverty."

"Poverty," the *Report* informs the reader, is a "relative" term. The dictionary defines "poverty" as "the state or condition of having little or no money, goods, or means of support." The "poverty warriors" of today take a broader view. Michael Harrington, whose *The Other America: Poverty in the United States* is billed as "the book that sparked the war on poverty," and whose catch phrases such as "the culture of poverty" abound in the *Report*, included in his "poverty estimate" all whose cash incomes were below $4,000 a year. This income, in 1962, was estimated by the Labor Department as necessary to sustain a "modest but adequate" budget for a family of four, one which would enable them to fill their "market baskets" with such purchases as golf fees, film developing, baby-sitters, parking fees, airline tickets, power mowers, and air conditioners.

The American poor, Mr. Harrington said, would not be considered poor in other countries. But that was beside the point.

> The American poor are not poor in Hong Kong—they are dispossessed in terms of what the rest of the nation enjoys, in terms of what society could provide if it had the will. . . . To have one bowl of rice in a society where all other people have half a bowl may well be a sign of achievement and intelligence. . . . To have five bowls of rice in a society where the majority have a decent, balanced diet is a tragedy.[8]

Time, which issued a cover story on "Poverty in America" some six weeks after release of the *Kerner Report*, harped the same ditty:

> The nation of the poor is often invisible to the rest of America. Unlike the destitute of other times and places, its inhabitants are not usually distinguishable by any of the traditional telltales of want: hunger-distended bellies or filthy rags, beggars' bowls or the lineaments of despair. Harlem's broad avenues—clean by Calcutta's standards—bop to the stride of lively men and women in mul-

tihued clothing; the tawdry tenements of Chicago's South Side are forested with TV antennas. ... In ... Watts, California's most notorious Slough of Despond, the orderly rows of one-story, stucco houses reflect the sun in gay pastels, and only the weed-grown gaps between stores along the wide main street—"instant parking lots" —hint at the volcanic mob fury that three years ago erupted out of poverty to take 34 lives and destroy $40 million worth of property.

Foreign observers of U. S. urban riots are frequently stunned at the vigor of the American poor. How, they wonder, can a looter claim to be hungry and oppressed, yet walk off with a color television set as easily as if he were hefting a loaf of bread?[9]

The latter is easy to answer. Said looter has U.C.L.A., among other prestigious institutions, to do his claiming for him. Poverty, according to a U.C.L.A. study, "may refer to a family's or a person's ability to purchase goods and services, to the opportunities open to individuals or groups for improving their economic position" but it also "has subjective dimensions ... determined by some kind of norms accepted by the society at large. People who fall below the norm do not necessarily consider themselves to be poor, and people above the norm may feel poverty stricken."[10]

There are two kinds of poverty, says *Time*: "physical and psychological." The poor, according to such definitions, are those who feel that they are poor. The *Kerner Report* concurs:

> "Poverty" in the affluent society is more than absolute deprivation. Many of the poor in the United States would be well off in other societies. Relative deprivation— inequality—is a more useful concept of poverty with respect to the Negro in America because it encompasses social and political exclusions as well as economic inequality. (p. 127)

The concept is useful—no doubt about that. In Kerner terms, anyone who has—or even feels that he has—less of anything than anyone else, may be excused for taking to the streets to remedy his lack.

The Terminology: A Patois of Prejudgment

Grasping the *post hoc* approach of the Kerner Commission's "search for truth" requires some study of its data, its methodology, and the statist-swollen roster of Commission witnesses. The *Report*'s slanted *terminology* hits the reader from the first page on.

The catch phrases and cant and clichés of the "war on poverty" abound, used without qualification or quotation marks. Why, for instance, "ghetto"? Why not "slum"? Why "deprived," not "poor"? The terms used in the *Report* are not the reasoned words of scientific inquiry, but trigger words intended to arouse emotions by selling the unwary reader intellectual package deals: two-concepts-for-the price-of-one offers in which the "free prize" at the bottom of the cereal box turns out to be a pellet of rat poison.

Take "ghetto," for instance. A "ghetto" and a "slum" are not the same thing—and the substitution of the first for the second has not been done casually.

The average adult American may well have been first exposed to the word "ghetto" in connection with the Nazi atrocities of the Second World War. It was the Warsaw Ghetto into which innocent people were herded, there to be slaughtered. Many were burned alive. The distinguishing characteristic of a ghetto is the legally prescribed, *forcible* confinement of members of a given racial-ethnic group (historically, Jews) to a designated section of a city. Dictionaries still give as the primary definition of "ghetto": "a section of a city in which, in former times in most European countries, Jews were required to live."

> The streets of the medieval ghetto were narrow and gloomy, and because of poverty and over-crowding, hopelessly squalid. Its houses were piles of crumbling masonry. Little sunlight ever penetrated there and usually the ghetto was separated from the rest of the city by high walls and a ponderous gate. . . . It was barred and bolted and made additionally secure at night by heavy chains and locks. No Jew was allowed to leave the ghetto from dusk to daybreak. Discovered outside the walls, he was subject to the harshest penalties.[11]

In a letter to *The New York Times,* British author Malcolm Muggeridge protested the misuse of the word "ghetto"—and exposed the purposes of the misusers as well:

> As ... a great lover of words and long-time .. vendor of them, I cannot forbear to protest against the widespread use of the term "ghetto" as a description of the quarter, or district, or, alas, in many instances slum, where Negroes live in some of the major American cities.
>
> No sane person, I think, will wish to contradict me when I say that the ghetto, as it existed in Imperial Russia and Poland, cannot be equated with, say, Harlem today. In some respects conditions were worse, in some better; they were in no wise the same.
>
> Why, then, has "ghetto" in this false sense come into usage? It would seem to me a perfect example of what Orwell was always going on about (for instance, in his brilliant essay "Politics vs. Literature")—the falsification of words to make them serve political ends.
>
> By equating Negro slums with a ghetto, white racialism—in itself bad enough in all conscience—is associated with the additional horrors of Nazi anti-Semitism. ... [12]

It is precisely such a connotation of *forcible* confinement, coupled with hazy associations of torture and murder, which the present-day users of "ghetto" wish to evoke. The term "slum"— "a thickly populated squalid part of a city, inhabited by the poorest people"—would not be nearly so useful in arousing feelings of horror *and guilt.* The *Report* uses "ghetto" (sans quotation marks) throughout.

A similar motivation underlies the ubiquitous use of "deprived" (and/or "disadvantaged") in place of "poor." The passive verb form, used here as an adjective, in itself implies someone *to whom* something has been done. To deprive a man of something is to take it away from him. The concept "deprivation" depends upon and presupposes possession—what one does not have cannot be taken away. A person who is poor—even "relatively" poor—has not been *deprived* of anything which is rightfully his—unless he is poor because someone has robbed him or is forcibly preventing him from claiming property which is his *by right.* It is precisely the connotation of theft, and hence of illegitimate possession and injustice, which those who use the term "deprived" are attempting to foist upon anyone who has what the "have-nots" have not. The two-fold purpose of such corruption of the language is the negation of property rights and the inculcation of guilt.

The statist-determinist orientation of the *Report* reveals itself in countless other words and phrases. Individuals? No such entities exist; human beings are mere cells of the body of "society," "human resources" to be parceled out at some bureaucrat's whim. Wealth, which someone, somewhere, at some time, had to produce? It's "national" wealth, belonging to everyone and to no one —sourceless, causeless—and inexhaustible. Taxes? Those are not someone's earnings. They are "government funds"—specifically, *federal* government funds. Government? It is the Philosopher's Stone by which nothing can be transmuted into something, and "programs" can be "funded" by some miraculous means.

THE VERDICT

It would be futile, and irrelevant to the purpose and theme of this book, to attempt to analyze and criticize, item by item, all the errors, the omissions, the *post hoc ergo propter hoc* pseudo-reasoning by which the Kerner Commission tailored its conclusions to fit its preconceptions. The fallacies involved are not original with the Kerner Commission—virtually nothing in the *Report* is. The recommendations of the Kerner Commission, and the foregone conclusions on which they were based, are part of the "conventional wisdom" which has been prevalent in our society for years. The Chairmen of the Commission, high priests of that "conventional wisdom," could have written the *Report*'s recommendations without leaving their tax-supported sanctuaries, without stirring from their tax-supported swivel chairs.

Given the premises shared by the Commission members, the witnesses, the press, the President—and the rioters themselves, to whose shrieked "demands" the Commission accorded a nationwide forum—the content of the *Kerner Report was* preordained.

It is the premises behind the platitudes which are responsible for the *Report* and the riots. It is the premises behind the "conventional wisdom" of statism, of which the *Report* is a mere distillation, which make analysis of the *Report* of crucial importance.

It is those premises—and their implementation through concrete proposals now being inflicted on lives and livelihoods—with
which the balance of this book will deal.

CHAPTER III

The Immoral Premises

The long, hot summers of the sixties have spewed up a torrent of words. Chewed and rechewed, ruminated and regurgitated, they poured from political podiums, from editorial columns, from television sets. Like the rest of that rancid tide, the *Report of the National Advisory Commission on Civil Disorders* (the *Kerner Report*) proceeds from two assumptions:

1. That needs are the equivalent of rights; and
2. That the succor of needs is a legitimate function of government.

Is the paint peeling from someone's porch, and the garbage piling up in front of it? Is someone too hot or too cold? Is his job not quite to his liking—its pay or its "status" too low? Is his toilet clogged? Has his wife left him? Has he sired more children than he cares to raise and support? Would those children like to go swimming, or picnicking in a park? According to the premises of the *Kerner Report* one has only to enumerate the "needs" of the "deprived"; to articulate their "demands"; to publish their "griev-ances" replete with a thicket of statistics and garnished with photographs of tearful children and tottering crones; in order to establish—beyond all question—the justice of the "deprived's" claim to "their share" of the "nation's" resources.

But the nation, as such, *has* no resources. The "national in-come" and the "national wealth" are merely convenient (but mis-leading) brief terms for expressing the aggregate sum of what the individual citizens of a nation have produced. To state that the "deprived" have a claim, *in excess of their production,* upon the "nation's" resources is to state that some men have a right to what other men's effort has created. To state that government should use the "nation's" resources to fill the needs of the "deprived" is to state that productive men's earnings should be transferred to the unproductive—or the less productive—by force.

One may question, and validly so, the existence of actual want among rioters with incomes of $5,000 and more a year, rioters who own automobiles and television sets, rioters whose main targets are liquor stores. According to the Kerner Commission's own data, 32 percent of the rioters in Detroit (well over half of whom were under 25) were earning $5,000 to $10,000 a year. (p. 7) In Newark, the establishments which suffered the greatest loss through looting were, in descending order, liquor, clothing, and furniture stores—a pattern borne out in city after city. (p. 67) But to confine one's criticism of proposed solutions to the riots of the sixties solely to the validity of the data or the extent of the rioters' actual "need"—to ask only whether the rioters were genuinely poor—is tacitly to concede that poverty in *some* degree consti-tutes a justification for plunder in the streets. To criticize govern-mental "welfare" programs solely in terms of their scope is tacitly to accede to the principle of plunder by statute. To ask only "how much?" is to evade the *fundamental* question involved in regard to tax-based "welfare."

That question is *not* "how much?" That question is "*why?*"

Because Americans have not asked this "why?" the whole tow-ering edifice of the "welfare state" has been built upon the backs of the men who produce, but who have never asked by what right any portion of their production should be given to others *without the producers' consent.* The foundations of the edifice were laid so

long ago, the walls have risen so slowly, brick by seemingly innocent brick, that today few Americans realize that the entire structure—from "public" schools to "relief" to urban "renewal"—rests
upon the immoral premise that need gives one the right to acquire
the property of another by means of legalized force.

Why should "need" be the sole unquestioned entree into other
men's pockets? By what right does any man lay claim to the
earnings of other men? Why should some men—by virtue of their
poverty, their ignorance, their incompetence, self-loathing, or
sloth—be entitled to receive what they, by their own admission,
have not earned? Why should other men—in proportion to their
intelligence, ability, rationality, ambition, productiveness, pride—
be expected to spend hours of their lives in forced labor, in order
to fill the "demands" of the "poor"?

A recipient of government "welfare," declares the *Kerner Report*, "should be able to regard assistance as a right and not as an
· act of charity." (p. 256) Thus the riots of the sixties, according to
the *Report*, were merely an expression (perhaps a bit excessive) of
the impatience of the "deprived" in the face of their legitimate
desire to "participate in the benefits of the national affluence."

But who *created* the "national affluence"? Who created the
abundance of a nation where even the "deprived" can afford
television sets to "arouse their expectations"? What—*who*—is the
unnamed source of that "assistance" to which the recipient is
declared to have an innate, unimpeachable right? Who expended
the hours of his life, the effort of his mind and muscles, to create
the "assistance"? What of *his* right to keep it? Have the men who
produced the "national" wealth no claim to the fruits of their
work? Why should *their* desire to participate in the *full* benefits
of their own labor be deemed irrelevant? Why should they have
only the leavings after the "deprived" have grabbed "their" share?

MYTHICAL "RIGHTS" AND LEGALIZED PLUNDER

The United States of America was founded upon the principle
that men—all men—were born with the right to life and the corollary rights of liberty and property. The contradiction of this principle within the original Constitution, which permitted chattel

slavery, was corrected when slavery was abolished. Since that time the rights of all men have been protected by law. (I do not intend to suggest that all men, at all times, received equal protection under the law, or that no laws were made which infringed men's rights. However, a legal foundation for protection of men's innate rights was established fully at this point, and means for redress of infringements was provided—through the courts.)

But at what point was the right of *all* men to "life, liberty, and the pursuit of happiness" transformed into the right of *some* men to live at others' expense? How have the "needy" magically acquired a "right" to insist that government be used as the instrument to force some men's work to be placed in the service of other men's needs? When so viciously perverted a concept as the "right to welfare" or to a "guaranteed income" inspires virtually no protest on *principle*, what has happened to Americans' understanding of the concept of rights?

"A 'right' is a moral principle defining and sanctioning men's freedom of action in a social context."[1] The source of all rights is the nature of man; the *fundamental, primary* right is the right to life. The rights of liberty and property, however, are not separate, expendable trimmings; they are part of, and derived from, man's right to his life.

Man came into existence on a planet hostile to his very survival, armed with no prior knowledge, no "instinct" to identify his goals or the means to achieve them; armed only with his reasoning mind with which to sustain his existence. In order to survive, man had to use his mind, to expend *effort*, intellectual and physical. To have food in consistent supply, he had to learn to grow it. To have shelter, he had to learn to build it.

In the industrial civilizations of the twentieth century, most men no longer grow their own sustenance, weave their own cloth, erect their own homes. But division of labor and specialization, upon which industrialization and its benefits rest, have not changed the principle involved. Man's right to his property—to the food he grows, to the shelter he wrought out of a wilderness, to the wages he earns by his effort, and to whatever he buys with those wages —is rooted in and inseparable from his right to perform the actions which sustain his life. Prerequisite to the simplest of those actions, as to the most complex, is *thinking*.

Because it is *thinking* which is the crucial, fundamental, indispensable action man must take in support of his life, the right to liberty can, no more than the right to property, be separated from the right to life. Man lives by a process of reason; to do so he must be free to exercise his own judgment—and to pay for his own errors if that judgment be wrong. Man must be free to take whatever actions *his* mind tells him are necessary to sustain and enhance his life, provided only that his actions do not infringe upon the rights of other men. To state that man must have liberty is to state that man must be free of *coercion.*

Coercion—force and its variant, fraud—is the only means by which men can be induced to act against their own judgment. No man has the right to *initiate* force against another in order to *compel* him to act, *whether the desired action be for or against his own interest. No one* has the right to wrest from others any values they do not choose to give him, whether the values be those of matter or of spirit.

When men are confronted by others who seek to make them suspend their judgment, who seek to negate their rights through initiated brute force, they have a legitimate right to answer that brute force in kind: to deal with those who would rob them of life or property as the predatory animals they have announced themselves to be. When men abandon rational persuasion and pick up guns, clubs, or Molotov cocktails to enforce their will, they thereby place themselves outside of rights; they place themselves outside of reason; they indicate that force is their chosen tool of discourse. They should be taken at their word; it is by force that men must answer them.

Man's right to his life—and, by extension, his property—is the source of his right to self-defense. But only chaos could result if each man undertook to defend his life and property himself, to punish real or fancied wrongs. To make civilized society possible (and to free their time for productive work) men delegate the *implementation* of their right of self-defense to an agent—government—agreeing that government shall have a monopoly on defining the legal use of force. (It should not be—but probably is, in today's context—necessary to state that when man delegates to government the implementation of his right to self-defense, he does not *relinquish* that right, nor the right to implement it himself if circumstances make it necessary that he do so.)

Government is legalized force; it derives its rights from the rights of the individuals it serves. Its function is to protect man's innate rights by enforcing contracts freely made by individuals, by arbitrating contractual disputes, and by prosecuting force and fraud (including contractual defaults) according to an objective code of law applied uniformly to all men within the government's jurisdiction.

One man's rights, however, necessarily end where another man's rights begin. Man's right to the actions which sustain his life does *not* include the right to actions on the part of other men. One man's right to the use and disposal of his property automatically precludes any "right" to the use and disposal of another's. Because each man has the right to his life, *no* man has a right to another man's; no man has a *right* to claim as his one second of another man's time, one ounce of effort on another man's part, or anything produced thereby—except by mutual agreement, by trade (in matter or in spirit) to mutual advantage. Nor has government any right to enforce such a claim for anyone. *Government has no rights beyond those of individuals.*

To assert a "right" to the fruits of the efforts of others is to attempt to secure goods without the voluntary consent of those who produced them, by force instead of by trade or rational persuasion. The test of any claimed "right" is this: *Is one claiming a right to the actions, or to the product of the actions, of other men?* What, then, on the basis of that test, is the nature of the "rights" which the *Kerner Report* implies in its enumeration of the "grievances" of looting mobs, "grievances" which the *Report* treats as claims against the "national" resources?

—Unemployment and underemployment
—Inadequate education
—Inadequate housing
—Poor recreation facilities
—Inadequacy of municipal services, such as trash collection
—Inadequate government welfare programs

The grievance of "unemployment and underemployment" implies the right, not to *work*, but to be provided with a job. Every man has the right to work; i.e., to use his abilities and efforts to produce the sustenance he requires. *No* man has the right to force another to provide him with tools (or a factory) with which to do so; to buy his services; to pay him more than—in the *employer's* judgment—his services are worth. "Employment"—*jobs*—connotes employers and places of employment. Jobs are not found in nature; it is men who create them. Individual entrepreneurs create jobs by inventing new products which other men desire and will accept in trade for theirs; by improving existing products or the means by which to make them; by forgoing present consumption in order to accumulate savings to be invested in factories and machine tools (capital); by having the vision to see what none before them had seen, and the courage to act upon their vision.

In the United States today, tens of thousands of dollars must be invested in plant and machines to create a single industrial job. Why should some men earn and then risk those tens of thousands only to have other men, who have invented and invested nothing, *because* they have invented and invested nothing, claim the "right" to use those achievements without the owners' consent?

The "grievance" of "inadequate education" implies the right, not to learn, but to be taught. The right to *learn* is inherent in man's nature. The right to be educated—to schools and textbooks and teachers' time and skill—is not.

The "grievance" of "inadequate housing" implies a right to a house or apartment. But "housing" does not spring intact from the earth. *Men* designed the buildings, produced rafters or steel girders, formed the glass for the windows, the shingles for the roofs, the locks for the doors. Men had to pour the concrete, lay the bricks, drive the nails. Should these men be forced to work for nothing, or should other men be forced to pay their wages, in order that the "needy" might have homes *their* production cannot pay for?

The "grievance" of "poor recreation facilities" implies a right to parks and swimming pools. "Inadequacy of municipal services" implies a right to have someone shovel up one's slops. But swimming pools, sliding boards, street lights, and trash removal trucks are built, maintained, and operated *by men.* If these facilities are provided "by the government," still they must be paid for by someone. It should be self-evident that if those who use such facilities do not pay for them, someone else must. What of *his* right to dispose of the fruits of his efforts according to *his* choice? Why should any portion of *his* earnings be taken from him, forcibly, in taxes, to buy for others goods and services which they cannot or will not buy for themselves? Suppose *he* prefers to buy (depending upon the amount of earnings thus confiscated) a swimming pool or a pack of cigarettes for himself? Why should the men who have *not* produced acquire, by virtue of their non-production, the "right" to his thought, his effort, and his time; while he, because he *did* produce, loses all right to his earnings? *It matters not whether the amount taken from him is large or small; it matters not how much or little he has left. By accepting the principle that some men have a "right" to any portion of other men's property, one abrogates all men's rights to everything they own.*

Once need is accepted as a right, there is no end to what men may demand. The "right" to government "welfare" implies the "right" to dentistry and diapers; to prescriptions, psychotherapy and Princess phones; to legal services, hot lunches, carfare, and condoms—and the "right" not to regard these as charity.

By means of such mythical "rights" the whole meaning of rights has been obliterated. Each proposal to enforce such mythical "rights" infringes, in one way or another, the *genuine*, innate rights of some men and thus of all. It is in the name of such mythical "rights" that men took to the streets in acts of overt plunder which the Kerner Commission sanctions by its premise that plunder is moral if committed by means of a statute.

No intelligent appraisal of the riots of the sixties—or of the Kerner Commission proposals—can be made until the premises underlying both the riots and the "remedies" are exposed as the root cause they are. Neither safety nor progress nor surcease from street chaos will be attained until the immoral premises that needs equal rights and justify riots are discarded; until the riots and the recommendations and the aftermath of both are assessed on the basis of the *only* premises by which the goals of liberty, justice, security, and progress for *all* men can be attained:

—That *all* men have the right to life, liberty, and property;
—That *no* men have the right to *initiate* force against others (and therefore neither has government);
—That the only proper function of government is the protection

of the lives and properties of the citizens within its jurisdiction, against the initiation of force by other men.

It is from these premises that the subsequent discussion of the *Kerner Report*'s proposals will proceed.

CHAPTER IV

Racism Institutionalized

Our nation, according to the *Kerner Report*'s most widely echoed pronouncement, "is rapidly moving toward two societies, one black, one white—separate and unequal. Reaction to last summer's disorders has quickened the movement and deepened the division." (p.1) "Disorders" is the mealy-mouthed euphemism used by the Commission to gloss over arson, assault, and pillage. It is typical of the intellectual orientation of the *Report*'s authors that they should blame *reaction* to the "disorders" on the part of the victims, and *not* the "disorders" themselves, for "deepening the division" of American society. Likewise it is typical of the *Report*, and of the "liberal" (statist) intellectual in-group whose dogmas the *Report* so flawlessly parrots, to interpret and vilify the intensifying pleas for law and order as expressions of antagonism between race and race. The citizens who express their revulsion for looting and for looters—the revulsion of the decent toward the criminal—are dismissed and reviled as "racists" because the looters of the riots of the sixties were individuals who happened to be Negroes. The citizens who beg for an end to mob rule would—we are expected to believe—condone murder, rapine, and arson if the perpetrators were white.

If it is true that the chaos in our cities is being thought of in terms of race warfare; if it is true that battle lines are being drawn between black and white; if it is true that Americans are becoming more race-conscious than ever before; if it is true that a false schism between Negro Americans and white Americans exists and is widening—and each succeeding day's headlines testify that these trends are a tragic reality—it is precisely the mode of thinking typified by the *Kerner Report* itself which is responsible.

Inveighing against "racism," which, they contend, is destroying the nation, the men of the Kerner Commission and their counterparts and cohorts throughout the culture are busily striving to make racism a way of life. Innocently or otherwise, depending upon their individual acuity and intentions, these men are pursuing the hopelessly contradictory and self-defeating course of attempting to destroy an evil by institutionalizing it. As an alternative to the "white racism" they claim to deplore (a "racism" indirectly and imprecisely defined as discriminatory *acts* directed against Negroes by, and for the supposed benefit of, whites), the Commission members offer proposal after proposal for providing alleged benefits to Negroes by means of legislative, i.e., forcibly implemented, acts of discrimination against whites.

Racism is, indeed, one of the major issues of our day, the subject of sermons and seminars and citizens' committees and car-card advertisements. Racism is, in fact, so universally accepted as an object of scorn and repugnance that those who bandy the term about seldom, if ever, ask themselves or anyone else just what racism *is*. Where, in the muddy turmoil of charge and countercharge, of slogans extolling "racial brotherhood" and "Negro aspirations," of discussions of "bussing" and "integration" and "civil rights"; where in all the torrents of invective directed at "racism" and "racists" by COPE and CORE and SNCC and SCLC, by the NCC and the NAACP, can one find the term intelligibly defined?

The *Kerner Report*, which presents "racism" as a virtual justification for chaos in the streets, identifies it as a national problem, and professes to offer solutions, is no exception to the general confusion. In common with current literature and political discussion, the *Report* implicitly interprets racism as color prejudice; more specifically, as prejudice of whites against Negroes. The converse is not termed racism. It is called "developing race pride," or "the Negro's assertion of his racial identity." (See below.)

THE ANATOMY AND IMPLICATIONS OF RACISM

Color prejudice, however, is only one of racism's manifestations. *Racism is a doctrine according to which men are judged, not by their actions, but by their ancestry: their genetic lineage. To practice racism is to use genetically determined differences as criteria for making distinctions among men in situations where genetics are irrelevant; i.e., in issues involving* volitional *activities or* volitionally acquired *attributes.* Racism attempts to link "blood" (body chemistry) with "good" (morality).

Metaphysically, racism is a form of determinism: a negation of causality, reason, and free will. Racism is a variant of collectivism; in common with his intellectual kin—the socialist, the fascist, the divine-right monarchist—the racist denies man's rational faculty and obliterates the concept of individual rights, lumping human beings together as indistinguishable, interchangeable, insignificant, expendable cells of a mystical organism with a "will" of its own. It is this organism, the collective (whether it be called "society," "the proletariat," "the state," or "the race"), whose "good" is claimed to supersede all individual needs or desires; and to which are ascribed the very capacities of reason and free will, and the very rights, whose existence in individuals the collectivist denies.

Psychologically, racism, like all forms of collectivism, is an attempt to attain a false self-esteem. By ascribing virtues to one group *as a group*, then proclaiming his membership in it; by ascribing vices to another group *as a group*, then proclaiming his superiority to it; the collectivist seeks an automatic self-esteem, an automatic self-identification, and surcease from the admittedly demanding task of forming one's own character and personality in accordance with a well-defined, logically defensible standard of morality. In the case of a racist, the rationale for dividing mankind into "good" and "bad" groups is genetic.

The racist seeks to establish an instant, effortless superiority over other men, not by means of *achievement*, but by means of mere *existence*. He lays claim to their respect on the basis of his genetic lineage, for which he has and can have no responsibility, thus absolving himself of the necessity of *earning* respect—*from others or from himself.* His search for self-esteem is entirely other-directed; his claim to superiority based, not even upon a comparison of his *virtues* with the *vices* of others, but upon a comparison of the virtues (real or fancied) of his *ancestors* with the sins (real or fancied) of *theirs*.

In his frantic pursuit of distinction divorced from effort, the racist uses many ploys. "Who am I to scrub floors?" whines some lounging sloven. "My grandmother's uncle's nephew's niece was a Hapsburg." "That man is no good," a mother tells her daughter. "His father drank like a fish." The racist thus may use the genuine achievements or imagined distinctions of his ancestors, or his children, or of others of his race or country of origin, to cloak his own secretly admitted inadequacies and defaults in borrowed glory. Or he may use the sins or errors or invented inferiority of another man's ancestors or descendants or compatriots as a means to "instant judgment" of *him*. In all such instances it is racism—whose distinguishing characteristic is the attempt to impute vice or virtue on purely genetic grounds—which is being invoked.

Crudest of all, however, is the racist who uses color differences as the quicksand foundation for his jerry-built self-regard. The black- or white-supremacist seeks his self-esteem totally outside volition and virtue—either his own *or* others'—and bases all his claims to distinction upon pigmentation and bodily conformation: on blood groupings, chromosome formation, and blind chance.

The color racist pretends that the moral worth and intellectual attainments of a man are predetermined by his ethnic origins; that any given individual's philosophy, habits, tastes, temperament, and achievements are dependent upon, and can be inferred from, his genetic heritage. A particularly ludicrous example of this sort of thinking (or, more precisely, *non*-thinking) may be found among those who regard themselves as most enlightened on matters of racism: sociologists. Not a few of them attribute American Negro individuals' adoption of American customs, manners, "democratic ideals," and desires for career achievement to a desire on the part of Negroes for "cultural whiteness." Negro Americans who work hard and keep themselves clean and neat, do so, according to these learned scientists, to "reject their African heritage." The assumption is that, because a man's skin is dark, he must have an inborn affinity with the customs and values of a primitive society in a land he has never seen. Kenneth Clark (*Dark Ghetto*) goes so far as to accuse Negro individuals who consider their color irrelevant and refuse to consider themselves inferior, of being hypocritical traitors to their racial obligations.[1] The pigmentation of a man's skin, the shape of his nose, the texture of his hair —all of which are *not* within his volitional control—are claimed by the racist to be instant, infallible indices of his rationality, his productiveness, his ambition, his morality—all of which *are* within his volitional control. Thus the racist proffers visual perception as a substitute for judgment, and physiognomy as a substitute for virtue.

Of the many guises in which the racist is found, the most grotesquely monstrous—the Ku Klux Klansman who viciously persecutes "niggers"; the "Black Power" demagogue who urges his followers to "kill Whitey"—are also, in any society of even partially rational men, the least dangerous *in a long-term sense.* Their very viciousness, their crudity, the patent perversity of their doctrines; the very overtness of their violations of human rights by means of acts which all decent men condemn, lead to their repudiation by the majority of their fellow citizens. Since the acclaim and respect of others are what the racist primarily (if subconsciously) seeks as a substitute for self-esteem, this contempt and disapproval on the part of the majority of others helps to hold him at least partially in check.

Overt, explicit racists have little philosophical influence upon a culture unless and until the groundwork is laid for them by the respectable and respected—by racist "philosophers" and intellectuals imbued with the sanctity of university positions or governmental office—and by the default or unspoken concurrence of normally decent men. It is these factors which unleash overt racists in number and in force, giving them first intellectual and, later, legal sanction. Nazi Germany is the symbol and the warning of what may happen then.

It is racism masquerading as reason, enlightenment, and science
—codified into law and placing the government's monopoly on
legal force at the racist's disposal—which can ultimately destroy
both individuals and nations. It is racism in precisely such dis-
guises, and proposals for precisely such legalization, which charac-
terize the *Kerner Report.* Posing as an attack on racism, the *Report*
—in its subtle, smug, and corrosive way—is fully as racist in orientation and purpose as any white supremacist or Black Muslim
screed.

The Rampant Racism of the "Anti-Racists"

The racist premises of the Kerner Commission are so pervasive,
yet so intrinsically part of each line of the *Report*, that the nearly
palpable aura they create is difficult to convey by means of single
and succinct examples excised from the text as a whole. The
Report deals with the riots of the sixties, not as riots participated
in predominantly by individuals who were members of the Negro
race, but as riots involving Negroes *as Negroes.* The references to
"race pride" and "Negro goals" are so tediously numerous as to
defy attempts to tally them. While the racism of "white America"
is repeatedly deplored by the Commission, the blatantly racist
attitudes of the interviewed rioters are neither identified as racist,
nor criticized as such by the Commission. Instead, they are pan-
dered to and even subtly praised:

> The . . . surveys indicate that rioters have strong feelings of racial
> pride, if not racial superiority. . . . To what extent this racial pride
> antedated the riot or was produced by the riot is impossible to
> determine from the survey data. Certainly the riot experience
> seems to have been associated with increased pride in the minds of
> many participants. This was vividly illustrated by the statement of
> a Detroit rioter:
> Interviewer: You said you were feeling good when you followed
> the crowds?
> Respondent: I was feeling proud, man, at the fact that I was a
> Negro. I felt like I was a first-class citizen. I didn't feel ashamed of
> my race because of what they did. (p. 76)

The Commission, which did not hesitate to deplore the "antagonistic attitudes" of ruined shopkeepers toward the rioters, had no adverse comment to make on the attitudes expressed in the above quotation. Instead, the Commission—in muted but unmistakable tones of approval—cites "the racial consciousness and solidarity reflected in the slogan 'Black Power' " as "[combining to] inspire a new mood among Negroes, particularly among the young. *Self-esteem and enhanced racial pride* are replacing apathy and submission to 'the system'." (p. 93, my emphasis)

Washington, D.C. television shop owner James Briscoe (a Negro) showed a discernment the Kerner Commission lacked. He was asked by *The New York Times* why he displayed no "Soul Brother" sign when mourners of "non-violent" leader Martin Luther King sacked Washington to express their grief. Said Mr. Briscoe: "I didn't really care to identify with that bunch."[2]

The extent to which racism permeates the Kerner Commission's basic attitude is perhaps most clearly illustrated by the following:

> An example will serve to illustrate how the [suggested] system [of community information "task forces"] might operate:
>
> Following the slaying last summer of a *Negro* teenager by a *Negro* detective in the Bedford-Stuyvesant section of Brooklyn, N.Y., a rumor that the youth had been shot by a *white* policeman . . . began to circulate through an already tense neighborhood. The situation became threatening. Yet, within an hour, three *white* members of the mayor's summer task force group were able to convince a group of black militants that [the policeman was a Negro]. Walking the streets that night and the next two evenings, they worked to dispel the rumor and to restore community stability. (p. 151, my emphasis)

The race of the participants was considered to supersede all other circumstances of the case: "black" policeman—no riot; "white" policeman—that's different. About this incident, the most tragic comment is: such tactics work.

As to the manner in which the Kerner Commission proposes to imbed racism permanently in our culture and laws, there are examples in sickening profusion:

On Education:

> [The Commission recommends] establishment of supplemental education centers: These centers would offer specialized facilities and instruction to students from different schools for a portion of the school day. *It is most important that courses be developed and scheduled to provide racially integrated educational experiences.* (p. 245, my emphasis)

> [E]ducational parks would consolidate or cluster existing schools, thereby broadening attendance areas to bring within the school zone a racially and economically heterogeneous population. (p. 245)

On Journalism:

> Finally, the news media must publish newspapers and produce programs that recognize the existence and activities of the Negro, both *as a Negro* and as part of the community. (p. 212, my emphasis)

> The Commission's major concern with the news media is not in riot reporting as such, but in the failure to report adequately on race relations and ghetto problems and to bring more Negroes into journalism. (p. 210)

> News organizations *must employ enough Negroes* in positions of significant responsibility to establish an effective link to *Negro actions and ideas.* .... (p. 211, my emphasis)

On Law Enforcement:

> Police departments should intensify their efforts to recruit more Negroes. ...

> In order to *increase the number of Negroes in supervisory positions,* police departments should review promotion policies to ensure that *Negroes* have full opportunity to be rapidly and fairly promoted.

> Negro officers should be assigned so as to ensure that the police department is fully and visibly integrated. (p. 166)

The years-long battle to free city police departments from political patronage and to institute valid standards for police force candidates should, in short, be negated. The examinations, the probationary periods, the studies, the rigid standards, and investigations of past records should be scrapped. They're passé. Hail to the new, scientific test for police officers' qualifications: A spectrometer.

On Politics:

> Respondents in the Newark survey were asked about relatively simple items of political [!] information, such as the *race* of prominent local and national political figures. In general, the self-reported rioters were much better informed than the non-involved. For example, self-reported rioters were more likely to know that one of the 1966 Newark mayoral candidates was a Negro. . . . The overall scores on a series of similar questions also reflect the self-reported rioters' higher levels of *information* [or racism?]. (p. 76, my emphasis)

> Self-reported rioters were also more likely to be involved in activities associated with *Negro rights.* (p. 76, my emphasis)

> The acquisition of power by Negro-dominated governments in central cities is surely a legitimate and desirable exercise of political power by a minority group. It is an American political tradition exemplified by the achievements of the Irish in New York and Boston [such as Tammany Hall?]. (p. 220)

Thus we find men who claim to oppose racism prating of "Negro actions and ideas" and "Negro goals," as though the mere fact of "Negroness" guaranteed a unanimity of philosophy, outlook, desires, and intentions among all to whom the physical description of "Negro" applies. Such men, consciously or not, are making common cause with, and providing intellectual ammunition for, those who propose to ship all Negroes "back" to Africa "because that's where they belong"; those who claim "Negro" laziness or "Negro" shiftlessness or "Negro" dishonesty as unvarying and inherent characteristics of black men—or "white" ambition, "white" cleanliness and "white" erudition as the unvarying and inherent characteristics of white men. When the Kerner Commis-

sion calls upon the news media to recognize Negroes "as a group";
when it urges the placement of Negro children, *because* they are
Negro children, in certain schools; when it urges employers to hire
Negroes *because* they are Negroes; when it advocates the social
mixing of black men and white men *because* they are black and
white, the Commission is playing the racist game as surely as any
advocate of segregated schools, "lily-white" hiring practices, or
the "would-you-want-your-daughter-to-marry-a-Nigger" school
of "thought."

Racism is racism, no matter by, for, or against whom practiced;
but *this* the Kerner Commission refuses to recognize—or admit.
And when the Commission urges that Negroes, *as Negroes,* seek
political representation, and that the racist practices the Commission advocates be enforced by law (as, of course, many such practices already have been), the Commission is accepting a premise
which (as it did in Nazi Germany) provides the philosophical
groundwork for the legitimized practice of racism in its most brutal and terrifying forms.

THE ROLE OF GOVERNMENT IN RACIAL ISSUES

One of the implicit premises of the Kerner Commission is that
government has a function in race relations *as such.* It was exactly
this principle—that it is within government's province to intervene in affairs involving individual relationships based upon individual choice—which supported the segregation laws. These laws
used government's monopoly of force to support discrimination of
whites against blacks. Today's "liberals" and "civil rights" leaders,
many of whom passionately fought segregation laws, are now invoking the self-same principle which spawned the laws they so
ardently and properly opposed. They now seek to use government
force on behalf of blacks and against whites.

In fact, *government has no proper role in race relations as such.*

Government's proper function is not the protection of "Negro
rights" or "white rights." Rights do not reside in groups; rights
reside in individuals; there *are* no exclusively "Negro" rights, just
as there are no exclusively "white" rights. Government, if properly constituted, protects *individual* rights—the individual rights
of all men. Government is legalized force which *should* always

(although obviously does not always) remain strictly retaliatory: governmental force should be used only after force has been initiated by individuals to deprive others of life, liberty, or property.

The pertinent question which must precede governmental action is not: "Has someone been discriminated against?" In racial matters as in all others, the pertinent question regarding governmental involvement is: "Have someone's *rights* been violated?" If so, government may and must act. If not, the issue is not within the province of government.

If a Negro buys a house, and his neighbors, who are white men, express their objections to his presence by throwing rocks through his windows, government (the police power) *must* act against those neighbors because a man's *rights* have been violated, *not* because the violators were motivated by racism. If a Negro desires to buy a house, and the legitimate owner refuses to sell to him, the government may *not* act against the owner; no one's rights have been violated, no matter how irrational or capricious the owner may have been in refusing the sale. No man has the right to the use and disposal of another man's property, which means that no man has a right to dictate in what manner another may sell his property. Those who disapprove of a bigoted owner's action should attempt to persuade him of the error of his thinking; they should subject him to social ostracism or to public criticism. But they may not rightfully use force, directly or through government, to compel him to sell against his wishes. His house is *his* property; he has the right to dispose of it as he sees fit.

Should a shopkeeper refuse to serve some men because of their race, that is his *right*, reprehensible though his action is. The shopkeeper's store is his property; he has the right to its use and disposal, as he has the right to decide with whom he wishes to associate. The fact that the public, with an owner's consent, enters his property and uses his facilities does not make a store, a train, a swimming pool, or a theater "public property." Laws regarding "public accommodations," whether the laws impose racial segregation or racial integration, have been responsible for some monstrous violations of property rights. "Public accommodations" laws have tended to lump together *private* property to which the public has access in the course of trade or other mutual-consent relationships with the property owner, and governmental, tax-financed, publicly "owned" facilities. Racial segregation of the latter *is* a violation of rights; racial segregation of the former, although a repugnant practice, is *not* a violation of rights.

The issue has been confused partially because more and more nominally private facilities are being financed, wholly or in part, with tax monies. Racial segregation of, for example, an apartment project built with government assistance is a double injustice—the first of which is the expropriatory financing.

Those who think a shopkeeper who practices racial discrimination wrong, should advertise their disapproval; they might subject him to economic boycott, or they might open a competing store. (Should they do the latter, and should he attempt to use force or the threat of force to intimidate his adversaries, to prevent suppliers or customers from dealing there, then and only then may government action be rightfully brought against *him*. But the issue in that event is one of rights, not of racism.)

Should racism motivate men to acts which are in themselves violations of rights, legal redress exists. Theft, murder, assault, fraud, and extortion are plainly violations of rights; there are laws against, and penalties prescribed for, them. Such laws and penalties take no cognizance of the color of the litigants, nor should they; it is irrelevant. Law must ignore color.

The current emphasis on "Negro rights" and on the acquisition of political power by Negroes *qua* Negroes is an outgrowth of the statist attitudes prevalent in our society. The gradual ascendance of statist ideas has resulted in the metamorphosis of the United States government, which was originally based (primarily) upon individual rights, into a "mixed economy" of pull and pressure groups. Statists regard government, not as a means for protecting individual rights, but as a vehicle for the forcible imposition of ideologies. Our present-day "mixed economy" of freedom and controls, in which the governmental power is wielded (in the name of the "public welfare") to secure special privileges and unearned values for some at the expense of others, has resulted in the formation of pressure groups, each attempting to seize the legislative reins or to lobby for its supposed interests. The solution to the inequities created by this situation, however, is not to be found in the formation of *new*, *racially*-oriented, pressure groups enlisting government force in their favor; the solution is to restrict government to its rightful province. The question of governmental action in racial matters has been wrongly posed. That question is not whether the United States should have a government "in favor of white men" or "in favor of Negroes"; the question is whether we are willing to replace a government of favor with a government based upon, and firmly restricted to, the protection of the individual rights of all men.

Laws which attempt to force men to sell to others, to eat with others, to go to school with or otherwise associate with others, are morally wrong—as are laws which attempt to prevent men from so acting. Such laws are an intrusion of force into areas of human intercourse which are matters of individual choice; they are violations of human rights—whether they are passed by the federal government, by state governments, or by local governments. They can and they must be struck down, *on these grounds and only on these grounds.* The injustices perpetrated by such laws cannot be remedied, nor can redress be found, in the passage of new laws which operate on the identical principle and differ from the old merely in terms of the pigmentation, nationality, sex, or profession of their victims.

The Remedy for Racism

There is no question but that Negroes in the United States have been, and often still are, the victims of viciously discriminatory practices, both in the form of individual, private discrimination, and in the form of discriminatory law. For the latter, redress may properly be sought through government; i.e., through the courts. But the answer to *private* acts of discrimination, so long as they do not involve violations of rights, does not lie in governmental action. Such discrimination is an individual matter and it is as individual, private citizens that men must act to eliminate it.

Racism must be fought at its root, by rejecting the premise upon which it rests. To urge "race guilt" upon white men because some of their ancestors may have held or sold black men as slaves; or because some white men now discriminate against Negroes; or because one white man shot a Negro; to encourage—virtually urge —Negroes to discriminate against white men; to condone or excuse Negroes who commit crimes against white men on such pretexts, is to preach fully as vicious a racism as that to which Negroes have so often been subjected. To encourage or extol the development of "race pride" in Negroes is to perpetuate the doctrines by means of which Negroes have been persecuted. Offering men "race pride" as an antidote to feelings of "race inferiority" is tendering them the opposite side of the same counterfeit coin. "Race pride" can only result, in those who profess it, in a psychological barrier to the development of individual character, to the achievement of the *individual* rationality, integrity, and productivity which are the only sources of authentic self-esteem.

In truth, in logic, in *reality,* there is no reason for any man to be proud that he is black. There is no reason for him to be ashamed that he is black. There is no reason for any man to be proud that he is white. There is no reason for him to be ashamed of it. There is no reason for any man to be honored because of the achievements of his forbears; there is no reason for any man to be vilified because of their sins. A man's color, his country of origin, his family history, are not matters of his choice or effort; they are totally irrelevant to his worth as a person—or his lack of it.

Those who attempt to demean a man, or to destroy his self-respect by derogatory remarks or humiliating practices based upon what he knows to be beyond his volition—his race—will be recognized by any man of *genuine* self-esteem for the scum they are. The man of genuine self-esteem will not allow his self-estimate to depend upon the good opinion of other men; least of all, of men who have revealed themselves as so lacking in intelligence, judgment, and self-respect as to judge him on the basis of his color. Should men, on such spurious grounds, refuse to deal with him, the man of self-respect will go his own way, knowing that it is not *he* who stands condemned, but those who condemned him without cause; knowing that any contempt he feels should be directed at his persecutors, not at himself.

The man who allows "harassment . . . together with contemptuous and degrading verbal abuse" to "strip [him] of the one thing he may have left—his dignity" (p. 159) has not fallen victim to racism, but to his own irrationality and self-loathing. If, in addition, he turns to violence and destruction as a means of "asserting his identity," he is guilty of making a false estimate true, with the result that the racists who persecute him will feel justified in their racism. The guilt for his acts is ultimately his, but the blame should be laid as well at the door of those who taught him—in pious official tones—that destruction is a source of self-realization instead of the total negation of self and existence which, in fact, it is.

The answer to the racial problem in the United States lies in our rejection of the collectivist premises upon which racism rests. It lies in the recognition that self-esteem and achievement are attained and maintained in and by *individuals*, and cannot be stolen or borrowed or extorted from others; that virtues are created by individual choice through individual effort; that rights do not reside in race or "society" or any other collective, but only in individual men; and that neither race nor any group affiliation gives men the right to impose their will upon others or to gain values from others by means of force.

Racism will have been eradicated as an influential force in the United States, not on the day that a Negro is elected President; not on the day that the political Waring Blendor of the "public" schools has finally achieved the exactly "right" homogenization of white with brown with tan with black; not on the day that all history texts uniformly proclaim that the first man to die in the American Revolution was a Negro—but on the day when race ceases to be a matter for concern or comment except by anthropologists and geneticists; on the day when a man's color is relegated to the status of the irrelevancy *it really is* in terms of his character and actions.

The attitudes and proposals of the Kerner Commission will by no means hasten the advent of that happy day.

Chapter V

A Fallacy Compounded:
The Economics of
Interventionism

It is phenomena such as the *Kerner Report* which lend the conditioned reflex theory its spurious plausibility. Push the button; sound the buzzer; flash the light: the "liberal" barks as "programmed." Be the trigger word "illness" or "old age" or "illiteracy" or "urban riots," the "liberal" yelps "Government Program!" Such are the automated mental patterns by which some men avoid the arduous process—and sometimes downright unsettling results —of genuine thought. The *Kerner Report* is a classic distillation of the consequences of such evasion.

Obviously, it has become impossible for the men of the Kerner Commission to conceive of solving any problem except by passing a law. This self-induced, self-maintained mental myopia inevitably renders the Commission—and the fulsome admirers who are daily echoing its pronouncements—utterly incapable of perceiving any cause-and-effect relationship between the very problems they decry and the laws *already* passed. Nowhere is this sorry state of intellectual atrophy more abundantly demonstrated than in the Commission's approach to economics.

Not only does the Kerner Commission hold it as an article of faith that the urban riots of the sixties are being caused by the "grievances" (mainly economic) of the "deprived." The Commission is equally dedicated to the dogma that only government "programs" (in this case, economic interventionism) can eliminate the conditions about which the aggrieved are grieving. So blindly and obdurately is the Commission devoted to its interventionist creed, that even when the *Report* admits—usually tacitly—that government has failed abysmally as a vehicle for creating instant paradise (an admission usually couched in some variant of the new cliché: "government alone cannot shoulder the vast task of . . ."), the participation of the "private sector" or "free enterprise" is invoked in terms of tax-financed subsidies and government controls. (See Chapters VI and VII.) The plethora of failures cannot shake the Commission's unshakable faith in what Bastiat called "the great fictitious entity by which everyone seeks to live at the expense of someone else": government—the state, the "benevolent and inexhaustible being" which has:

> . . . bread for all mouths, work for all hands, capital for all enterprises, credit for all projects, ointment for all wounds, balm for all suffering, advice for all perplexities, solutions for all problems, truths for all minds, distractions for all variety of boredom, milk for children and wine for old age, which provides all our needs, foresees all our desires, satisfies all our curiosity, corrects all our errors, amends all our faults, and exempts us all henceforth from the need for foresight, prudence, judgment, sagacity, experience, order, economy, temperance, and industry.[1]

Several centuries of disasters wrought by government "programs" have taught the Commission and its fellow "liberals" nothing; why should a few additional decades, a few recent examples, be any more convincing?

The riots of the sixties are not, of course, *caused* by "grievances." They are caused by the irrationality of those who riot, an irrationality in which they are sanctioned and encouraged by the prevailing philosophy that "need" constitutes a right to grab whatever one needs—by force. Moreover, even if there *were* a direct causal connection between the economic "grievances" of the rioters and their acts of depredation, the alleviation of their needs via governmental "programs" would not be morally justified. Those who *initiate* force to gain goods or services from others forfeit, by their actions, any right to a hearing for their claims. Moreover, government "aid" is force-supported; "government" funds are force-extorted; taxation-financed "poverty" programs *at any governmental level* are immoral. These legalized abrogations of people's right to do what they want to with their own property cannot be made moral by any quantity of subsequent amendments, extensions, exemptions, revisions, or other legislative tinkering. A fallacy compounded does not equal a truth; injustice compounded remains injustice still.

Interventionism could not be morally justified even if it "worked." But, of course, it does not work even when, in a limited, out-of-context, short-term sense, it *seems* to work. The immoral is the impractical as well. In a manner which the *Report*'s authors refuse to recognize, the data in the *Kerner Report* itself bear this out. The rioters and their non-rioting fellow "deprived" *have* been the victims of injustice, but not necessarily—and certainly not primarily—from those whom the rioters victimized. Nor have the "deprived" been victimized by the free enterprise system, by the "capitalism" their self-appointed leaders so glibly condemn. The "deprived" have been victimized by legal, initiatory governmental force. To the extent that the "grievances" of the "deprived" actually exist, they are largely caused—and invariably aggravated—by the very forms of economic interventionism which the Kerner Commission proposes to extend.

The "Death" of the American Dream

Despite abundant evidence to the contrary within its own findings (see Chapter II), the Kerner Commission persists in basing its recommendations on the premise that "poverty" and its corollaries (or, more precisely, its alleged corollaries) of "inadequate" housing, "inadequate" recreation, "inadequate" education, divorce, and dirt, are—together with racial discrimination—the primary cause of "disorders." The rioters were, in a catch word, "deprived"; the "victims" of rat-infested housing, overcrowded living conditions, broken homes, and filthy streets. From these tragic conditions today's urban Negroes (urban "deprived" white men, who have not been rioting lately, naturally get short shrift from the Commission) are—unlike the immigrants of earlier years —"unable" to rescue themselves. Moreover, to suggest that they try is to give heartless sanction to "oppression," as explained by one of the Commission's pet sociologists, Dr. Kenneth Clark:

> One ["Negro middle-class"] ... woman leader, in a talk to a Negro church in Harlem [after the summer "revolts" of 1964] urged Negro women to organize for community reform. On every block in Harlem, she said, a committee should be rallied to buy brooms; squads of women and children would be recruited to sweep the streets. She argued that people who live on dirty streets could not hope to gain the respect of others. Negro children, she said, should be taught to respect cleanliness and this would in turn give them pride in their parents and in themselves.
>
> She did not understand that it is not the job of the people to sweep the streets; it is the job of the Department of Sanitation. . . . To lecture the miserable inhabitants of the ghetto to sweep their own streets is to urge them to accept the fact that the government is not expected to serve them. . . .
>
> *Most disturbing of the implications of her advice was that Negroes are responsible for their own condition, that dirt reflects defects in the inhabitants. She was buying the position of many middle-class whites that social victims are responsible for their plight.* She was in error, but even more important was the fact that she was, in effect, presenting an apology for oppression.[2] (my emphasis)

The so-called "Protestant Ethic" of hard work and self-determination is *out*; the "Social Ethic" is *in*. "What the American economy of the late 19th and early 20th century was able to do to help the European immigrants escape from poverty is now largely impossible," declares the *Report*. "New methods of escape must be found *for*"—not, one notes, *by*—"today's poor." (p. 145, my emphasis)

In the self-same section of the *Report* the Commission contradicts its own assertion. The percentage of "non-whites who are employed in white-collar, technical, and professional jobs" rose, the Commission states, from 10.2 percent of the "non-white" population in 1950 to 20.8 percent in 1966; it is, moreover, predicted that the 1970 census will show a further increase of nearly 5 percent from the 1966 figure. "The proportion attending college," says the Commission, "has risen an equal amount." The percentage of Negroes aged 25 to 34 who are high school graduates will have nearly doubled, from 22.4 percent in 1960 to 43 percent in 1970—a percentage about the same as for whites of the same age group (46.5 percent). The percentage of college graduates among Negroes aged 25 to 34 has more than doubled, rising from 4.3 to 9.5 percent over the same period.[3]

"Indeed," says the Kerner Commission, "the development of a small but *steadily increasing* Negro middle class . . . is creating a growing gap between Negro haves and have-nots." Daniel P. Moynihan's widely discussed study, *The Negro Family: A Case for National Action* (the "Moynihan Report") had stated that a "stable middle class group" in the "Negro community" is "steadily growing stronger and more successful." Statistics compiled both before and since the *Kerner Report* have borne this out. In the decade between 1960 and 1970, the number of Negro families with incomes between $5,000 and $7,000 had nearly doubled; the number of Negro families with incomes between $7,000 and $10,-000 had tripled; the number with incomes between $10,000 and $15,000 had more than tripled—while the number of Negro families with incomes below the $3,000 "poverty line" had decreased by about half. The number of Negro families with incomes of $15,000 or over had multiplied by *twenty*; there were more Negro families with incomes over $7,000 than families with incomes below $5,000 and more with incomes of $10,000 or over than families below the $3,000 "poverty line." (In 1960 there had been nearly *nine times* as many Negro families with incomes below $3,000 as families with incomes of $10,000 or more).[4]

Presumably the families included among Moynihan's steadily growing, "stable middle class group" of Negro families, and those lumped together by the Kerner Commission as Negro "haves" were subject to the same environmental deprivations and the same racial discrimination which, according to the Kerner dogmas, make "escape from poverty" impossible. But asking *why* the "Negro middle class" is "steadily increasing" would be irrelevant—

even detrimental—to the Commission's purpose: "proving" that the "deprived" cannot help themselves and should not be asked to do so. Moynihan—a witness before the Kerner Commission, and now a member of the Nixon Administration—evidently considered such a question irrelevant to *his* "case for national action" also. A single sentence was all the "middle class" got.

To some extent, however, what the Kerner Commission calls a "dead end lack of opportunity" *does* exist in today's American economy. The pertinent question is "*Why?*" The Commission asks the question, in phrasing more in keeping with its preconceived reply. "Why," the Commission asks, "has the Negro been unable to escape from poverty and the ghetto like the European immigrants?" Having conveniently ignored the achievements of the Negro "haves," the Commission based its "why" on the premise that Negroes, *qua Negroes*, have been unable to escape from the "ghetto." Having asked its "why," the Commission devotes an entire chapter—"Comparing the Immigrant and Negro Experience"—to providing an anti-answer. But in the course of its anti-explanation the Commission inadvertently furnishes a number of clues to the cause of such "dead ends" as do exist.

"The immigrant who labored long hours at hard and often menial work had the hope of a better future," says the Commission,

> if not for himself, then for his children. This was the promise of the "American dream"—the society offered to all a future that was open-ended; with hard work and perseverance, a man and his family could in time achieve not only material wellbeing but "position" and status.
>
> For the Negro family in the urban ghetto, there is a different vision—the future seems to lead only to a dead end. (p. 145)

But why the "difference" in the vision? The immigrants, too, acknowledges the *Report*, "were immersed in poverty, they, too lived in slums, and these neighborhoods exhibited fearfully high rates of alcoholism, desertion, illegitimacy, and other pathologies associated with poverty."

In common with the present-day "social-ills" school represented by Dr. Clark, the Commission nimbly bridges the conceptual gap between pathologies *associated with* and pathologies *caused by* poverty, consistently referring to the former as though they were the latter. The "social-ill" credo that alcoholism, marital discord, illegitimacy, and dirt are the products of poverty is a sacred, not-to-be-questioned cliché. Yet it is far more likely that the irrationality and short-term thinking which incline men to drink themselves into stupor, to shirk responsibility for the consequences of their actions (including children), and to make unwise or downright self-destructive choices in romantic partners, likewise cause them to perform poorly at school and at work. The result, naturally enough, will be poverty—which may compound their other problems. Poverty is not the *cause* of their misery; rather, it is one of a number of tragic effects of faulty thinking.

The immigrants suffered the same "deprivation" as today's urban Negroes; conditions in the teeming immigrant slums were actually worse than those in the "ghettos" of today. Why did the pathologies "caused" by their social environment fail to immure the immigrants hopelessly and perpetually in the "culture of poverty"? "The changing nature of the American economy," says the Commission,

> is one major reason. When the European immigrants were arriving in large numbers, America was becoming an urban-industrial society. To build its major cities and industries, America needed great pools of unskilled labor. The immigrants provided the labor, gained an economic foothold, and thereby enabled their children and grandchildren to move up to skilled, white-collar and professional employment.
>
> Since World War II especially, America's urban-industrial society has matured; unskilled labor is far less essential than before, and blue-collar jobs of all kinds are decreasing in number and importance as a source of new employment. The Negroes who migrated to the great urban centers lacked the skills essential to the new economy, and the schools of the ghetto have been unable to ... qualify them for decent jobs. The Negro migrant, unlike the immigrant, found little opportunity in the city; he had arrived too late, and the unskilled labor he had to offer was no longer needed. (p. 143)

The myth of the "maturing" economy is a standard statist shibboleth. What makes an economy "mature"? Are there no cities, no highways, no industrial plants left to be built? Is there no work, anywhere, to be done by unskilled labor? Are there no products left to be invented; no human desires to be met by new production? If so, how come we're talking about poverty?

As for the "Negro migrant" thesis: one of the Commission's apparently sacrosanct articles of faith is that the large influx of southern Negroes into northern urban centers is a cause of "disorders." However, according to the Commission's own studies, most self-admitted rioters were not recent émigrés desperate with disillusionment: most were born in the region where they rioted. *Non*-rioters, on the other hand, were more often Negroes from the South. Besides, if Negroes who migrated to the cities lacked essential skills, the immigrants who crammed the steerage compartments of ships bound for America at the turn of the century lacked industrial skills also. And *they* had the added impediment of a language barrier to overcome. The schools of the immigrant era no more "provided education in job skills" than do the "ghetto schools" of today, and the education of many immigrant children was of necessity short-lived, as the biographies of Edward Rickenbacker, Moss Hart, David Sarnoff and numerous others illustrate.

The immigrants, asserts the Commission, came to America from much poorer societies, with a low standard of living, and they came at a time when job aspirations were low:

> When most jobs in the American economy were unskilled, they sensed little deprivation in being forced [*sic*] to take the dirty and poorly paid jobs. Moreover, their families were large, and many breadwinners, some of whom never married, contributed to the total family income. As a result, family units managed to live even from the lowest paid jobs and still put money aside for savings or investment, for example, to purchase a house or tenement or to open a store or factory. Since the immigrants spoke little English and had their own ethnic culture, they needed stores to supply them with ethnic foods and other services. . .
> Although Negro men worked as hard as the immigrants to support their families, their rewards were less. The jobs did not pay enough to enable them to support their families, for prices and living standards had risen since the immigrants had come, and the

entrepreneurial opportunities that had allowed some immigrants to become independent, even rich, had vanished. Above all, Negroes suffered from segregation, which denied them access to the good jobs and the right unions. . . .

Generally relegated to jobs that others would not take, they were paid too little to be able to put money in savings for new enterprises. In addition, Negroes lacked the extended family characteristic of certain European groups; each household usually had only one or two breadwinners. (pp. 144-45)

What emerges from this lugubrious lament for lost opportunities? A muddle of contradictions; a distinction without a difference; and one *genuine* difference—the crucial one—left unremarked.

Negroes have been "relegated to jobs that others would not take"; the immigrants were "forced to take the dirty and poorly paid jobs." Negroes suffer from racial discrimination; the immigrants (although the Commission appears oblivious to the fact) were called "Hunkies," or "Wops" or "Kikes" or "Shanty Irish"; subjected to verbal abuse and sometimes to physical violence; and confronted with signs saying "No Jews Allowed" and "No Irish Need Apply." The immigrants came from "much poorer societies"; Negro migrants to the cities came from the rural South, whose "unspeakable" living conditions the Commission spends several pages deploring. If living standards had risen, it was because productivity had risen due to mechanization: mass production had placed former luxuries within the reach of all. Indeed, the immigrants of the nineties might have been a bit bewildered to see Negroes "unable to support their families" and "crushed by the burden of poverty" being photographed in "substandard" hovels equipped with refrigerators, gas ranges, and bathtubs. They might wish they had been as "poor" as the families below the $3,000 poverty line: 73 percent of whom own washing machines, 65 percent of whose homes have hot running water; 46 percent of whom own automobiles; 79 percent of whom own television sets[5] —"the universal appliance in the ghetto" according to Kerner and Company, who quote a survey showing that 95 percent of the lowest-income residents of New York's "ghetto" had television.

Since the Commission believes that entrepreneurial opportunities have vanished, it seems pointless (not to say inconsistent) for the Commission to bemoan the Negro urban immigrant's "inability" to save for new enterprises. But as for the alleged lack of entrepreneurial opportunities afforded by a yearning for "ethnic foods" (a term which one *hopes* the Commission uses to denote foods indigenous to a particular region, not foods innately craved by members of given ethnic groups)—stores selling native Southern foods, lately called "soul food," abound in areas such as Harlem.

"In a casual walk through Harlem," writes Michael Harrington, best-selling crusader grown affluent through his concern for the poor, "you will see advertised some of these things: chitterlings, ham knuckles, hog maw, pig's feet, pig's tail, pig's ear; and fish is everywhere. This food—and some of it can be fairly costly—is the diet of the poor South, brought North by the migrations."[6]

Tiny *bodegas* selling delicacies popular in Puerto Rico have sprung up all over Spanish Harlem. "Almost as soon as the Puerto Ricans arrive," says Harrington, "Spanish-speaking shops dot the avenue. And this was true even before the big migration of Puerto Ricans in the post-war period." The Puerto Ricans coming to America were less than rich; they were, as a matter of fact, desperately poor. Unable to speak English, as most of them were; subjected to racist discrimination as vicious as that displayed against Negroes; the Puerto Rican immigrants—some of them, at least—managed to start tiny enterprises: most of the Puerto Rican "ethnic food" shops described by Harrington had Puerto Rican proprietors. If most "Negro ethnic food" shops had white proprietors, it was not because entrepreneurial opportunities in this area had vanished—but because few Negro individuals chose to cater to this particular demand.

As for the "extended family"—Negroes have, on the average, chosen to have larger families than have whites. If the immigrant families required the contributions of several breadwinners, and got it, but Negro families of today cannot—*why?* The teenage children of immigrant families went to work, if necessary; got their education when and where they could, and their job training on the job. If the unskilled immigrant laborer wished to learn a trade, he did not require "access to the right unions" to learn or practice it; unions did not then have a government-enforced stranglehold on skilled jobs. If the immigrant wanted to start a small business, he did not first have to breach the red-tape barricades—most formidable in the cities—and beggar himself to purchase a license before he could sell candy, cut hair, or peddle bananas. If he saved his money to buy a horse and a hackney (or, later, a car), he did not also have to save some $30,000 to acquire someone else's hack license. He must, today, in New York City, where the number of licenses issued is limited *by government* (at the 1937 level) and any suggestion that the number be increased is met with agonized yowls of protest from those who hold a monopoly which only government can guarantee them.

Here, then, we have come to the crux of any difference between "the Negro and the immigrant experience"—between the late nineteenth and early twentieth centuries and today. The economy which enabled the immigrants to escape from poverty was *a relatively free economy*—and *therefore* a growing economy. The economy of today is *a largely controlled economy*, an increasingly statist economy—and *therefore* an increasingly stagnant economy.

One need trace only a few of the effects of interventionist measures to comprehend how the statism and the stagnation are interrelated; to perceive that the interventionist panaceas of the Kerner Commission cannot remedy—indeed, must aggravate—the very economic maladies they were concocted to cure.

Minimum Wages and Make-Work

The typical rioter, according to the *Report*, was Negro, aged 15 to 24, poorly educated, unskilled, un- or "under"-employed, and so desperately despairing at his lack of useful occupation that he was impelled to run rampant, loot liquor stores, hurl bricks at policemen, and burn down buildings by the block. Ten-odd years of incarceration in the "free public school system" had left him singularly unprepared to seek employment. In spite (or, perhaps, because?) of the ministrations of a "progressive," state-controlled educational system, he had failed to "be motivated" in the direction of any salable pursuit. He preferred, it seemed, to stand on the corner and watch the girls go by, or to lounge in his rat-infested home, envying the "affluence" taunting him on the TV, waiting for the government to solve his inactivity problem. (For some, it does —sometimes forever—by dragooning them into the Army.)

In reality, neither unemployment, nor "under"-employment, nor lack of job skills causes rational, productive men to riot. It is illuminating, however, to scrutinize the means by which the Kerner Commission intends to aid the stalwart young worthies, criminalized by "the system," whose plight the *Report* so lachrymosely strives to depict.

Make-Work ...

To remedy unemployment, especially among "ghetto youth," the Kerner Commission proposes an array of government make-work schemes, with the cautionary proviso that these must not jeopardize any existing jobs, and must provide a "meaningful work experience" fraught with "dignity." The latter is highly unlikely. (See Chapters VI and VII.) The former is a rank absurdity.

Government is by nature non-productive; governmentally "created" jobs produce no wealth. Government's only source of income is the production of private citizens—*earnings*—extorted via taxation or inflation of the currency, or both. Monies which are grabbed by Washington cannot be paid as wages in Waukegan. Nor can those whose money is confiscated through taxation invest in the new enterprises, the expansion of existing enterprises, the development of new products and production methods which are the only possible sources of *real* new jobs.

Neither is the proposition a simple one of *quid pro quo*—one private job lost; one government job gained. Monies sucked into the government maw seem to be mysteriously diminished by the time they trickle back to the alleged beneficiaries. The "porous and absorbent hands" of the state, said Bastiat, always retain a part, and sometimes the whole, of what they touch.[7] The scandalous goings-on in the government's Job Corps, for example, amply bear out this truth. The bureaucrats outnumber the trainees; the costs per trainee actually placed in a job reach fabulous sums; and the only "upgrading" attained is attained by slews of OEO officials

who never had it so good. It's "the government's" money, after all
—and no one worries much about how much of it is spent.

In her exhaustive study of the Job Corps and similar programs,
Poverty Is Where the Money Is, Shirley Scheibla of *Barron's*
quotes a House Education and Labor Committee Report as follows:

> The cost of this single anti-poverty program is appalling. . . . The
> combination of high property rentals, excessive salaries and under-
> estimated site rehabilitation costs has resulted in a cost per enrollee
> that has been variously estimated as $9,210 to $13,000 per year. . . .
> When costs are evaluated on the basis of cost per graduate the
> results are even more astounding.

Mrs. Scheibla continues:

> Even figured for enrollees, costs exceeded $13,000 at some cen-
> ters. According to Senator Strom Thurmond, they came to $22,000
> at Camp Atterbury, and Representatives Fino and Goodell found
> the costs per graduate came to $39,205 at St. Petersburg, Florida.
>
> A Congressional investigation in late 1965 showed that Atter-
> bury had 500 staff members and only 300 corpsmen. . . . The enrol-
> lees at Camp Breckenridge outnumbered the staff by only a narrow
> margin of 358 to 350.
>
> A study by the House Republican Poverty Subcommittee re-
> vealed that over one-third of the staff at five urban Job Corps
> centers received salary increases of over 20% when they went to
> work for the Job Corps.[8]

Naturally, some recently elevated "anti-poverty" officials found
their new salaries, also, inadequate to their "needs." Job Corps and
Youth Corps scandals were soon so common that they were relegated to the back pages as being no longer "news." One Harlem
Youth Corps official was arrested and indicted for issuing rigged-
computer checks—a cool half-million dollars' worth—to "fictitious enrollees at nonexistent work sites" and cashing them
himself.[9] It takes more than a $10,000-a-year salary to keep one-
self in Fifth Avenue duplexes and new Cadillac Eldorados. Investigators estimated that $2.7 million or more was "liberated" from
New York's Neighborhood Youth Corps alone by such enterpris-

ing employees. Officials of the program, however, hastened to calm indignant taxpayers with the assurance that the amount stolen was "much lower." The fictitious enrollees and nonexistent job sites no doubt enhanced the program's glowing "employment" statistics no end; a number of the lately "deprived" learned computer-programming of a sort and acquired, in the process, some instant—if ephemeral—"dignity." And that's what the program is for.

... and Minimum Wages

All government interventions in the economy interact in such complex ways that it becomes exceedingly difficult to trace the course of their ill effects. Statistics, in themselves, are not necessarily sufficient evidence to prove a cause-and-effect relationship. But the parallel between the increases in statutory minimum wage rates and increases in unemployment provides some illuminating empirical data to substantiate the consequences of interventionism which classical economics predicted, and logic can infer.

The Kerner Commission gives much emphasis to the statistics for unemployment rates among Negroes—and Negro teenagers in particular. The unemployment rate for the latter, the Commission frequently reiterates, is two-and-one-half times that of the equivalent age group of whites. The Kerner Commission does *not* mention that the unemployment rate for Negro teenagers (as for all teenagers together) has risen—astronomically in the case of Negroes—over precisely the period in which legislated minimum wage rates have been raised and raised again.

Professor Yale Brozen, of the University of Chicago, has done an extensive study of the relationship between minimum wage increases and unemployment levels. "Although the various upward moves in the statutory minimum have increased the incomes of some people (temporarily . . .), they have decreased the incomes of a great many others by causing them to lose their jobs," he writes. Brozen continues:

> When the minimum was increased in 1956, for example, unemployment among teenagers and women over 45 rose despite the fact that total unemployment was falling. Usually, when total unem-

ployment falls, unemployment in these two groups falls twice as rapidly. However, this usual relationship was reversed by the rise in the minimum wage from 75¢ to $1.00 an hour in 1956. . . .

The incidence of unemployment caused by increases in the statutory minimum wage is falling most heavily on one group—Negro teenagers. Before the Fair Labor Standards Act [a prime example of the "name game"—see Chapter VII] raised the minimum wage to $1.00 in 1956, non-white and white male teenage unemployment both were approximately the same, oscillating between 8 and 14 percent of those seeking jobs, depending on the state of business. In 1956, when the $1.00 minimum wage went into effect, non-white male teenage unemployment surged to levels 50 percent greater than white. . . . White male teenage unemployment has stuck at high levels since 1956, approximating or exceeding 14 percent . . . in most years. *That is a figure in excess of the maximum unemployment among white male teenagers in any year before 1956.* Negro male teenage unemployment, however, has gone to even higher levels than white . . . since 1956, exceeding 21 percent . . . in every year in the last decade.[10] (my emphasis)

In 1965, wider application of the $1.25 minimum wage was imposed; non-white male teenage unemployment promptly rose to double that for whites. In February, 1967, the minimum wage was raised to $1.40; non-white male teenage unemployment reached levels of two-and-one-half times that of whites. (The *white* levels were, as Professor Brozen points out, rising, too.) In 1968 the minimum wage *and* Negro teenage unemployment jumped again. Moreover, the *rate* of increase in unemployment has been greater than the rate of increase in the minimum wage rates. Between 1951 and 1968 the minimum wage approximately doubled—after allowance for inflation, the rate has less than doubled. During the same period, the unemployment rate for Negro teenagers almost *tripled.*

A 1964 study by David E. Kaun, of Stanford University, of 14 low-wage industries, concluded that increases in the minimum wage had "adversely affected employment opportunities for certain classes of labor, namely, Negroes, females, younger workers, and workers living in rural farm areas."[11]

According to a Cornell University Study, imposition of a $1.00 minimum wage rate on New York retail stores resulted in lower profits to stores. Accordingly, stores reduced their hours for part-time help; laid off "inefficient" workers (defined by the study as elderly, handicapped, and part-time help); reduced store hours; and instituted "more careful recruitment of employees," which the study explains meant excluding "the elderly, Negroes, and other 'less acceptable' employees."[12]

The sequence is exactly what any old-fashioned economist—or logician—could have predicted. When wage rates are pushed arbitrarily above economic levels (pushed above levels at which employers can pay them and still make a profit, which they must, in order to survive and provide *any* employment to anyone) some workers may gain raises in the short run—at the expense of other workers, who will simply be out of a job. Were the wage rates imposed by minimum wage legislation economic, the legislation would be a dead letter. No one asks for minimum wage legislation except with the intention of imposing wages *above* the economic level.

Those who suffer most from uneconomic legislated increases in wage rates are precisely those whom the Kerner Commission's recommendations are supposed to help: the unskilled, marginally productive workers—and those who are victims of race prejudice. It is particularly pertinent in relation to the *Kerner Report*, which so emphatically stresses race prejudice as a factor in un- or "under"-employment, that —despite the known existence of prejudice against Negroes—the differences between white and Negro teenage unemployment were negligible or nonexistent during periods when the minimum wages imposed by law were low enough so that teenagers (the unskilled, inexperienced young) could be profitably employed and were therefore in demand as workers. As increases in the statutory minimum wage made unskilled, inexperienced help less and less profitable—and, finally, a losing proposition—employers who happened to be prejudiced against Negroes were better able to indulge their irrational whims when hiring help: the uneconomic wage rates had flooded the job market with unemployed teenagers, black and white.

Inevitably, increased competition for the few remaining jobs not subject to the minimum wage (or, at least, not subject to strict enforcement of it) tends to depress wages in those jobs. Were the minimum wage laws actually uniformly and universally enforced and applied, teenage unemployment—like the unemployment of other unskilled, marginally productive, or inexperienced workers —would zoom to even greater heights. "If the law covered everyone in the economy," writes research chemist James Blair, "those who were 'saved from the sweatshops' " by the law "would have nowhere to go to find jobs. It is all very well for the 'liberal' theorist to claim that a man is better off unemployed than working in a 'sweatshop,' but shouldn't the decision rest with the man in question?"[13] Blair continues:

> One additional observation on this point: often a low-paying job gives a person the chance to learn the business or demonstrate his ability, and can lead to a higher-paying position. Consider the number of company presidents and high officials who started their careers in low-paying jobs, and imagine where they might be today if they had been "protected" against being offered their first job by a minimum wage law.[14]

The Kerner Commission, which bewails the "death" of the "American Dream," the unemployment rate for Negro teenagers, and the "poverty" of workers in marginal industries, *proposes increases in—and expanded coverage by—the Federal Minimum Wage.*

GOVERNMENT BULLDOZERS AND BUREAUCRATIC BUILDING CODES

Third on the priority list of "grievances" to be alleviated with the "nation's" resources is that of "substandard, inadequate" housing, in which, the *Report* claims, nearly six million families live.

> Negro housing in large cities is significantly better than that in most rural areas—especially in the South. Good quality housing has become available to Negro city dwellers at an increasing rate since the mid-1950's when the post-war housing shortage ended in most metropolitan areas.
> Nevertheless, in the Negro ghetto, grossly inadequate housing continues to be a critical problem. (p. 257)

What constitutes "inadequate" or "substandard" housing depends, of course, upon one's standards. The State of New Jersey, for example, designated *one fifth* of the housing units in the State (approximately 421,000) as "substandard" and an additional tenth (about 242,000) as "blighted" in a report issued in September, 1968. The definition of "substandard" is not included in the press release announcing the New Jersey report and its recommendations. The Kerner Commission, however, *did* condescend (in a footnote) to define "substandard" to this extent:

> The Department of Housing and Urban Development classifies substandard housing as that housing reported by the U. S. Census Bureau as (1) sound but lacking full plumbing, (2) deteriorating and lacking full plumbing, or (3) dilapidated. (p. 257, footnote)

The Kerner Commission does not elucidate. But "full plumbing" means a private toilet and bath and inside running water. "Deteriorating" dwelling units are those which exhibit any four of the following: slightly cracked masonry or chimneys, peeling paint, loose or missing shingles, broken gutters, crooked or sagging porch railings, or slight wear of doorsills or window frames.

The New Jersey report defines "blighted" housing units as those which are "individually sound but threatened with blight by their location in neighborhoods which are *environmentally* substandard" (my italics). The plot thickens! "Blighted" housing includes that "surrounded by dumps, noisy industry, or major highways; those without adequate municipal services, and housing built on overcrowded sites." Housing built on "overcrowded" sites means housing which, by some planner's arbitrary estimate, is located in an area of too high "densities"—too many dwelling units per net residential acre (land left after subtracting streets). According to conventional planning dogmas, Philadelphia's fashionable Rittenhouse Square, San Francisco's Nob Hill, and New York's presently fashionable Greenwich Village and Yorkville sections have densities which are "too high"; Brooklyn's Bedford-Stuyvesant "ghetto" and much of Harlem have lower densities than these.[15]

"Overcrowded" dwelling units, as opposed to "overcrowded" sites are, according to standard planning criteria, dwelling units lived in by 1.01 or more persons per room. By this yardstick, a young couple and infant living in a two-room apartment would be "overcrowded" and would narrowly escape being "seriously over-crowded": 1.51 persons per room.

By mixing and matching the appropriate combinations of "standards," and compounding the confusion with such terms as "environmentally substandard" and "blighted," it is, of course, possible to manufacture "inadequate" housing to order. More succinctly described, "inadequate housing" is housing that someone feels is not what he ought to be living in, even though he can afford nothing better.

Even on the Kerner Commission terms, however, the number of substandard housing units in the United States has been shrinking rapidly. Between 1950 and 1960, occupied *standard* dwelling units *increased* from 27.7 million to 44.2 million. During the same period, the number of occupied "deteriorating" units *decreased* from 11.3 million to 6.4 million. The number of *occupied* "dilapidated" dwelling units *decreased* from 3.9 million to 2.4 million. The percentage of substandard dwelling units occupied by non-whites declined from 72 percent to 44 percent. *And virtually all the gains were effected by private building and rehabilitation:* the amount of "public" housing built over the period was insignificant.[16]

Private building and rehabilitation, however, is not exactly what the Kerner Commission recommends. The Commission proposes to eliminate the "substandard" dwelling units which blight the landscape and reduce the "deprived" to lives of crime by: bigger and better urban renewal, stringent enforcement of housing codes, and a uniform national building code cooked up by HUD.

Government Bulldozers . . .

The study hatched in September, 1968, by New Jersey's "Human Resources [!!] Planning Project" should be just to the Commission's taste. Typically, the study calls for a massive demolition program to reduce 200,000 units to rubble. Simultaneously, the report called for approval of a bond issue (since passed) for $12.5 million dollars of so-called "seed money" intended to "draw out" private investment of $90 million. "Seed money" plus the shy "private investment" to be drawn out of hiding total 102.5 million dollars which, according to the plan, will provide housing for *five thousand* families. At $25,000 a house, the drawing-board dwelling units doubtless will be "adequate"—at least for a time. Where the remaining 195,000 families to be evicted from the 200,000 units earmarked for demolition are to live is not stated.[17] As for that "seed money": Dr. Martin Anderson's comprehensive study of the urban renewal program[18] indicates that an optimistic estimate of net private funds drawn by such projects is 50 cents for every government dollar spent.

In the decade between 1950 and 1960, the urban renewal program was responsible for destroying 126,000 dwelling units. It built approximately 28,000. By 1956, *nearly one million people* had been "relocated" by the program; i.e., forced to leave their homes. Fifty thousand places of business had been destroyed— more than twelve thousand of these never reopened anywhere. Most of the homes destroyed, of course, were those of the "disadvantaged"—it was "blighted" areas which the federal bulldozers "improved." Most of the businesses destroyed were small ones; perhaps this is what the Kerner Commission had in mind when it mourned that "entrepreneurial opportunities are vanishing" in the twentieth century.

Four billion dollars in tax monies were spent over a decade (a cost of over $100,000 per dwelling unit actually erected). Of the dwelling units which *were* constructed, most were high-rise, high-rent apartments renting (in 1962) at a median of $195, a low of $100, and a high of $350 a month. The nearly nine hundred thousand involuntary relocatees shoved summarily out of their "blighted" low-rent homes would understandably have found it difficult to squeeze into the three thousand low-rent dwelling units constructed under the program. Three hundred persons per dwelling unit is overcrowding indeed. The remaining "blighted" low-rent housing available to the "disadvantaged" naturally becomes more crowded and more costly as supply shrinks and demand increases.

Nor were the tax billions spent the only cost of urban renewal projects. Land for these projects is acquired through eminent domain; that is, by government seizure for "the public good." Once bulldozed clear, streeted, streetlighted, sewage-disposaled, and sometimes libraried, parked, and schooled—all at taxpayers' expense—the land is sold, usually at a considerable loss, to *private* developers. Professor Anderson points out the basic issue:

> There are many important issues in the urban renewal question, but there is one which is both the most important and the easiest to understand. The local government must have the power to take by force the private property of one man—his home, his land, his business—with the intent of turning it over to some other man for his private use and gain. It is on the acceptance or rejection of this principle that the fate of urban renewal rests, for without the power of eminent domain local governments could not force people to surrender their homes, their land, and their businesses.[19]

The Constitution of the United States decrees that private property shall not be taken for public use "without just compensation." How "just" is the compensation received by businessmen ruined by urban renewal? A report made by management expert Anthony J. Panuch to the City of New York gives some inkling:

> The direct consequence of the exercise of the power of eminent domain on the commercial tenant is drastic and often ruinous. When the government condemns property it is required to pay only for what it *acquires* for itself and not for what it *takes* from the owner.
> The government is *not* in condemnation acquiring a business, but only the premises. It need only pay for the premises. The proprietor gets nothing for the loss of his business or goodwill, nor even for his unexpired lease. . . .
> Although his entire property and his full investment is taken from him, he receives substantially nothing.
> [For example] a druggist purchased a drug store for more than $40,000. A few years later, the building in which his store was located was taken in condemnation. The total sum which he eventually received was an award of $3,000 for fixtures and that sum had to be paid over to the chattel mortgagee. Thus his total investment was completely wiped out. (Italics in original)

Commenting on the Panuch Report, planner Jane Jacobs writes, "This is one reason these schemes are fought so desperately by site businessmen. They are subsidizing these schemes, not with a fraction of their tax monies, but *with their livelihoods, with their chil-*

dren's college money, with years of their past put into hopes for the future—with nearly everything they have."[20](Italics hers)

Yet Mrs. Jacobs, whose now-classic book on planning, *The Death and Life of Great American Cities*, has devastatingly demolished conventional planning myths and made many of her fellow "liberals" hate her, remains a "liberal"; never questioning the right of governments to "plan" where and how people should live even as she incisively deplores the results. Thus she makes the incredible error of referring to the tax funds used for urban renewal as "voluntary subsidy" while calling the losses of ruined site businessmen "involuntary subsidy."

Redevelopment officials, Mrs. Jacobs writes, "blanch when it is suggested" that the *full* expense of reimbursing site businessmen be borne by "the public" for whose "good" they have been uprooted and expropriated. Doing this would make the projects so overtly expensive that no one would stand for the cost. So much for morality.

As for accomplishment:

> There is a wistful myth [writes Mrs. Jacobs] that if only we had enough money to spend—the figure is usually put at a hundred billion dollars—we could wipe out all our slums in ten years, reverse decay in the great, dull, gray belts that were yesterday's and day-before-yesterday's suburbs, anchor the wandering middle class and its wandering tax money, and perhaps even solve the traffic problem.
>
> But look what we have built with the first several billions: Low-income projects that become worse centers of delinquency, vandalism, and general social hopelessness than the slums they were supposed to replace. . . . Cultural centers that are unable to support a good bookstore. Civic centers that are avoided by everyone but bums, who have fewer choices of loitering place than others. . . . Promenades that go from no place to nowhere and have no promenaders. . . .
>
> Under the surface, these accomplishments prove even poorer than their poor pretenses. They seldom aid the city areas around them, as in theory they are supposed to. These amputated areas typically develop galloping gangrene. To house people in this planned fashion, price tags are fastened on the population, and each sorted-out chunk of price-tagged populace lives in growing suspi-

cion and tension against the surrounding city. When two or more such hostile islands are juxtaposed the result is called a "balanced neighborhood." ...

That such wonders may be accomplished, people who get marked with the planners' hex signs are pushed about, expropriated, and uprooted much as if they were subjects of a conquering power. Thousands upon thousands of small businesses are destroyed, and their proprietors ruined, with hardly a gesture at compensation. Whole communities are torn apart and sown to the winds, with a reaping of cynicism, resentment and despair that must be heard and seen to be believed. A group of clergymen in Chicago, appalled at the fruits of planned city rebuilding there, asked,

"Could Job have been thinking of Chicago when he wrote:
'Here are men that alter their neighbor's landmark . . .
shoulder the poor aside, conspire to oppress the friendless.
'Reap they the field that is none of theirs, strip they the vineyard wrongfully seized from its owner. . . .
'A cry goes up from the city streets, where wounded men lie growning. . . .' "[21]

In Detroit 8,000 low-income housing units were demolished for urban renewal in the seven years prior to the riots of 1967; over a longer period, only 758 public housing units had been built. In the "model" urban renewal city of New Haven, 6,500 homes fell before the federal bulldozer; about 951 were built. The Douglas Commission Report on HUD (which HUD tried desperately to suppress) revealed that in New Haven, which spent $800 per capita for its "model" renewal program, "community hostility" to the renewal program ran so high that police were stationed inside and outside renewal hearings as a precautionary measure.[22] The riots in Newark, New Jersey—an extremely "blighted" city in which acre upon acre has been cleared for "renewal," and left clear of anything but rubble for years on end while the "deprived" crammed into the houses which were left—erupted shortly after residents learned that a new renewal project, which would displace more than 22,000 persons with a clean, pristine medical school, was to go through despite their protests. Twelve thousand people had been uprooted by previous projects. (The Kerner Commission attributes resentment of the medical school project to a feeling that it would "dilute Negro representation on City Council"!)

The net result of all this suffering has been *less* low-income housing than before. Does anyone profit? Yes, indeedy. But not the "disadvantaged." The spoils accrue to the bureaucrats, the social workers, the city planners, and the mixed-economy-type businessmen, who draw huge salaries from their "non-profit" or "limited-profit" housing corporations. And, of course, the spoils accrue to slum landlords. Not only can they raise rentals when the renewal projects shoe-horn the "relocated" poor more tightly into the remaining dwellings. Renewal projects *in themselves* benefit the exploitative "wheeler-dealer" landlords just as surely as the tax laws penalize the landlord who improves his properties.

As to the latter, the *Kerner Report* itself observes that property taxes in Newark, for example, "had increased, perhaps, to the point of diminishing returns." Taxable property kept decreasing "as land, cleared for urban renewal, lay fallow year after year." By the fall of 1967, taxes reached $661.70 on a $10,000 house and "as a result, people were refusing to either own or renovate property in the city." In New York City, by early 1969, the city was pushing the panic button as increasing numbers of property owners abandoned properties rather than pay the taxes on them.[23]

As to the former, Jane Jacobs writes:

> . . . slum landlords, unlike the drugstore proprietor of the Panuch report, benefit handsomely from blanket use of the powers of eminent domain. When a building is bought under the powers of eminent domain, three factors are customarily taken into account in setting the award (the sale price). These are the assessed value of the property, the replacement value of the building, and the current earning power of the *building* (as distinguished from the earning power of a business which may be conducted within it). The more exploited the building, the higher its earning power, and the more the owner is given. So profitable are such condemnation sales for slum landlords that some of them make a business of buying up buildings in areas already condemned, overcrowding them, and raising rents, less for the profits to be made in the interim than for the profits to be made by the buildings' sale to the public.[24]

"We recognize," states the Kerner Commission, "that in many cities [urban renewal] has demolished more housing than it has erected, and that it has often caused dislocation among disadvantaged groups. *Nevertheless, we believe that a greatly expanded, though reoriented, urban renewal program is necessary to the health of our cities."* (p. 262—my italics)

"Expansion" is the key word. "Reorientation" is the sop. No amount of "reorientation" can make the urban renewal program morally defensible. The Kerner Commission's interpretation of "reorientation" is to have HUD "promulgate policies" giving "top priority" to projects that "directly assist low-income households in obtaining adequate housing," and "low priority" to "projects aimed primarily at bolstering the economic strength of downtown areas, or at creating housing for upper-income groups." On the prospects of modifying urban renewal, Martin Anderson comments that if modifications of the foregoing sort were made, "project activity would slow down considerably. This illustrates what happens when one attempts to modify an inherently bad program. It becomes obvious that the program cannot work without its bad aspects," including the eminent domain expropriations, "and any attempt to lessen the costs associated with the program does nothing more than slow down the program."[25]

But when faced with the blatant failure of one of his schemes, a "liberal" doesn't think—he twitches. And the twitch always triggers protestations that the program did fail, all right, by golly. BUT, if only more money can be milked out of the taxpayers and poured down the same drain, the failure will magically be transmuted into success. This modernized version of the medieval belief in the philosopher's stone might be touchingly naive, were it not so dangerous. The medieval alchemists did not have powers of confiscation and eminent domain to assist them in their attempts to turn dross into gold.

. . . and Bureaucratic Building Codes

"A high proportion of residential and other structures" in disadvantaged neighborhoods contain, according to Kerner, "numerous violations of building and housing codes. Refusal to remedy these violations is a criminal offense . . . [yet] in most cities, few building code violations in these areas are ever corrected." (p. 259) Were the "violations" corrected, the "disadvantaged" might not merely be poorly housed, they might be homeless. Explained architect William Altenburg in an interview on rent controls and building codes:

> The distinguishing characteristic of a slum is that it is filthy. Neatness, or its lack, is the differential that makes one house a slum unit and its counterpart in another neighborhood "a nice place to live." Neatness is an attribute of effort, not income or education. If slums were neat and clean but still in poor repair, it would be the slumlords' fault in a free society. But the cost of repairing and maintaining a building inhabited by systematic vandals at a rent they can afford is impossible. Therefore, the landlord collects what little rent he can squeeze from the tenants (between visits by vast hordes of social workers organizing "rent strikes" and developing "revolutionary consciousness") and lets the building rot.
>
> Slums are composed (usually) of older buildings that are not modern in many aspects of their plumbing, wiring, heating, and bathrooms. When a city adopts a code that regulates any aspect of construction, it also outlaws the "old way." However, a "grandfather clause" permits existing buildings to continue in violation as long as they stay the same. As soon as they are altered in any substantial way a permit must be obtained, and it will not be granted unless *all* code violations are corrected. The landlord who can afford to fix only the heating soon discovers he must also redo the wiring, plumbing, fire exits, etc.—all or nothing. The heating, as you might guess, remains in disrepair.[26]

Rent controls, which discourage new construction and frequently make it unprofitable even to extract the last dregs in rentals while letting buildings rot, operate to *decrease* the housing supply. In the classic manner of interventionist evils, codes and controls interact and compound one another's damage.

A tale of the aegis of New York Mayor (and Kerner Commission Vice Chairman) John Lindsay will illustrate how building codes benefit the "disadvantaged." In the fall of 1968, His Honor, afire with good intentions no doubt kindled anew by his stint on the Kerner Commission, announced that the city would remorselessly enforce a 1967 law that single-room landlords provide one bathroom per six tenants. Building owners who did not throw in the towel completely, served eviction notices to their roomers in order to renovate the buildings and keep themselves out of court. As the January 1, 1969, deadline neared, evictions intensified. "It soon became clear," stated *The New York Times*, "that tenants had almost no other place to go, except to other buildings that would soon be inspected and found in violation." Between the evictees from buildings abandoned and under renovation and those unable to pay the higher rents the improvements necessitated, it appeared that some 40,000 tenants (mostly poor, widowed, or single) would be benefited right onto a park bench.

Mayor Lindsay, the "liberal" White Knight, mounted his charger and rode into battle. "Mayor Signs Bill to Help Roomers," was the headline in the *Times*. And "help" the roomers the Mayor did—by signing a bill postponing enforcement of the bill he had "helped" them with before. Oh, yes—the Mayor also created a "special division" of the Housing and Development Administration to "study" the problems of single-room renters, and appointed a social worker to head the new division at a salary of $20,000 a year.

In New York City alone, the Kerner Commission notes, *"rigorous code enforcement has already caused owners to board up and abandon over 2,500 buildings rather than incur the expense of repairing them."* (p. 259, my emphasis) It continues:

> There are economic reasons why these codes are not rigorously enforced. Bringing many old structures up to code standards and maintaining them at that level would require owners to raise rents far above the ability of local residents to pay.

Meanwhile, owners who *do* want to renovate their homes or rental properties in "blighted areas" cannot get mortgage money because banks—thoroughly indoctrinated by "renewal planners" in the techniques of recognizing "blight," and aided by the latest "renewal maps," which grace their inner-office walls—refuse to lend money for improvement of properties likely to be demolished. And twelve thousand older apartment buildings in New York City, containing 350,000 dwelling units (more than ten times the number erected *nationwide* in a decade of urban "renewal") have been abandoned in recent years. At controlled rents allowing a 6 percent return (computed in current mini-dollars) on an original investment computed in pre-1947 dollars, owners could not afford even to "drain" their buildings. Meanwhile, construction of new privately built rental units creaked to a near-standstill rate of 3,000 (expensive) units per year—a rate at which the abandoned units, mostly inhabited by the "deprived," might be replaced in a century, give or take a few years. Perhaps these more "adequate" domiciles will be enjoyed by the evictees' grandchildren, if they can afford the rents.[27]

The Kerner Commission urges stricter enforcement of housing codes. Obviously, no home at all is more desirable—to the Commission, if not to those evicted from boarded-up buildings—than housing not up to "standard." However, the Commission neglects to explain how the abandonment of still more dwellings and eviction of still more tenants upon rigid code enforcement will provide additional housing for the "disadvantaged" or anyone else.

Thus are the "deprived" deprived.

As for building codes—i.e., construction regulations:

> Approximately 5,000 separate jurisdictions in the United States have building codes. Many of these local codes are antiquated and contain obsolete requirements that prevent builders from taking advantage of new technology. Beyond the factor of obsolescence, the very variety of requirements prevents the mass production and standardized design that could significantly lower building costs. (p. 263)

In a breathtaking example of describing a problem and simultaneously urging more of the same, the Commission recommends "reform" of local building codes in conformance with a "model" national code to be drawn up by the Department of Housing and Urban Development.

The rationale behind building codes, of course, is that they supposedly protect the unwary homebuyer from leaky plumbing, dangerous wiring, sagging floors, and vanishing paint—by describing precisely, to the finest detail, how his house should be constructed. What codes actually *do* protect is the divine right of stagnation of building materials manufacturers and building trades unions. Architects' journals regularly inveigh against the obsolescence and absurdity of building codes (without, naturally, ques-

tioning the *principle* of blueprints-by-bureaucracy). Let any local-
ity dare attempt to revise its codes, however, and an impassioned
outcry immediately arises. The hearings last for years, while the
proposed new codes become obsolete. Are homebuyers afraid
their roofs may cave in on them? No. But representatives of
plumbers', electricians', carpenters', and painters' unions, and
public-spirited representatives of the manufacturers of the building trade equivalent of buggy whips swarm to the hearings to
protest that the public health and safety will be horribly endan-
gered, should these gentlemen be tumbled from their cushy
featherbeds by competition.

As for the homebuyer's protection from being bilked—the protection is all on the side of the bilkers. Aside from the occasional
(and minor) expense of squaring a few building inspectors, the
unscrupulous operators can wheel and deal securely behind the
screen of false confidence the codes induce in potential buyers,
who trustingly believe that "the government won't let" anyone sell
them shoddy houses. In a minor variation on the same theme, Jane
Jacobs has written:

> Most cities have legal requirements that rats be exterminated in
> any building demolished; in New York, the going rate in 1960 for
> a lying certificate of extermination, paid by corrupt owners to cor-
> rupt exterminators, is $5. How public agencies, like the Housing
> Authority, evade the law I do not know, but to know that they do
> evade it, one need only go look at the fearful rat festivals and
> exoduses at twilight from their sites in process of demolition. New
> buildings do not get rid of rats. Only people get rid of rats. . . . Our
> building was overrun with rats—big ones—when we got it. It costs
> $48 a year to keep it thoroughly rid of them and all other vermin.
> A live man does it. . . . We expect too much of new buildings [and,
> Mrs. Jacobs might have added, of new regulations] and too little of
> ourselves.[28]

Meanwhile, honest builders, who do not take their friend the
building inspector out to lunch, and who must compete with the
fast-buck boys, usually oblige the latter by going quietly bankrupt
(the more scrupulous the builder, the sooner he obliges)—leaving
the fast-buck boys and their bureaucratic buddies a clear field.

The idea of eliminating building codes entirely; of letting buyer and seller (or renter) alone decide whether the plumbing shall be copper or cast iron or polyvinyl chloride; the trusses wood or steel; the toilet "noiseless" or "silent"; the walls the latest in prefab laminates or good old fake brick; never occurs to the Kerner Commission. Building codes may demonstrably hamper technological progress and increase costs; nevertheless, faith in the *principle* of codes as a viable means of ensuring standard, adequate housing for all remains unsullied by dirty reality. Just widen the scope and jurisdiction of the codes, and all problems will automatically disappear.

The Kerner Commission—true to form—pins its hopes on a *national* bureaucracy as an antidote to the boobery of *local* bureaucracies. HUD, with its all-seeing eye and superhuman clairvoyance, will comprehend all possible conditions and foresee all technological improvements. HUD bureaucrats will be of a stripe ineffably superior to the local yokels. Serene in their devotion to rectitude and "progress," the HUD code-makers and enforcers will resist the importunings, cocktail parties, campaign contributions, and call girls proffered by the crafts unions and by the pull-peddling breed of manufacturers spawned in profusion by "mixed" economies. (Those familiar with the history of the National Labor Relations Board and its tendency to equate the "public" interest with that of the labor unions might feel some slight trepidation on this score.)

HUD will be competent to specify the number of coats of paint, the thickness of insulation, and the placement of electrical outlets required by any and all comers in any and all cities from Philadelphia, Pennsylvania, to Fairbanks, Alaska.

Thus shall the "deprived" be provided—on paper, at least—with suitable, safe, "adequate," and affordable homes.

THE FALLACY CONTRAVENED

It does not matter what governmental intervention is being discussed. In the midst of describing a program's failure to achieve its intended results—even in the midst of describing the *detrimental* effects of some scheme—the Kerner Commission courageously refuses to allow the faintest glimmer of light to penetrate its mental fastnesses. The failure of a program is deplored in one sentence; expansion of the program is called for in the next.

The policies of interventionism have been tried again and again. Yet all the hoary techniques—subsidies, doles, controls—are solemnly exhumed by the Kerner Commission and paraded before the reader, gaudily tricked out in the latest nomenclature ("Income Supplementation," "Project Breakthrough," "Project OWN," "Upward Bound") to obscure the fact that these schemes are literally as old as the Pyramids, about equally useful, and, like the Pyramids, erected by slave labor.

If droves of "deprived" young men are poorly housed, "under"-employed, and nearly illiterate, it is not for lack of interventionist ploys. Compulsory "free" schooling has failed to educate them. Restrictions on "child labor" discourage, or completely prevent, employers from hiring them. The truly meaningful, relevant, *practical* on-job training they might once have acquired *on the job* is precluded in no small part by minimum wage laws which make such training uneconomic for employers (even with subsidies—see Chapters VI and VII), and by confiscatory taxation which curtails investment in the productive enterprises where *actual* "job opportunities" lie.

The standard answer of the "liberal" to these and all other problems caused or aggravated by interventionism is to devise still more enormously complicated, fantastically expensive, ludicrously ineffective, force-supported, and therefore immoral, plans for achieving what could have been achieved quite simply and naturally by a fully free economy.

To the extent that the American Dream of the urban poor has been killed by evils not of their own making, it has been legislated to death.

The corpse will not be resurrected by a compounding of the fallacy which killed it.

Chapter VI

The Obscene Currency: Incompetence

Once upon a time—not nearly so long ago as we are taught to believe—the politico-economic system of the United States was one which rewarded ability. The system was based upon trade— a trade of *values.*

It was then—as it is now and always will be—clearly impossible for everyone to have everything he might need or desire. In the days of the "American Dream," who got what and how much of it was determined by what he had *earned.* To a significant extent, though not wholly (for the market was distorted by interventionism from the start), a man's financial rewards were determined by his productivity: by the market value of his work as determined by the uncoerced judgment of those to whom he offered his product or his services. The system of the "American Dream" was one of voluntary trade to mutual advantage; it rested upon rational self-interest; competition within the system was a competition of productivity, of creativity, of ability, of *value.* The tangible currency of that system was gold. The intangible currency was competence.

The system of the "American Dream" was called capitalism.

It was based upon justice.

It exists no longer, neither in the United States nor anywhere on earth.

The capitalist system exists no longer because generations of men called the system "inhumane," and sought to pervert and destroy it. It exists no longer because men like the men of the Kerner Commission—who are now bemoaning the "failure" of the American Dream—called the capitalist system cruel. They called capitalism cruel because under that system the unreliable, the unambitious, the incompetent, did not receive the unearned fulfillment of their "demands" and "needs." They called capitalism cruel because, when an employer sought to hire workers, he did not investigate their need for the job he offered; he investigated their ability to do that job. They called capitalism cruel because, when a man sought employment, he was not asked for a list of his needs or his traumas or his troubles: he was asked for a list of references, for evidence of his ability to do or to learn the job which he sought. They called capitalism cruel, unjust, and unfair because, in an employment transaction as in any market exchange, *both* parties to the transaction were required to bring a value to the trade. The employer brought the wages he offered, and he asked, in return, for the employee's currency of competence.

But the brothers-in-spirit of the Kerner Commission called the currency of competence evil. They preached and they shouted and they wrote that to give a man only what he had earned was immoral. And in place of the currency of competence, the exchange of *values*, they sought to substitute an obscene antipode, a new currency: ineptitude. But they did not dare to call their currency by its name, to identify the exchange for what it is—a system based upon the exchange of *dis*value, a system in which the honorable currency of competence is driven from the market by an obscene counterfeit.

Such is the economic system proposed by the *Kerner Report.* And nowhere is its nature made more starkly plain than in the proposals now being hawked the length and breadth of the land by the Kerner Commission, by the government, by prominent politicians, and their advisers (some of whom, at least, ought to know better). The Commission and its pimps in business and industry—notably something calling itself the National Alliance of Businessmen—are frantically peddling the prostitution of great enterprises to the public and to their reluctant and "reactionary" confreres under the misleading label of "a private enterprise solution to the problem of the hard-core unemployed."

Such is the intellectual cowardice of the Kerner Commission, and such is its contempt for the intelligence of the public, that it is attempting to sell its obscene alternative to capitalism by labeling it with the name of the system it despises.

By all reports, its tactics work.

THE "GREEN CARDS": ADMISSION TICKETS TO THE UNEARNED

Theory . . .

Like savages stumbling upon the nearly obliterated ruins of some vanished civilization, prostrating themselves momentarily in dimly felt, almost visceral awe of that which they cannot begin to comprehend, the men of the Kerner Commission pay lip service to the product and remnants of the capitalist system before proceeding to describe their alternative:

> Free enterprise, with its system of incentives and rewards for hard work, ability, ingenuity and creativity, has made this nation strong and produced the highest standard of living the world has ever known. (p. 313)

Then, as though seeking to placate some unknowable god by means of an obligatory rite, the neo-savages of the Commission repeatedly apply the term "free enterprise" to the *dis*value-based employment system they propose.

In common with other apologists-for-plunder in and out of government, the Commission repeatedly touts the theory that the urban riots of the sixties erupted because the city "ghettos" are chock-full of a strange breed of young men who, although they hunger and thirst for the "dignity of employment," mysteriously fail to "be motivated" to look for work:

> The Commission has received ample testimony [see Chapter II of this book, "The Foregone Conclusion,"] that unemployment and underemployment are among the most persistent and serious grievances among many Negroes in the central cities which have experienced disorders in recent years.
>
> It is estimated that some 500,000 unemployed persons may be characterized as hard core in the sense that they lack eighth grade literacy and mathematical skills, have only intermittent work histories at most, and *often lack motivation to hold and perform a job*. (p. 315, my emphasis)

The Commission neglects to explain why people who lack motivation to hold and perform a job should be persistently and seriously aggrieved by unemployment. Instead, the Commission leaps to the conclusion that it was a frustrated desire to work which led these young men to run riot:

> The evidence before the Commission suggests [to the Commission, that is] that it is this group of late teenagers and young adults who are often the initial participants in civil disorders. (p. 314)

The skeptical may observe that such young men have no difficulty in exerting themselves to find and grab a piece of the action when the action involved—stoning police stations and looting liquor stores—is to their taste. "Motivating" them to head for the employment office, however, is a bit more tricky than "motivating" them to head for the street. "Motivating" them to read a sheet of instructions for the manufacture of Molotov cocktails is one thing; "motivating" them to read a want ad is quite another. "State employment agencies and other job listing groups," says *Newsweek*, ". . . are precisely where the hard-core unemployed hardly ever go."[1] "These people aren't easy to locate in the community," explained James D. Hodges of Lockheed Corporation (head of that company's "hard-core" hiring program). "We don't advertise because hard-core people don't respond."[2] (Mr. Hodges has since graduated to a ranking position in the Nixon Administration's Department of Labor.) "It must be recognized," sighs the Kerner

Commission, "that a sure method for motivating the hard-core unemployed has yet to be devised."

The unreconstructed among us might observe that, under the "cruel" capitalist system, those who lacked positive motivation to produce received ample negative motivation from the prospect of an empty grocery cupboard. When there were no "manpower development and training programs," no subsidized high-rises and meal tickets, no "aid to dependent children" provided by suckers fool enough to work, mass starvation among the "hard-core" of that day did not result. The unreconstructed might also observe that "motivation" is self-generated and self-maintained. Such observations, however, are utterly incomprehensible to the prophets of the new era.

Since the so-called hard-core have failed to motivate themselves to seek work, and since all the King's horses and all the King's men have so far failed to accomplish the impossible, the Kerner Commission proposes to place a premium on incompetence, in order to encourage business to try its hand at "motivation." And thus has evolved the proposed "green card" scheme which, with minor variations, is being implemented across the nation.

"First," says the Kerner Commission, "the hard-core unemployed should be defined and identified by a government agency." This government grading process is intended to make sure that the identificatees—candidates for instant status and other goodies—are really, truly, deep-down, rock-firm "hard-core." Indeed, one wonders why the Commission members, environmental determinists down to their shoe-soles, fail to suggest such identification at birth. Surely a set of defining criteria ("member of minority group," "drunken father," "broken home," "environmentally substandard home," "unidentified father," "parents on welfare," "parents and grandparents on welfare," "parents, grandparents, and great-grandparents on welfare," etc.) could be developed. Under this negative grading system, any child receiving a specified number of anti-points could automatically be classified at birth as "hard-core," "medium hard-core," "soft-center hard-core," and so on—much as toothbrushes and mattresses are now labeled as "firm," "medium," and "extra-firm" upon manufacture. Tattooing would appear to have definite possibilities as a simple means of providing permanent proof of classification.

Not having thought of, or not daring to suggest, tattooing (yet), the Commission proposes, instead, a system of "green cards." "Second," says the Commission, "an unemployed person once certified as hard-core should be issued a green card or other similar identifying document which he would present to the employer. Third, for each new employee furnishing a green card added to his payroll, the employer would receive substantial credit against his corporate income tax for the year in which the employee was employed."

> In order to stimulate efforts by the employer to devise techniques for motivating green card employees to remain on the job, the tax credit would not be allowed to the employer unless the employee were retained for at least six months. If he remained for six months, the employer would be entitled to a tax credit in the amount of 75 percent of the wages and fringe benefits paid to the employee during that period. From the outset, the employer would be required to pay the higher of the minimum wage or the prevailing wage for the occupation in question.
>
> To encourage continued retention of the employee, the employer would be entitled to a credit against tax in the amount of 50 percent of the wages and fringe benefits paid to the employee during the second six months of employment. .... For example, an employer paying the minimum wage of $1.60 per hour, or $3,328 per year to a full-time employee, and no fringe benefits, would receive ... a total of $2,080 as a credit against tax for the first year. ... Of course, over [a] 2-year period the employer will incur the cost of training and other supportive services and the cost of wages and fringe benefits paid and would therefore also receive the usual deduction from gross income for these costs as business expenses.
>
> The premise of the plan is that, given the tax benefit only if the employee *is motivated to remain on the job,* the employer will attempt to create the conditions necessary to keep the employee motivated, through the provision of training, job ladders, and the supportive services ... so necessary to motivation and retention of the hard-core unemployed. *In order to avoid abuse of the premium which the green card confers upon the job applicant,* no green card holder would be entitled to use the card for more than two years of cumulative employment and in no event for a series of less-than-6-month periods with different employers. (p. 316, my emphasis)

So much for the rock-bottom hard-core. The moderately hard-core are not forgotten:

> In our recommendations we propose to deal primarily with the 500,000 hard-core unemployed who have not yet been reached or placed in permanent employment by existing programs. By so zeroing-in, we do not intend to ignore the remaining approximately million and a half jobless whom the U. S. Department of Labor estimates also need help with regard to employment [the medium-hard core]. Nor do we intend to ignore the approximately 10 million underemployed, 6.5 million of whom work full time and earn less than $3,000 annually, which is the federally defined poverty level.

The $3,000 poverty line (which has been raised since the *Kerner Report* was published) was for an urban *family* of four. The 6.5 million figure above refers to *individuals* who earn $3,000 or less annually. Their *family* income might be much higher. Mixing apples and oranges is a useful means for making a situation look worse—or better—than it is, depending on one's requirements. (See Chapter II, "The Foregone Conclusion.")

> Many members of these latter two groups, the unemployed who are not hard core in the sense of extreme disadvantage, and the underemployed, would undoubtedly also benefit from the kind of training which our recommendations would encourage for the hard core. . . . In addition, we recommend consideration of extension to these two groups of the program we recommend for the hard core, perhaps with modifications. (p.316)

The *Report* does not elaborate on the specific nature of the "modifications" proposed for the less-than-rock hard-core. The general trend of recommendations, however, suggests that the "modifications" would consist of slightly fewer "incentives," i.e., bribes, to employers who hire the less than totally worthless.

The employer who hires his employees on the basis of competence, however, receives no goodies at all. He is left with the dubious pleasure of paying the extra taxes which will buy the premiums placed on *in*competence. The system, in short, is one of a hierarchy of non-values, in which the premium placed on a prospective employee increases in inverse ratio to his ability; in which the only real "disadvantaged," the men who are ignored and forgotten, are those who are cursed with competence.

For the benefit of those cloistered innocents who may naively cry that such a system couldn't be, not here, not in the United States, the following evidence is offered! A "hard-core" training project, federally assisted, has been put into effect at, among other places, the Lockheed Corporation. The hiring criteria are de-scribed thus:

> Because it wants only the hardest of the hard-core in the pilot program, Lockheed has set up five *negative standards* and requires that prospective trainees meet four of them.
>
> To qualify, a trainee has to be a school dropout, unemployed, with no consistent record of work of any kind and an annual family income of $3,000 or below.
>
> Among recruits, a "certain percentage" must have arrest records, and a heavy proportion are drawn from minorities. Most are Negro.
>
> According to a Lockheed official: "We intended to make sure they were the hard core. *Some men were weeded out at the start because they didn't meet the low standards. There were some who didn't get jobs because they were too well qualified.*"[3] (My emphasis)

The Lockheed program differs from the Kerner proposals in detail, not in intent. The major difference is that the company does not receive a tax credit—it is reimbursed directly by the government for the wages, the training costs, and the "supportive ser-vices" of its program, to a maximum of $3,500 per trainee.

... and Practice: The "Hard-Core" Hunt in Action

For those with the stomach to laugh, the situation has its comic aspects. The employment "creation" efforts of the Kerner Com-mission and the National Alliance of Businessmen smack of noth-ing so much as a lunatic big-game hunt conducted on a nationwide scale. The trappings of more traditional safaris are missing. Pith helmets and mosquito boots have given way to Brooks Brothers suits. Pack mules, elephants, and bearers have been supplanted by the company Chrysler. The staked-down goat of Bengali tiger hunts has been replaced by less overtly sacrificial bait. Swarms of Organization Men converge upon the cities, busily beating the back alleys of the "ghettos" in hopes of flushing out the elusive and wary fauna identified by Kerner Commission zoologists as "hard-core unemployed."

"Some employers, notably the automakers," burbles *Newsweek*, "are foraging the ghettos on their own to find workers. The city of Atlanta uses Jobmobiles, rented church vehicles often staffed by reformed ghetto hustlers. Recruiters prowl the dusty slum streets and, in some cases, practically strong-arm reluctant men and drag them to the Jobmobile to talk about working."[4]

The "War on Poverty" has already enabled owners of 4-room, $30-$35-a-month shacks to collect $140 to $400 a month for use of their domiciles as "Head Start Centers." Now one wonders how many worthy divines will be able to repeat the miracle of the loaves and the fishes by parlaying one or two beat-up Sunday school buses into "hard-core" hunting vehicles at rentals Hertz and Avis would envy. As for those "reformed" hustlers—government hustling undoubtedly pays better than the illegal variety. And it's safer.

The intrepid trackers of the "hard-core" hunts are not, of course, armed with rifles. The quarry is not intended to be shot; it is intended to be shanghaied. Once run to ground in its native habitat, the catch is dragged to the appropriate bureau for certification as bona fide, authentic, simon-pure "hard-core."

> Some companies have sent recruiting teams into the ghetto to interview, screen, hire, and process new employees as a one-step operation. [Note: Whittaker Corporation of Los Angeles calls this tactic "Instant Hiring."] Other firms may find this an effective means of locating candidates, but recruits must be certified as eligible, i.e., hard-core poor, by the Employment Service if they are to count toward the company quota.[5]

Only when the official government grade stamp has been affixed to their catch may the brave hunters of the "hard-core" collect their bounty money—complete with strings.

There are still some businessmen who ask whether, government subsidy-goodies notwithstanding, men who have to be "strong-armed" into talking about working are a good employment bet. Despite the oft-repeated assertion that "only the most benighted companies still define their roles in the narrow terms of a product and a profit,"[6] the government's industrial front men are having some difficulty in convincing the "benighted" that they exist for the purpose of providing instant status to a bunch of erstwhile bums. Wrote *Newsweek*:

> The idea of giving jobs to black people who may have little more to offer than their bodies is a wrench to American industry, built as it is on the principle of the survival of the fittest. In place of their highly sophisticated placement tests and searching performance records, businessmen were being asked to rewrite the rules—overlooking prison records, excusing inferior work, forgiving tardiness. One Eastern executive who made an appeal to a group of fellow businessmen for their help has recalled: "It was the most shattering experience of my life. In the middle of my presentation, I suddenly realized that these guys had been trained for their whole life in business to screen people out—and here I was asking them to screen people in. Fifty percent of them were negative and 50 percent said nothing."[7]

Possibly the recipients of this gentleman's pitch were also "shattered" to hear that thenceforward it was the competent they should "screen out." Their more enlightened confrere did not say.

What such benighted reactionaries as the Eastern Airlines executive's reluctant audience fail to grasp, of course, is that such rigid and arbitrary hiring standards as placement tests and performance records should be applied only to the competent, the "middle class," the "non-deprived." (When the jets repaired by such screened-in protégés crash due to "mechanical failure," the passengers can take comfort from the knowledge that they are plummeting to earth—and to probable death—in a good cause: standards for some and status for all.) In this dawning new age of justice for all except the able, men who insist on applying standards of performance to the incompetent "hard-core" risk finding themselves accused of treason (or at least restraint of trade). They are not, in current parlance, "with it." One Leo Beebe of the Ford Motor Company *is*:

I used to sit in my office at Ford and receive memo after memo from Mr. Ford telling me I'd better hire some Negroes. I kept throwing the memos away. Mr. Ford was dedicated to that approach, but I wasn't. I looked at it this way: I said I refuse to hire any man for a job on any other criteria than his competence to do the job. And I was right. But I was stupid for the times. Hiring the most qualified man is a good philosophy—the right philosophy— so long as you give everybody the opportunity to be qualified. That simply has not been possible for many Negroes.[8]

Mr. Beebe's touching mea culpa for the sin of rewarding competence should be an inspiring example to his unreconstructed fellows—as it is to us all. He is now running the National Alliance of Businessmen's pimping ("employer recruitment") operation.

In the Alice-in-Wonderland world of the N.A.B. and the Kerner crew, it is not the *employee* who should prove *his* willingness to work. Hell, no!

The militant leaders of the nation's largest cities assert that business, unlike other segments of the society, has a "show-me" credibility. They say that the black man wants a good job and he believes industry and business have the knowhow not only to produce that good job, but the ability to train him to meet the qualifications of that job. Their only questions concern the willingness of industry to tackle that job.[9]

When some meekly hat-in-hand businessmen came around to his gang headquarters to ask what they could do to help his cause, one Frank Ditto, a "black militant leader in Detroit," laid it more succinctly on the line than the N.A.B. "If you cats can't do it," quoth Ditto, "it's never going to get done. The government can't lick this problem [of producing jobs], so business has to."[10] Most of them cats scurried right out to start trying.

It is, in other words, the employer's duty—the duty of the productive in our nation—to justify the touching demand-and-it-shall-be-given faith of belligerent barbarians. It is the employer's duty to seek out the men he would once have turned down flat. It is the employer's duty to proffer earnest entreaties to lure them into the hiring office. It is the employer's duty to grovel humbly before assorted skeptical bums, punks, and hoods; to implore them to believe that, yes, boys, he really means it, he will *so* give them jobs—and not washing dishes, either. Won't they please, please step this way? Or better yet, he'll send a taxi for them, or pick them up in his private limousine (*Newsweek* illustrates its "hard-core job" article with a photo of a "Chrysler executive picking up workers" in his shiny new Imperial) so that they needn't strain their brains reading bus schedules or get their feet wet at the bus stop in the rain. That might be good enough for the competent. For the incompetent, getting there should be half the fun.

Despite the frenzied efforts at "recruitment," certifiable 24-carat specimens of worthlessness have proven hard to capture and harder to keep. Columnist Henry J. Taylor has reported that only 35,000 applicants showed up to fill 162,500 jobs pledged to the N.A.B. in 1968. The response of then President Johnson was to urge his minions to "hunt harder."[11] Although 1,238 job-training contracts were signed in the 1968-69 fiscal year, even the Labor Department admitted in the fall of 1969 that only 26,000 of the 77,000 trainees were still on the job as of June 30, 1969. Labor's response has been to up the subsidy ante by shortening trainee-retention requirements.[12]

Strong-arming the foot-dragging applicants, moreover, is only a small portion of the job-creation process. The fun and games are just beginning when an "applicant" has been trapped and hired.

> Tardiness and absenteeism are major problems for this group, who have previously found little social or economic benefit from conformity with the usual standards of commercial life. A number of experiments, including the substantial experience of the Job Corps training centers [see Chapter V] indicates that it is difficult to motivate hard-core youths to remain on the job for more than a few weeks. (p. 315)

> Business has found that hiring and training people at the bottom of the ghetto barrel—"making the transition from the street corner to the job," as a Los Angeles training executive puts it—is tougher than it sounds.[13]

> Turnover is high—holding more than 50 percent of the trainees

is pretty good. Absenteeism, tardiness, a general lack of responsibility are common failings.

"Mondayitis is almost epidemic," says one supervisor.

"They have a tremendous number of grandmothers and grandfathers who keep dying month after month," another supervisor complains.[14]

The yearning of the "hard-core" for the dignity of employment should obviously not be misconstrued as an eagerness to face the grim realities of *work*.

Herbert R. Northrup of the Wharton School (University of Pennsylvania), puts it this way:

> One group of newly recruited people from the slums is being taken through an automobile plant. Now, an auto-assembly plant is a noisy place. It can be a frightening experience to a person who's never been in one, especially a person who has never worked eight hours a day, five days a week—and whose friends have never done that either.
>
> You tell this person: "I want you to be here eight hours a day." And he says, "Man, you mean eight hours every day?" And, of course, everybody thinks that's funny—but it's really a very natural reaction.
>
> Now, you say to this fellow: "If you have trouble getting to work, call us." But it never occurs to you that he may never have used a telephone. Or he may think, "Gee, I'll be in trouble if I'm late, so I'll just disappear." You might even have trouble finding him to give him his paycheck for the days he has worked.[15]

Even in those who have no phones, such utter innocence of the ways of the working world, in this day when television is "the universal appliance in the ghetto," passeth all understanding. (Looks as though Mother Bell is wasting her TV ad funds.) After all, the fellows *do* seem to learn how to get the cash out of pay-phone coin boxes, leaving as many as one third of big-city pay phones out of order at any given time. But that behavior such as Mr. Northrup describes *does* occur is not news to anyone who has ever employed (or attempted to employ) the so-called "disadvantaged."

"The first day is the first hump," says Northrup:

Then the first week is another hump. Then there's Monday morning —you see, he's got that first week's paycheck, and it's more money than he's ever had in his life, so he's likely to blow it on a big weekend.

Then, first thing you know, this new worker is going to buy a car, probably a jalopy that is likely to break down on the expressway the first time he drives it to work. Well, you would probably phone the company and explain the circumstances and it would be an excused absence. But that's the first time this fellow ever had such an experience. He might just leave the car on the expressway and disappear.

To cope with this sort of nonsense, companies are urged to institute "buddy systems" under which established employees undertake to wet-nurse their less advantaged co-workers through such traumatic procedures as setting their alarm clocks, getting to work and back again, and, of course, working. And companies *do*! "We help with problems," says Stanley W. Hawkins of Lockheed, "on shift and off—getting people into hospitals and out of jail, getting gas and electricity turned back on, towing cars off the freeway, fighting off finance companies, arguing with car dealers."[16]

In New York, the Citizens Committee on Metropolitan Affairs, Inc. instituted a "buddy system" where new employees from the ghetto received on-the-job assistance from established employees. Among other things, they make sure the recruit gets to work on time, understands the job, and has a person within the system to whom he can talk.[17]

General Motors, among other firms, has developed a buddy system in which established employees counsel and cajole new employees from the ghetto.[18]

Chrysler's Virgil Boyd recalls the puzzlement around one of his firm's Detroit plants when a number of new hirees—the ones who signed with "X's"—didn't report. "The answer, in many cases, was childishly simple," he said. "If you can't read, how do you know what it says on the destination signs of . . . buses. . . . And a grown man isn't going to get on—and be sent off—the wrong bus very many times before he stops getting on buses any more. So, we

showed these people, one by one, how to recognize the right bus
to take, and in some cases how and when to transfer. ..."[19]

The United States has had "free," "public," compulsory education for decades. Grown men still sign with "X's." Advocates of
coercionary cure-alls might (but probably won't) draw some conclusions from this sorry sequence: namely, that *minds* cannot be
forced, or, in the more homely idiom much favored by teachers of
another day, "You can lead a horse to water, but you can't make
it drink."

> "Quite basically," said Inland [Steel Corporation] vice president
> William Caples, "we tried to explain ... such things as why time
> is important ... why absenteeism is wrong. What you're doing is
> taking somebody with a completely different sense of values and
> trying to persuade him that your values are valid. And these kids
> need a good deal of sustaining. They feel awfully left out and
> alone."[20]

What of the other employees at Mr. Caples' plant? What of the
men and women who got their jobs the hard way, who have
painstakingly accumulated their currency of competence over
many years of diligent effort? When they observe the newly
nabbed scum of the street corners being "motivated" with money
and mothering, free taxi rides and free teeth, being instructed in
the intricacies of flush toilets and alarm clocks and "forgiven" for
all kinds of peccadilloes—might not the older employees also feel
somewhat "left out and alone"? Mr. Caples did not say. The
competent, after all, don't count.

It is those forgotten men and women, the competent workers—
each to the extent of his competence—who are the unseen victims
of the "hard-core" employment schemes.

THE SIGNIFICANCE ...

The 300-odd pages of the *Kerner Report* read like a veritable
pharmacopoeia of snake-oil nostrums which—like castor oil—can
prove fatal if swallowed in large doses and mightily discomforting
if swallowed in small ones. To date, the general public—no doubt

fed up to here with being shaken down for handouts to every bum, slut, and slouching punk with a loud whine and a limber brick-throwing arm—has received the Kerner Commission's hush-money riot remedies with less than the wild enthusiasm desired by the mass media shills who have been pushing the *Report*. But if polls and press reports can be believed, a considerable portion of the public has been misled by the "private enterprise" label into swallowing the "job-creation" philter whole, thinking that this, at least, is no handout. It has been fed a lie.

Like all schemes based upon false premises and accomplished by immoral means, the Kerner proposals for motivating the "hard-core" cannot and will not—in the long-term sense—work. Inno-cently or otherwise, the pitchmen selling these schemes point to instances where they have *seemed* to work as justification for making the obscene currency the coin of the realm. They point to the ten or ten hundred or ten thousand men employed under the "hard-core" programs. And they say, "See? But for these pro-grams, these men would remain bums, burdens to society, threats to us all. Yet these men have been made useful citizens. We have produced value from non-value. We have made jobs where there was none."

Those who say this—and those who believe them—are wrong.

Nothing can justify a program based upon the use of force. But, in truth, these programs create no jobs—no values—at all. So long as no actual market necessity for hiring the so-called hard-core exists; so long as the "incentive" to such hiring is a mixture of subsidies and not-so-subtle blackmail threats ("Give us jobs, buddy, or we'll bash your head in!"), each job "created" in nomi-nally private business by government bounty money and govern-ment bullying must wipe out a genuine job elsewhere just as surely as would a job "created" with government as the overt employer. (See Chapter V.) Oh, yes, the Kerner Commission demands that "the already employed must not lose their jobs to make room for the hard-core unemployed." Much verbiage is expended on the insistence that the medium hard-core and the soft-center hard-core must not be done out of jobs by the hard-core programs, but must be "moved up" to cushier, higher-status jobs "created" for *them*. Such verbiage is a disingenuous smokescreen to befuddle the economically brainwashed.

When incompetence becomes the accepted currency, when men

are hired because a premium has been placed on their incompetence by means of a government bounty, it is the competent who must pay for that premium. *There is no one else to pay for it.* When someone, somewhere, gets something for nothing—or for less than nothing*—someone else, somewhere else, must balance reality's scales. He will be hidden from sight; he will not be seen in magazine spreads; he will not be pointed to on guided factory tours and paraded before a pre-sold press. But that someone, and his suffering, will be real.

That someone will be the unskilled, untrained worker who nonetheless achieved a steady work record, but who cannot compete with the bounty money paid for hiring his street-corner-slouching neighbor. That someone will be the unskilled worker who made himself skilled; who pulled *himself* out of the "ghetto," studying by day and working by night, year after arduous year, and who must now forgo the pleasures he has earned, in order to pay in taxes for the bounty money itself. That someone will be the long-term steady worker—the skilled man passed over for promotion when the government pressures his employer to promote the "disadvantaged" who "need" the status *he* has earned. That someone is the man who, because of the curse of competence, never got the job at all:

> If we have a choice between hiring a qualified white man for a particular job and an untrained and unqualified Negro, we have to discriminate against the better-prepared man and hire the Negro, solely because the Government says that's what we've got to do.[21]

It is the victims, always the victims, who must pay—and pay, and pay, and pay—for the implementation of the schemes which destroy them.

The whole hard-core employment safari might be merely a hilarious farce, were it not for the nature and source of the bait. The space-age substitute for the staked-down goat is *us*. The alchemy of transmuting incompetence into the obscene new coin of the realm will, and must, be paid for by human sacrifices.

*"Less than nothing" is what the typical "hard-core" prospect has to offer: not only has he no value to give the employer in trade for his wages, but employing him will actually result in losses traceable to his incompetence—botched work, slowed production, etc., not to speak of the "counselling and cajoling" costs.

It is the competent, the diligent, the conscientious, whatever their level of achievement, who are being forced to fork over a portion of their lives as bait to trap the "hard-core" into working. It is every man who works for his living, who obtains his job through honest qualifications and keeps it by honest effort, who will be taxed for the bounty money, the bureaucratic salaries, the ink for the green card "tattoos."

It is those who believe that employment is a trade of value for value who will now find themselves turned away in favor of those who offer no value at all.

It is to this obscene system—the converse of all that capitalism achieved and stood for—that the Kerner Commission has the incredible audacity to apply the term "free enterprise."

CHAPTER VII

The Disqualifying Adjective: "Black" Capitalism

'Tis but thy name that is my enemy.
... O, be some other name!
What's in a name? that which we call a rose
By any other name would smell as sweet.
                    —*Romeo and Juliet,* Act II: Scene 2

"What's in a name?" queried Shakespeare. Modern politicos know the answer to that one: "Plenty!" That which we call interventionism, for instance, by any other name would smell a darn sight sweeter. Take racism-based government handouts—subsidies, and such. Drench them liberally in *eau de liberté.* Call them "private enterprise" or "Negro entrepreneurship" (Kerner nomenclature). Better yet, call them "Black Capitalism" (current nomenclature). *Voilà!* Hitherto chary "conservatives" and lately leery libertarians will sniff and holler "Hallelujah! A great new day has dawned!"

Lacking the resistance to intoxication which firmly grasped, non-contradictory political principles would provide, such folk are readily seduced by an artful synthesis of semantic perfumery and their own premature optimism. Dreamily lapsing into self- and scent-induced euphoria, they'll do their bit—while the rosy glow lasts—to help palm the pottage off on the peasants.

Eventually, of course, the trip is over. Some cold, gray morning the celebrants discover, with aggrieved surprise, that underneath the Air-Wick was the same old garbage. But, in the meantime, presidents have been elected; government "programs" have been programmed; staff headquarters have been staffed; "funding" has been funded. What might once have been preventable folly is now *fait accompli*, rapidly congealing into status quo, and tricked out with all the formidable accoutrements of deep-rooted entrench-ment, prolific puffery, and payrolls full of the loyal voters which government programs invariably acquire.

This, in essence, was the procedure by which the "hard-core employment" game was foisted upon a gullible population. And, almost before the inevitable morning-after symptoms of disillu-sionment had reared their nauseating heads, a new happy-gas labeled "Black Capitalism" was wafting over the land, eddied hither and yon by the turbulent breezes of presidential campaign rhetoric.

The primary infatuation of the Kerner Commission had been overt interventionist programs, vast in scale, all-encompassing in scope, and staggering in cost. Still, the United States is (nominally) a capitalist nation. It did seem meet and right to devote a portion of the *Report*—mostly the Appendix and sundry halfhearted asides—to "private" enterprise involvement in alleviating the grievances of the "ghettos." An Advisory Panel on Private Enter-prise composed of (or was it stacked with?) university business "experts" and businessmen with sizable government contracts was duly assembled. Heading the Panel was Charles B. Thornton, the representative of "business" on the balanced ticket which formed the Kerner Commission proper, and chairman of the board of Litton Industries—a Job Corps contractor. Also present were John Leland Atwater, president of North American Rockwell Corpora-tion—a busy defense contracting firm and trainer of the "hard-core"; Martin R. Gainsbrugh of the National Industrial Conference Board—a "business lobby" of the sort prevalent in mixed economies; Walter E. Hoadley of the Bank of America; Louis F. Polk, vice president of international development and finance at General Mills; and Lawrence M. Stone, professor of law at the Berkeley campus of the University of California.

The Advisory Panel obligingly warmed up a stew of "incentives" to "private" rehabilitation of the "ghettos" and "ghetto"-ites: a stew composed, understandably enough, of ingredients conforming to the panel's standards of "enterprise" and "private." The hard-core-hunting proposals were the principal component of the recipe, and elicited most of the initial salivation from the Pavlovian press. But also sprinkled into the tepid goulash were a few paragraphs devoted to stimulating "Negro entrepreneurship."

It wasn't much. But, given the temper of the times, it was enough. In the months that followed, the Advisory Panel's relatively unsung portion of the *Kerner Report* formed the nucleus for a full-blown political puff-job called "Black Capitalism."

Describing "social problems" as "too big for private enterprise to handle" and billing government programs as the cure had, not long since, been the cliché of the day. But by the late sixties a few of the peasants were remarking that, as government programs multiplied, so did "social problems"—riots particularly. A right-about-face from the excuses of yore seemed indicated; it became expedient to designate problems as "too big for *government* to handle unaided," and labeling new government programs as private enterprise solutions became the "in-thing" to do.

While the Kerner Commission and their programmed parrots of the press prated of "national commitment" and "Marshall Plans for the cities"; while they screeched for the allocation of ever more of the "national resources" as blackmail tribute for the riot-prone "deprived"; while they labored to close the purportedly yawning "schism between black and white America" by filling it up with cash; a goodly number of the so-called middle class cavalierly dismissed as "haves" (perhaps dimly recognizing that "the national resources" meant *them*—voters, that is) were beginning to reject the smear of "racism" which had been splashed on their unwillingness to leap upon the sacrificial chopping block for further decimation of their lives. They interpreted the American schism somewhat differently than had the Kerner Commission. To many of the "middle class" it appeared that America was indeed becoming increasingly divided into two societies: one society asking for handouts and the other forced to do the handing. To the exasperated, harassed, and tax-burdened handers-out, any proposal smacking of *self*-responsibility, *self*-improvement, *self*-motivation—of private enterprise—for the handout collectors had a most enticing aroma.

And at least one of the presidential candidates of 1968 knew it. Adopting a dim official view (at least prior to his election) of the *Kerner Report* theme and those of its variations readily recognizable as handouts, he meanwhile quietly appropriated a choice selection of the *Report*'s proposals which he and his advisers deemed superficially more appealing to America's "forgotten men"—the *producers* of the "nation's" resources. Having sprayed the schemes generously with an intellectual Airwick called "Bridges to Human Dignity," he wrapped them up in a glistening new package tagged "Black Capitalism" and hawked them across the land. They sold.

By March of 1969, when a "progress report" on the nation's commitment to Kerner (which came across more as a dirge to the "inadequacy" thereof) was released by the Urban Coalition, "Black Capitalism" alone rated nearly five pages of a document much, much less wordy than the original *Report*.[1] Incubated by the hot political pantings of Richard Nixon, "Black Capitalism" had blossomed out into a lusty national mystique. Drenched in the sure-fire fragrance of "private enterprise," another pail of statist garbage had been hustled past the public nose. All it took was the name game.

The process had happened before; it will, sadly, happen again. One more name-game snow job would hardly be worth analyzing —except that many an erstwhile advocate of free enterprise fell headlong into this particular garbage pail.

THE NAME OF THE GAME

"Black Capitalism" is not used by its advocates to plump for the establishment of a capitalist politico-economic *system*. The Kerner Commission, the Nixon crowd, and most politicians who get anywhere these days find it useful to preserve the polite public fiction that a capitalist system is what we already *have* in the United States today—and that all it needs is "improvement" via their particular prescription for "modernization." (Lest the reader receive the impression that I am nastily attributing disingenuous motives to all and sundry politician-extollers of American "free enterprise," let me hasten to say that all of them may not be dishonest—some may just be dumb.)

"Capitalism" is used interchangeably with "entrepreneurship" by advocates of the "black" variety, to denote business enterprises —*private* business enterprises. "If our urban ghettos are to be built from within, one of the first requirements is the development of black-owned and black-run businesses," said Richard Nixon in one of his widely heralded "Black Capitalism" speeches.[2] "It's no longer enough that white-owned business enterprises employ greater numbers of Negroes, whether as laborers or as middle-management personnel. This is needed, yes—but it has to be accompanied by an expansion of black ownership, of black capitalism," he said in another.[3] The "emerging pride" of the "black American" and his "demand for dignity" are, says Mr. Nixon, a "driving force" to build upon; jobs are needed within a "new economic structure" which must be built in the "ghetto" to "create . . . [a] rebirth of pride, individualism, and independence." But jobs must be "provided within a framework that establishes dignity and the pride of the black man as well as the white." And this framework is only provided by jobs in enterprises owned and managed by "blacks."

From the economic standpoint this pitch is pure hogwash. An improved standard of living—in the "ghettos" as anywhere else— can only be achieved through the channeling of capital (money, accumulated through past labor and risked in an enterprise) and labor (present effort expended in an enterprise) through the free market on the basis of productivity—not pigmentation. Moreover, one might question the value of an "emerging pride" which "demands" a dignity to be derived from the race of one's employer as a driving force for the achievement of anything but self-destruction and self-disgust. Some might suggest that the "black capitalist" pride-demanders have the cart before the horse. Pride, dignity, individualism, and independence are achieved from within and cannot be applied from without; it is self-attained, self-maintained pride, dignity, individualism and independence which enable men to advance in their jobs and to create new enterprises, new products, and new economic structures—not vice versa. And the "blacks- (or whites-) to-have-dignity-must-work-for-other-blacks (or -whites)" pitch is a naked appeal to racism. But we'll let that pass.

"Capitalism," defined as starting one's own business, might be a viable means for achieving financial success and the joy of productive accomplishment in the case of a man of ability unable to find employment because of the irrationality of potential employers—for example, a Negro of ability denied employment because of his race. But suggesting entrepreneurship as a solution to the "grievances" of a mass of rampaging rioters appears, to put it politely, asinine. The majority of individuals lumped together as "ghetto blacks" are at present—as the Kerner Commission and the "militants" keep reminding us—poorly skilled, poorly educated, poorly "motivated," and plain poor (relatively deprived, that is). A man who has to be comforted and cajoled into setting an alarm clock and showing up for work two weeks in a row (see Chapter VI) would seem a poor prospect for proprietorship—or for a "meaningful" executive position.

Contrary to the pipe dreams of the street-corner "deprived," real-life capitalists work longer and harder than most eight-hours-less-coffee-breaks employees. Those running small-scale enterprises or embryonic, innovative endeavors generally receive far less return (at least immediately) per hour put in than do their employees. And, despite the popularity of the corporate "togetherness, " Organization Man myth, management personnel in major industries—the ones who get anything "meaningful" to manage—put in longer hours and invest more effort, intellectual and, often, physical, in their jobs than do the boys on the assembly line.[4] At any given level of ability, it is not "the system," but the willingness to put in that extra hour—and then another—instead of going to the bar for a beer or to the sofa for television, that separates the achievers from the also-rans.

"OK," say the "militants," the Kerner Commission, and Mr. Nixon in ear-splitting chorus. "We know all that, man." The "militants," Mr. Nixon tells us, know that "profits are the great motive power of our fantastically productive economy." All the "militants" want is "a chance to apply the principles" of free enterprise to their own communities; to get "a share of the wealth and a piece of the action" for themselves.

Only a spoilsport would ask, "Who's stopping them?" Only a racist reactionary would ask, "If free enterprise is what you want, fellows, why wait for a government program?" Only the hardhearted would cavil that, when Henry Ford wanted "a chance" to mass-produce cars, he did not acquire his assembly line at Molotov-cocktail point; that when "the system" at Eastman-Kodak refused to recognize the merits of Polaroid snapshots, Edwin Land didn't burn down Rochester.

A rational observer will find his gorge rising at the racist miasma surrounding the "Black Capitalism" pitch. A common-sense economist will detect the giant-sized fly lurking in the entrepreneurship-for-the-incompetent ointment. But if the aggrieved "deprived" really want to give proprietorship a whirl; if the "black businesses" the "militants" claim to lust after are private enterprises which are truly private; if the militants' "piece of the action" includes no extorted piece of anyone's paycheck—well, go to it, fellows, and good luck to you! Glad to have you off our backs!

But is it private enterprise, as those "conservatives" and pro-capitalists who drool over "Black Capitalism" understand it, that the boys are really after?

THE GAME AS IT'S NAMED

"Capitalism" is not a physical entity. The attribute of "blackness" cannot, therefore, be accurately applied to it. From the implicit definitions given by those who use the slogan, however, one can infer that the "black" in "Black Capitalism" is used to refer to "blacks"—the appellation by which (according to their self-anointed spokesmen) millions of Americans who happen to possess "Negroid" physiognomy suddenly, and fervently, desire to be described. (The Kerner Commission, which uses "Negro," slipped up that time.)

"Negro," we're told, is a "racist" term. Now, "Negro"— adopted from the Spanish and derived from the Latin *niger*—

means "black," of course. But "ghetto" schools are pretty lousy (see Chapter VIII), so perhaps the "militants" never learned that. And, anyway, today's "militants" *feel* that "Negro" has racist connotations, just as yesterday's self-styled "Negro spokesmen" *felt* that "black" had racist connotations, and agitated for the substitution of "Negro." After all, it's what's felt that counts.

"Black Capitalism" is supposed to mean "capitalism" practiced by "blacks."

Now, "Black Capitalism," remember, is a program cooked up to combat "racism." Yet by affixing the qualifying adjective "black" to "capitalism," one implies that there is some essential, inherent, significant difference between capitalism (private entrepreneurship) practiced by "blacks" and capitalism practiced by, say, whites: a peculiar tack for anti-racists to take. Is "Black Capitalism" merely an ill-considered shorthand phrase for advising "black" individuals to become capitalists? Or is the brand of "Black Capitalism" currently being peddled different from capitalism plain?

It is and it ain't.

It is different. And it ain't capitalism.

Strictly speaking, it is not possible to conduct a totally private, capitalist enterprise in the United States today. The politico-economic system of today's United States is *not* a capitalist system. It is a "mixed economy" of freedom and controls—less and less freedom and more and more controls. As in all mixed economies which attempt to achieve a "balance" between the healthy tissue of capitalism and the cancer of statism (this is usually called "achieving a balance between freedom and security"), the healthy tissue must—unless the malignancy be diagnosed and excised in time—be consumed, ultimately, by the cancer. No nominally private enterprise in America today is totally free of statist controls (wage and price regulation, zoning and planning laws, licensing, race-sex-age hiring quotas), whether these be actually enforced or merely potentially enforceable.

However, a "private" enterprise, as the term is generally understood (or, more precisely, has come to be misunderstood)—and as it is *intended* to be understood by the "Black Capitalism" peddlers —is an enterprise which is private (non-governmental) in ownership, and which operates without using tax funds or initiatory governmental force.

The fundamental, significant differentiating characteristic of a private enterprise is voluntary trade to mutual advantage in accordance with the freely made (uncoerced) decisions of all parties to the business transactions conducted by the enterprise. The primary goal of a *capitalist* private enterprise is to make a profit; to do so the enterprise must produce a product or service which men desire; i.e., for which there is demand; to profit over the long term it must produce that product or service efficiently. If the primary goal of an enterprise is not profit—if providing employment or helping the poor are *ends*, not *means*—the enterprise is not capitalism; it is organized charity. (Lacking the sure indicator of success or failure which profit provides, the latter enterprise will invariably achieve its stated aims less successfully—if at all—than if the "benefits" sought had been peripheral to a prime goal of profit.)

In an enterprise properly designated as private and capitalistic, capital is raised on a voluntary basis; the risks of the enterprise are assumed voluntarily by the entrepreneurs; the profits *and the losses*—the rewards for success and the penalties for failure— accrue to the entrepreneur(s), who has assumed the responsibility for both. If a portion of the capitalization (the money invested in plant and facilities) is borrowed from banks or from other lenders, the money is voluntarily lent in return for interest at rates determined by supply and demand (and degree of risk), and freely agreed to by borrower and lender; the loan is secured by the borrower's assets and/or his credit (reputation for repayment acquired in previous business transactions); transactions among buyers, sellers, lenders, borrowers, and investors in a private enterprise are conducted on the basis of the uncoerced judgment of each party involved as to his rational self-interest; the profits of the enterprise are determined by its *productivity*: by the entrepreneur's ability to ascertain the demands generated by a free market and the most efficient methods for meeting those demands.

In capitalist enterprises, business decisions such as the location of plants, the product or service to be produced and sold, the criteria by which the labor force and the managerial personnel will be hired, are based upon the entrepreneur's assessment of (1) the demand, actual or potential, for the product or service he proposes to produce and sell, and (2) the most efficient (and therefore the most profitable) methods of producing the product. The goal of a capitalist enterprise is profit; the means to that goal is *ability*—it is the most able entrepreneur who receives the greatest profit.

In a capitalist (free) economy, the maximum profits will accrue to the most productive business enterprises as determined by the market: by the sum of the value choices of individual buyers and sellers. In a mixed economy, the function of the market is distorted and impeded by governmental interventions, "redistributions," and controls. Scarce resources are thus wasted in uneconomic enterprises, to the ultimate detriment of all; and the maximum money profits frequently accrue, not to the most efficient producer, but to the most skillful manipulator of interventionists and controllers.

Despite the prevalent fiction that "welfare state" interventionism helps the "have-nots" at the sole expense of the "haves," it is precisely the poor, the unskilled, and the least competent who have the least money to pay the "inefficiency tax" inevitably imposed by interventionist diversion of resources into uneconomic enterprises and "redistributory" discouragement of the productivity and thrift of the "haves."It is precisely the "have-nots" who benefit most *in relation to their own productive ability* from the vast increase in productivity made possible through mechanization *in a free economy* where the profit motive encourages investment in the tools of production.

Within the context of a mixed economy, a private, capitalistic enterprise is one financed by the savings of individuals who have deferred current consumption to invest in the tools of production. It is an enterprise whose owners are conducting the business as private citizens—not as government employees endowed with legalized force—for the purpose of making a profit. It is an enterprise whose owners, although subject (as are all businessmen) to the strictures and injustices inherent in an interventionist economy, do not *seek and use* additional legal tools of government coercion to obtain capitalization, to augment profits, or to shift losses to other, involuntary bearers. It is an enterprise whose owners do not attempt to expand the scope of immoral governmental force (interventionist legislation and its implementation) to assist them in gaining competitive markets by violating the rights of others.

A private, capitalistic enterprise has profit as its primary goal, and is neither started nor conducted by the expansion of initiatory governmental force, direct or indirect.

THE NAME WITHOUT THE GAME

But scrounging around for capital, earning money and forgoing present consumption to save for future investment; using rational persuasion to convince potential financiers of the merit (profit potentialities) of the proposed enterprise and the abilities of the would-be enterpriser, are not precisely the brand of "capitalism" that the would-be "black entrepreneurs" (the ones, that is, who are making all the noise instead of quietly producing) have in mind. The immigrants of an earlier day, and impoverished newly arrived Puerto Ricans of the present—as well as the mysteriously ignored, steadily growing, despised, and inexplicable (in Kerner terms) "black middle class"—might have done things that way. But starting small and working up would be impossible (Kerner version— see Chapter V) and/or unpalatable ("militant version"—see television) to "ghetto" Negroes: the "ghetto Negroes," that is, that the "Black Capitalism" crowd is desirous of assisting. To keep up with the great expectations of the "Black Capitalizers," the assistance had better be on a sizable scale.

"The Nixon Administration," complains the *Black Capitalism Newsletter*, "appears to define Black Capitalism in terms of 'mom' and 'pop' shops, not as big corporate structures. . . . The type of Black economic power that must be developed requires the massive cooperation of many big businesses."[5]

"Typically," laments the Urban Coalition, black private businesses "are small, marginal businesses: retail and service firms which cater to a constricted market. . . . black enterprises [must] move beyond the traditional small retail and service pattern with its limited neighborhood market and into light manufacturing and other ventures aimed at the general economy."[6]

Great oaks might grow from little enterprises; the massive industries of today were marginal enterprises once (not, in the case of many of them, too long ago). But the boys ain't got time to wait, or to fertilize and cultivate. Moving "beyond the present pattern"

by starting with a pushcart and working up to A.&P.; by rising at
5 A.M. to sell newspapers before school and staying up till midnight for telegraph key practice, to end up running R.C.A.; starting
with a bathtub, long hours, lean rations, and patience to end up
with Polaroid Corporation—well, that isn't what the new breed of
"capitalists" have in mind. Henry Ford and them cats might start
by layin' on greasy garage floors. David Sarnoff might start by
emptying wastebaskets. Sidney Poitier might wash dishes by day
and learn reading by puzzling out newspapers on a tenement roof
by night. But that ain't got no status, baby! It's instant aerospace
or nuthin! And don't let no Charlies get too uppity tellin' us how
to do it:

> Often, white businessmen find themselves walking a treacherous
> path when they aid black entrepreneurs. Fledgling black business-
> men are eager to learn what their white counterparts know about
> business, but they are quick to resent the slightest hint of dictation
> or paternalism. . . . In Pasadena, California, a black group leased a
> service station from Mobil and ran it $8,400 in the red. When Mobil
> tried to straighten things out, the group resisted, because they
> "didn't want some honkie looking at the books."[7]

So much for anti-racism. As for raising the green . . .
The change from "Mom and Pop" enterprises to "frozen food
processing, men's and boys' apparel, and commercial printing," let
alone computer components and aerospace parts, "requires contacts and knowhow that many potential black businessmen just
don't possess," the Urban Coalition points out—neglecting to ask
how businessmen who do possess "knowhow" happened to acquire it. (The "militant" anti-racists apparently assume that white
businessmen are born with contacts and knowhow; "blacks" who
do acquire wealth and "meaningful" managerial positions are con-
temptuously dismissed as "Oreos": black on the outside and white
on the inside. That's "race pride"? Sounds more like race contempt.) Floyd McKissick, erstwhile CORE man now selling "community relations" and "liaison" services to nervous corporations
and to eager mayors seeking Model Cities programs ("Black Capitalism" in action), says, "Blacks have not, as a people, been allowed by the system to accumulate wealth."

"Lack of capital," says the Urban Coalition, is an "impediment" to black entrepreneurship. "Establishing new enterprises," says Mr. Nixon astutely, "requires both capital and knowhow."

Now, a common-clay, run-of-the-mill "potential" businessman might be expected to acquire knowhow by working days at a low-status job and going to school nights; or by finding a job and working his way up in an established business of the type he proposes to start, in order to learn the ropes. He might amass some capital by restraining himself from blowing his whole paycheck on short-term goodies in order to accumulate some savings. And he might acquire the rest of the necessary capital by approaching would-be investors and selling them stock in his enterprise, or by negotiating a loan with a bank or other lender. In order to raise funds from sources other than his own savings, he would have to furnish *facts* to convince others that he is competent to run a business enterprise; that the likelihood of future profit from his venture outweighs the risk of loss. The higher the risk of loss, the greater the rate of return he will have to offer (interest and/or potential dividends) to make his project a more inviting one for investors and lenders than other projects competing for their funds.

Such an entrepreneur risks his own time, knowledge, and effort: past time and effort in the form of the capital he has personally saved, present time and effort in the form of his entrepreneurial services. The stockholders risk their past time and effort in the form of savings used to purchase stock. And the banker risks the savings voluntarily entrusted to him by his depositors, plus his own principal business asset—his reputation, knowing that, should he make too many poor-risk loans, he will lose the confidence of his depositors and be a banker no more.

"Black capitalists" and their political buddies find that sort of enterprising too risky by a long shot. "American businessmen," whines Floyd McKissick, "have made loud pledges about what they intended to do. A great deal has been said about the amounts of money which were to be invested in the ghetto. *Yet, the banks tend to follow the same investment rules for lending money to Black entrepreneurs as to white.*"[8] (my emphasis) The selfish, racist, reactionary bastards, in other words, balk at pouring money into losing ventures, even when the venturers are black.

Mr. Nixon, more practiced at the semantic-spray game, put the proposition more smoothly. "Too often, the normal [translate: voluntary] sources of capital are unavailable for ghetto enterprises. The risks are considered too high." Now, if men, in their rational, uncoerced judgment, consider a risk "too high," the alternative is obvious.

"As the President's Riot Commission [the Kerner Commission] has recommended," said Mr. Nixon, "the Small Business Administration's loan program should be substantially expanded in these areas. Beyond this, additional loan-guarantee programs can be combined with active efforts to enlist traditional lending institutions in ghetto development." (Mr. Nixon did not elucidate as to what he meant by "active efforts." Doubtless it's coincidence that a number of the "traditional lenders" most ardently pursuing "ghetto loan programs" have anti-trust suits pending.)

Indeed, the Kerner Commission had suggested exactly what Mr. Nixon proposed: continuation and expansion of SBA "minority loan" programs for "ghetto loans" to "stimulate Negro entrepreneurship."

In August, 1968, the SBA launched something called Project OWN (Only Wants Negroes?) to "create" minority-owned businesses at the arbitrary rate of 10,000 a year. (If governmental fiat can produce "minority-owned businesses" on a planned production basis, why stop at 10,000 a year—a rate at which it would take two centuries to make "entrepreneurs" out of the 10 per cent of Americans who are Negroes?) The OWN program was billed as a vast gain for "private" involvement: "direct" SBA "minority" loans were to be phased out in favor of "private" bank loans backed by a 90 per cent SBA guarantee. While all the ardent anti-racists, in government and out, were busily invoking regulations which made it illegal to use the tax funds of white and Negro citizens to guarantee FHA mortgage loans for "whites-only" housing projects (a procedure which might be termed an immorality-within-an-immorality), they were busily working up programs for using tax funds extorted from both white and Negro citizens to guarantee "blacks-only" "minority loans." (The latter isn't racism —it's combatting racism. Only a racist would ask, "Why?")

The purpose of Project OWN, according to the Urban Coalition's paper on the progress of the Kerner Commission's recommendations, "is not only to free more funds, but to bring about greater overall involvement of the private sector." One would think everyone would have caught on to the loan-guarantee ploy by this time—but evidently it's still good for a few more go-rounds.

The distinction between "public" and "private" sector funds is a spurious one.[9] All wealth is produced by the "private" sector, i.e., the productive activities of individual citizens; the "public" sector—government—is by nature non-productive. In an interventionist economy, however, the implication that "private funds" exist in practice is an expedient nicety. Once property rights have been abrogated by promulgation and acceptance of the myth that the "public sector" has a "right" to any part of anyone's money for redistribution in the "public good," all money becomes—in practice—the government's. What the "private sector" (the individual citizen) keeps, is kept by government's permission.

Under the present politico-economic system in the United States, if the government wants more "minority loan" funds, it can easily grab them and redistribute them to the capital-shy "potential" entrepreneurs. The natives, however, are currently getting a bit restless at the enormity of what government openly claims as its portion. For the "public sector" overtly to grab more just now would be impolitic. To keep the milch cows complaisantly producing the milk of human grievances, it is advisable at least to pretend that people's earnings (property) still belong to them.

Accordingly, loans made "directly" by SBA are phased out; loans made by "private" sources and "guaranteed" by the taxpayers are phased in. This will, of course, have the effect of channeling funds, and consequently scarce resources, away from non-guaranteed enterprises—the ones likely to be successful—and into "guaranteed" ones whose "potential" proprietors have proven to the SBA's satisfaction that they have few enough qualifications for running them. The actual capitalists—the *productive* enterprisers—are penalized twice: by a "shortage" of loan funds for *their* ventures, and by the taxes grabbed to pay for the defaulted loans of the non-productive. The bankers, meanwhile, relieved of risk, can merrily relax their credit standards, safe in the knowledge that every taxpayer in the nation has no choice but to pick up the tab for their mistakes.

Nor did the SBA confine its efforts on behalf of would-be "ghetto" enterprisers to "private" loans-cum-guarantees. SBA, says the Urban Coalition triumphantly, "has relaxed its own loan criteria [for direct SBA "minority loans"] in line with the concept of 'compensatory capitalism' [that's what the boys call it] based on the premise that higher risks can be accepted when high priority social objectives are at stake." Accepted by whom? Discreet silence.

SBA raised the ceiling on its "minority" loans to $350,000; decreased the equity investment standard from 50 to 15 percent (making it possible to borrow more with less), and elongated the easy, easy payment terms. "Calmly anticipating a rise in the default rate from 3 percent to as high as 7 percent," says the Urban Coalition approvingly, SBA "stressed 'character, not collateral' " for "minority" loans, and encouraged private banks to do likewise. It also speeded up its loan approvals for "guaranteed" loans: wouldn't want the fellows to get too impatient waiting for their "chance"—they might burn down the bank.

It's easy, especially for a starry-eyed coterie of bureaucratic "ghetto" salvagers, to be "calm" about losing other people's money. But one does wonder why, if "character" as defined by the SBA is as good as collateral, the default rate should be expected to rise.

SBA was not left to fight the good fight unaided. The Economic Development Administration was doing its bit all the while. Among its capitalistic projects was "funding" (using guess whose funds?) the administrative costs of a consortium of eight socially conscious Philadelphia banks that formed a Job Loan Corporation to make $2 million available to "minority" borrowers only. The EDA "funding" enabled the banks to make the loans at the prime (most favorable) interest rate usually reserved for blue-chip corporations and similarly excellent credit risks. Normally, "administrative costs" come out of the interest charged. And higher (not to say astronomical) administrative costs—tracking down disappearing defaulters, for example; or sending reminder notices; or auctioning off repossessed assets—are a principal reason for the higher interest rates on higher-risk loans. These higher costs attributable to higher risks are normally borne by the high-risk borrowers. The EDA "funding" program, however, made certain that the costs would be public-spiritedly borne by the taxpayers. The costs did not disappear; they were simply shifted to *involuntary* bearers so that poor-risk borrowers might collect the unearned, in the form of low interest rates.

In addition to "non-normal" loan programs and "active efforts" to secure instant capital, the Kerner Commission and Mr. Nixon proposed to furnish "knowhow": "A New Enterprise program," Mr. Nixon suggested, "should be established [by whom, Mr. Nixon forbore to state] to serve the Negro in the central city, helping black employees to become employers. Under such a program, successful businessmen and business school teachers could provide training in the techniques of business management. . . ." The knowhow-providers would be "induced" by tax incentives and other goodies. But naturally. The amount involved is scarcely small change: government-assisted "counselling" of 22 "black"- owned Brooklyn businesses came to $41,850 each in 1968. (The loans they got besides were extra.) Negro employees in the sub- urbs—and white employees anywhere—who hanker to become employers will, of course, be expected to *pay* for acquiring *their* knowhow (plus the cost of their competitors' counselling). Per- haps some philanthropic industrial firm will take pity on these new-style deprived and teach them without tax incentives. It might be a better deal at that.

Tax "incentives" (permission to keep more of one's own money) for businesses that locate in "poverty areas" are part of the pack- age, too. The Kerner Commission (and Little Sir Echo) recom- mends a "tax credit" for "the location and renovation of plants and other business facilities in urban and rural poverty areas." Such tax incentives, however, are slated only for businesses which have no *economic* reason to renovate or relocate in "pockets of poverty." "Protections would have to be provided," cautions the Commission, "against subsidizing 'runaway' plants from urban areas," i.e., plants which relocate to take advantage of inexpensive labor. Efficient enterprises are out, too: "Protection would also be necessary to avoid abuse of the credit by automated operations which involve few employees." Of course, the "dead end" un- skilled jobs of labor-intensive industries are precisely the jobs the status-hungry "hard-core" and aerospace-avid "potential" entre- preneurs want no part of. Consistency!

"BLACK CAPITALISM" IN ACTION

To savor the full aroma of a "Black Capitalism" project, it is advisable to take a typical example and follow it on its merry free enterprise way. Take those "Black Capitalism" projects paternally initiated by private (well—semiprivate) corporations motivated by social consciousness, the hope of government contracts, and/or a desire to please the powers-that-be. These are the projects hailed across the land in glowing, slick-paper, four-color-process handouts extolling corporate "commitment" to the "ghettos." These are the projects billed as "The American Way" at work. And since huge private companies start them, they must be capitalistic to the core. *Sure* they are.

To illustrate, let's take widely heralded Watts Manufacturing Company and trace its tortuous path to "Black Green-Power." As an itinerary for our journey, let's take the definition of a capitalistic enterprise:

In a capitalist enterprise, business decisions . . . are based upon the entrepreneur's assessment of (1) the demand, actual or potential, for the product or service he proposes to produce and sell; and (2) the most efficient (and therefore the most profitable) methods of producing the product. A private capitalistic enterprise has profit as its primary goal, and is neither started nor conducted by the expansion of intentionally-sought assistance of initiatory governmental force, direct or indirect.

After the Watts riot of 1966, a California company called Aerojet General was fired with a burning wish to aid the desperate "deprived." The way to do it, the company decided, was to provide them with jobs. It was imperative, in order to do so, to start a manufacturing operation in Watts. The wish was father to the deed—and Aerojet promptly filed papers to set up Watts Manufacturing Company as a wholly owned subsidiary. What was Watts Manufacturing to manufacture? At this juncture, and for some time thereafter, Aerojet didn't know.

Taking first things first, the company set out "to find a Negro to head the operation."[10] Looking among successful Negro managers of similar production firms would be unfeasible—no one had the foggiest notion what Watts' product would be. Besides, it would be unthinkable—a successful Negro corporate executive would be, by definition, an "Oreo" who might not have "the respect of the Negro community," that part of the "Negro community" which burned down Watts, anyway.

Decisions! Decisions! Outside consultation was indicated. And, like all good capitalists, Aerojet executives sought the advice of an expert in the field—in this case, anti-production, or the "art" of making production ultimately impossible by coercion, confiscation, and controls. Incumbent Governor "Pat" Brown was duly consulted, and, consequently, James Woods, owner of a Watts building firm, was named president of the newly hatched company. His son, 23, and one year out of college, was named general manager in charge of production. Production of what, no one knew.

Everyone knew, though, the criteria for hiring the production workers to produce the unknown product. Only unskilled "hard-core" workers were to be hired—by company policy.

Having set up the company, located its Negroes, and announced its hiring criteria, Aerojet began to "mull over a choice of product lines" to decide what Watts Manufacturing should manufacture. A $1,300-per-man "training" subsidy was negotiated with the federal government to "train" the hard-core workers to make whatever the company might make. Since a war was going on—and on and on—tents seemed a likely enough product. A $2,500,00 tent-making contract was "negotiated" with the Department of Defense. Having done the important part of the work, the triumphant capitalists scuttled home to set up a plant for tent-making.

Watts Manufacturing, its corporate pappies figured, was sure to make a "profit." There were those training subsidies, for one thing, and those Defense Department "set-asides"—contracts kept just for "ghetto" businesses. How could one lose? That remained to be found out.

Watts Manufacturing made tents, but not profits. Having lost money, subsidies and all, on its first tent contract, the company tried furniture frames, wood pallets, clothing—nearly anything. It made no profits on those, either.

In the first year of operation, 1,200 of the hard-core were hired to keep an average of 500 on the job. Not even by compromising its principles and hiring a few experienced men did the company manage to make out. Aerojet, instead of collecting the subsidy profits it had confidently expected, poured "hundreds of thousands of dollars" into Watts Manufacturing. The reason for their failure was explained to *Fortune* magazine by the capitalists in charge:

Their 23-year-old General Manager, having "little" previous production experience, "naturally" made mistakes. (There's nothing like learning by doing.) But he and the Aerojet capitalists hadn't expected that *they* would have to pick up the tab for their earning-while-learning management training project. "More support from the government" had been expected. Take those $1,300-per-man training subsidies: "comforting and cajoling" the hard-core takes more than that, man! Four to five thousand dollars per man would have been nearer the mark, Woods felt. And of the anticipated set-aside contracts, only $1.5 million worth had materialized. Stranded amidst his shattered "expectations," Woods, sympathizes *Fortune*, "felt a bit like cannon fodder in the war on poverty."

Watts Manufacturing, when last heard from, was still staggering along. Whenever it appears that it might have to fire its non-Oreo manager, lay off its hard-core protégés, and quietly fade away like any common-run capitalist project whose management loses millions, the Defense Department comes to the rescue with another set-aside.

That's capitalism?

No. But it is the definition of capitalism which the Urban Coalition used when it praised Aerojet General as a firm which, through "partnership," encouraged "ghetto enterprise."

Translated, the "compensatory" "Black Capitalism"-through-coercion programs are just one more version of the ancient argument of the "public good." In essence, it means that the "good" of the gang-of-the-moment (the one with the most votes or the most Molotov cocktails) becomes, by mystic metamorphosis, a "high priority social objective." "Gang-of-the-moment" may sound, at first, like too excessive and unkind a metaphor. But listen to the Urban Coalition: "A particularly hopeful surge of ghetto entrepreneurship has been among youth organizations in cities across the country, many of which [one presumes the UC means the "organizations," not the cities] started as gangs and are now involved in a variety of businesses from film-making to soul food shops. They have names like the Conservative Vice Lords (Chicago), the Mission Rebels (San Francisco), and Thugs United (New Orleans), and they also have a national organization, Youth Organizations United, which tries to round up money and technical advice." (p. 17) "Failure for the black youths" of Thugs United, warns the Urban Coalition, "could bring a special kind of disillusionment with the American system." Getting the boys to go straight (or at least semi-straight: some of the methods used to "round up money and technical advice" might not sound so worthy if judged by the standards applied to the rest of us) was "an uphill effort" and "the stakes are high." If their "capitalist" enterprises don't pay off fast and well, the boys just might (the Coalition hints, none too subtly) revert with a vengeance to their former ways.

Those who fell for the "capitalism" half of the "Black Capitalism" label did not, perhaps, foresee that the program meant using their money (i. e., tax funds) to bribe the members of "Thugs United" into a semblance of good behavior. Getting money by threatening mayhem is an enterprise of ancient tradition: it used to be called "blackmail." Now it's called "Black Capitalism." And for *that* sort of business the brickbat-brandishing "militant" entrepreneurs are undoubtedly more qualified than any old-fashioned accumulators of collateral.

Common-run capitalists set up their enterprises for the purpose of making profits. Watts Manufacturing and Thugs United have different goals—and who's to say they aren't meeting them? All they needed was a "chance." They're getting it. And no doubt their enterprises will be as successful as all getout—"socially," that is. Just keep their subsidies and "salaries" coming, and they'll turn out their anti-product of not bashing us over the head.

Those advocates of a free enterprise system who bought a "capitalism" with a racial coloration failed to grasp the significance of the disqualifying adjective.

CHAPTER VIII

The Inherent Contradiction

In Detroit, grown men registered for job-training programs by signing their names with "X." They could neither read nor write. In Rochester, New York, a supervisor asked a high school graduate to drill holes a foot apart. "What's a foot?" asked the baffled trainee. And in the Ocean Hill-Brownsville section of New York City an elderly woman, tears streaming down her face, stood in the street and told a reporter: "He can't read . . . my little grandson can't read. He's been in school three years; he's nine years old. *And he can't read!*"

Tax-supported compulsory education is one of the oldest and most widely accepted intrusions of government force into American lives. For many decades, education in the United States has been both "public" and "free." During those decades the scope of the system has constantly expanded, the period of schooling required by law has constantly lengthened; the expenditures for schooling have soared in both absolute and per-pupil terms. Yet

today we are bombarded with empirical evidence, and with statistics thrust upon us from all sides, showing that a considerable
portion of the population emerge from the schools as disaffected
illiterates, unable—or barely able—to read, write, and cipher; possessed of no useful skills in terms of today's job market; "unmotivated" to work; and anxious to take to the streets to express
their hostility to hard work, the rule of law, "affluence"—and the
school system.

"Education in the slums and ghettos," says the Urban Coalition
flatly, "is a failure."[1] If this is true, it is because the end was
inherent in the means.

Although the focus and the method of her protest were in error,
the Ocean Hill grandmother's problem, her anguish and her frustration, were real. In the field of education—as in no other—the
"deprived" have been deprived indeed. They, and all of us, have
been literally robbed of choice; deprived of solutions by the very
agency to which many now appeal for aid: the government. In no
other field has the iron hand of a force-perpetuated bureaucracy
been so dominant for so long. In no other field have the avenues
of choice been so effectively blocked by a genuine, i.e., coercion-
supported, monopoly; a monopoly which not only starves out,
suppresses, and regulates the activities of its pitifully hamstrung
competition, but literally forces its "customers" to accept its
shoddy wares: the government monopoly of the training of our
children's minds.

If the Ocean Hill grandmother cannot see that the root of her
problem lies in the very system to which she now cries for help
—well, neither can whole commissions of learned men. The
Kerner Commission proposes to remedy the ills of the educational
system by extending its monopoly over still greater portions of our
children's lives.

The Kerner Commission proposals on education are stamped all
over with what the reader will by now recognize as the Kerner
(and "liberal") trademarks: the foregone conclusion, fiercely clung
to in the face of all facts which might contradict it; racism, so
pervasive and rampant as to take one's breath away; the immoral
premise that "needs" equal rights, and its corollary premise that
government force is a legitimate tool to satisfy those needs. In a
typically Kerneresque chapter of its *Report*, the National Advi-

sory Commission on Civil Disorders proposes to minister to the "grievances" of those functional illiterates who have been taking to the streets to express their hunger for knowledge. How? By incarcerating them both earlier and longer in the schools they itched to get out of; by spending more and more and *more* of other people's money to do so; by making the curricula of "ghetto" schools more "relevant" to the "goals and values" of the anti-work, anti-mind "deprived"; and by stuffing helpless children into a sort of educational cement mixer inside which, it is hoped, a process of education-by-osmosis will occur through sheer physical proximity to those of another "race and class." This last, by the way, is offered as a means of combatting racism.

THE FOREGONE CONCLUSION REVISITED

In introducing its (nominally) educational panaceas the Kerner Commission trots out its *post hoc* shibboleths all over again.

> The hostility of Negro parents and students toward the school system is generating increasing conflict and causing disruption within many city school districts.
> But the most dramatic evidence of the relationship between educational practices and civil disorder lies in the high incidence of riot participation by ghetto youth who have not completed high school. Our survey of the riot cities found that the typical riot participant was a high school dropout. (p. 236)

The implication, of course, is that more schooling would have made the rioters less riot prone. Typically, the Commission ignores those portions of its own data which cast doubt upon the foregone conclusion to which the Commission's "liberal" (statist) intellectual orientation predisposed it from the start: that "grievances" of the "deprived" are the primary cause of riots; and that smothering those grievances in vast heaps of greenbacks will magically satiate the insatiable and thus cause "disorders" to cease.

The Commission's actual "supportive" data are placed elsewhere in the *Report* from the recommendations—indeed, the survey statistics and methodology themselves are buried in the back of the book. The discrepancies between those statistics and the conclusions the Commission has derived from them lead the cynical to wonder whether the Commission didn't fervently hope that everyone would ignore the supporting "facts" and concentrate on the recommendations. (Virtually everyone seems to have done exactly that.)

Such a jaundiced view is doubtless unjustified. Most likely, the Commission's intellectual myopia enabled it to read into its ambiguous figures a stunning validation of what the Commission members already held as an article of faith.

At any rate . . .

The Commission itself states (on page 75—a safe distance from its educational proposals) that "those with some high school education were more likely to riot than those who had only finished grade school." (For purposes of clarification it may be pertinent to note at this point that "more likely to riot" is the Commission's interpretation of the "fact" that more "rioters" than "non-rioters" in its minuscule sampling exhibited a given characteristic—in this case, "some high school" education.)

Also strangely missing from the section on educational recommendations is the information that a nearly equal percentage of "non-involved" and of "rioters" (38.9 percent and 34.9 percent, respectively) in Newark had *finished* high school. And that approximately equal percentages of rioters (5.7 percent) and "non-involved" (6.3 percent) in Newark had had some college. And that 2.2 percent of the rioters surveyed in Detroit had had some graduate school.

If those youths with "some high school" rioted, and those with no high school did not, and if one accepts the Kerner conclusion that "level of schooling is strongly related to riot participation," what remedial measures come to mind? Perhaps "ghetto" youth should be yanked out of school after eighth grade as a riot-prevention measure? Absurd? No more so, *on the basis of the Kerner Commission's own data,* than the sweeping proposals of *more* schooling as an answer to urban chaos. Should we conclude, on the basis of the grade school, high school and college riot-participation figures, that a little learning (grade school) is fine, a little more learning (some high school) is a dangerous thing, and a lot of learning (some college) is fifty-fifty? Or should we conclude that there is something damn fishy about those first few years of high school, and maybe the "deprived" had better skip them?

And what about the figures showing that between 50 percent and 55 percent of those *not* involved in riots were dropouts, too? Might we conclude that some factor other than sheer years of exposure to schooling (one hesitates to say, "level of education") is critical in the making of a rioter? And that all those ponderous statistics, based upon interviews with only 600 of all the thousands who rioted in 1967, don't prove a damn thing?

THE IMMORAL PREMISES REVISITED

No one, surely, will quarrel with the contention that "ghetto" children, like all children, *need* education. The specific content of any given child's education, its duration, and its aims, will vary, as human beings vary from one another in their intellectual capacities, their interests, their plans, their goals, their dreams. But, for all human beings, learning is an inescapable necessity of life and growth. Like other necessities, education is not given man by nature; it must be earned by man's own effort.

During his childhood, man, by his nature, is as yet incapable of providing for himself the essentials required for the sustenance of his life. Since a child exists as a result of the choices and actions of his parents, it is his parents who logically are responsible for providing his food, his shelter, his clothing—and his education. The need for education does not constitute a right *to be educated.* Nor does it constitute a right to have one's children educated at others' expense. The right to life, which is every man's, must, by man's nature, include the right to learn. It does not and cannot include a right *to be taught*, for inherent in such a "right" would be the right of a man to determine what use other men may make of their talents, their earnings, their time: their *lives*.

The *concretes* of the Kerner Commission proposals for education are based upon the false premise of a nonexistent "right" to "free public education," which means an education provided by someone else's effort, at the expense of other men. Carried to its logical conclusion, this false concept of rights must include a "right" to be clothed, a "right" to be fed, a "right" to be housed, a "right" to be amused. It is no accident that the Kerner Commission and their fellow spokesmen for the "deprived" claim these rights as well. Once one accepts the premise of men's "right" to *anything* provided by other men, there is no sane end to the road. It is a road which can lead to nothing but cannibalism, overt or indirect:

> Modern cannibals are more efficient than the old-fashioned ones. Instead of feeding on a man's body, they feed on his labor and property. The feast lasts longer that way.
>
> Socialism is the fiction that everyone can feed off everyone else. The Great Society is a society of cannibals, where men feed off each other in a glorious feast of brotherhood. The left-wing politicians are all cannibals running for the office of chef so that they can be put in charge of the menu, so that they can decide who is fat enough to roast and who is needy enough for a free meal. . . . Society [has been] reified and deified . . . as an entity greater than man, as a kind of super-being whose diet requires human individuality. . . . People accept the idea of higher forms preying upon lower ones. They think it natural that a higher form, society, should devour men as [men] devour lower forms, plants and animals. In reality, since society is not a higher entity but only a group of individual men, [the doctrine of "public needs"] means that some individuals prey upon others, under the banner of society.[2]

There is no right to be fed. There is no right to be housed. There is no right to be educated. There is only the right to *be*. "Free, public" education is based upon needs, not rights; implemented by force, not reason; it is an immoral system which should not exist. Regardless of their out-of-context validity (or lack thereof), the Kerner proposals for education are proposals for the perpetuation and expansion of a system built upon an immoral base. They cannot be justified. No amount of empirical effectiveness can justify educational methods rooted in the initiation of force, via government, to wrest values from men.

No man has the right to *initiate* force against another, no matter how demonstrably desirable, in themselves, the ends he thus seeks to achieve may be. The specific educational proposals of the Kerner Commission may, however, be taken out of this larger context for purposes of evaluation. While doing so, one must bear firmly in mind that it is from the foregoing *fundamental* premise that judgment of the Kerner recommendations as a whole must ultimately proceed.

RACISM RAMPANT: THE CEMENT-MIXER SCHOOLHOUSE

A substantial portion of the Kerner proposals for "ghetto" *education* is actually devoted to presenting schemes for forced racial *integration*, as though precisely the proper blend of shades of difference were a sort of magic formula for instant erudition. Placed first among the recommended "educational" practices is "Increasing Efforts to Eliminate de Facto Segregation"—with the assistance of the federal carrot backed up, sooner or later, by the federal club.

> We have cited the extent of racial isolation in our urban schools. It is great and it is growing. It will not be easily overcome. Nonetheless, we believe school integration to be vital to the wellbeing of this country. (p. 243)

> We believe that the Title IV program should be reoriented and expanded into a major Federal effort to provide comprehensive aid to support state and local desegregation projects. ... As an additional incentive to integration, the Title IV program might well be modified to provide substantially increased support upon attainment of specified levels of racial integration. ... It is most important that courses by developed and scheduled to provide racially integrated educational experiences. (p. 245)

"Successful implementation," the *Report* states, will require "assistance to support and encourage desegregation through *assignment of students to public schools in order to overcome racial imbalance*." (Emphasis mine.) The popular term for this ploy is "bussing." In other words, the racist practice of shuttling children from hither to yon to achieve forced *segregation* is to be supplanted by the racist practice of shuttling children from yon to hither to achieve forced *integration*.

So far, the thrust for racial integration has focused upon achieving the proper ratio of "blacks" to "whites" in each school. The difficulties encountered in attaining the proper (or popular) mix are formidable enough, since neither geneticists, anthropologists, nor politicians have ever agreed even among themselves just what proportion of "Negro blood" constitutes legal "Negroness." But at least there would appear to be enough "official" Negroes and "official" whites to go around. When the Chinese, Indians, Eskimos, and Polynesians start demanding their rights to racial/ethnic quotas, however, the problem will be compounded indeed. One can readily envision the day when little Eskimo boys and girls will be jetted from city to city so that they may spend an hour or a day in each of the many schools which will demand their statistically proportionate presence in order to qualify for federal aid via proof of "racial" heterogeneity.

The only plausible rationalization for *forced* integration is that integration combats "attitudes toward race, on both sides, produced by centuries of myth, ignorance, and bias." According to this rationale (which is given short, racist-oriented shrift in the *Report*), children in integrated schools can see for themselves that people of other races are *individuals*, to be judged as such. In practice, the sudden, arbitrary, artificial infusion of a flotilla of "unmotivated," "educationally deprived," perhaps psychologically disturbed "ghetto" children into an educationally "enriched" suburban school system is unlikely to accomplish this laudable aim. Faulty intellectual integration (i.e., erroneous concept formation), compounded by children's acceptance of irrational parental attitudes, will tend to cause some children in forcibly integrated classes to link the unadmirable traits of disturbed or unintelligent "ghetto" children to their race. Resentment of forcible racial (and "class") integration is likely to intensify whatever irrational antagonism parents feel. Thus the tactics of forcible "race"–"class"–competence mixing are quite likely to *reinforce* whatever race prejudice may *already* exist among the forcibly integrated children (in the "white middle-class" children *and* in the "ghetto" newcomers, who may be cruelly ostracized as interlopers). Moreover, by advancing its halfhearted anti-prejudice argument from a collectivist, anti-individualist base of "interaction between the races" per se, the Kerner Commission nullifies its claim to even this dubious, out-of-context excuse for tolerance-via-force.

The Commission states at the outset that its insistence on inte-

gration is *not* based "on the effect of racial and economic segregation on achievement of Negro students," but rather upon the
premise that Negroes will blow the country to bits if integration
is not immediately forthcoming. (The Commission was behind the
times. Even as the *Report* was published, all "with-it" militants
worth their press clippings were threatening to blow up the country if *segregation* were not immediately forthcoming.) However,
it is precisely against the supposed ill effects of segregation on
educational achievement that the thrust of the *Report*'s erudition-
via-integration proposals is directed.

In the course of its attempts to substantiate its pleas for the
cement-mixer schoolhouse, the Commission advanced arguments
which any white supremacist would be delighted to borrow. "Class
and race factors," says the *Report*, "have a strong bearing on
educational achievement."

> In the critical skills—verbal and reading ability—Negro students
> fall further behind whites with each year of school completed. For
> example, in the metropolitan Northeast Negro students on the
> average begin the first grade with somewhat lower scores than
> whites on standard achievement tests, are about 1.6 grades behind
> by 6th grade, and have fallen 3.3 grades behind white students by
> the twelfth grade. (pp. 236-7)

These are *averages*—and they can mislead, as averages will. In
Harlem, for example, 30 percent of third-grade pupils placed "below grade level" (according to standard achievement tests); but
21.6 percent placed *above* grade level in "reading comprehen-
sion," leaving 48.4 *at* grade level. (By sixth grade, when 77.5
percent scored below grade level in "word knowledge," 10.6 percent scored *above* grade level and 7.4 percent *at* grade level.)[3] The
Commission neglects to speculate upon why students reading below grade level are *in* the twelfth grade, as it neglects to explain
why "many of those who graduate" from high school—having
ostensibly fulfilled the academic requirements of their schools—
are "not equipped to enter the normal job market." (New York
City schools offer a "general" diploma to any student who sticks
out the 12 years of school. Students who actually have passed their
courses are given an "academic" diploma. About half the city's

high school "graduates" have "general" diplomas; more than 75 percent of Harlem high school "graduates" have "general" diplomas.)[4]

> The failure of the public schools to equip these students with basic verbal skills is reflected by their performance on the Selective Service Mental Test. During the period June 1964 to December 1965, 67 percent of Negro candidates failed the examination. The failure rate for whites was 19 percent. (p. 237)

Which Negro candidates? Of what level of intelligence? From which schools? The *Report* does not say. The Selective Service Mental Test is not strictly an achievement test; it is a test of "aptitude," an attribute which armed forces tests have so far failed dismally to measure.[5] If such an outsized percentage of individuals of a single racial/ethnic group failed the test, the record might suggest, especially to those familiar with the questionable record of "aptitude," "personality," and "I.Q." tests in general, that this test, too, is a less than reliable instrument for measuring what it is purported to measure. The much-touted "Moynihan Report"[6] quotes statistics to "prove" that children with "no father in the home" have lower I.Q.'s (i.e., are less intelligent) than children whose fathers live at home. Children raised by non-parents are "proven" less bright still. The conclusion reached is that a national effort should be instituted to keep fathers in all homes. No one questioned the validity of I.Q. tests themselves as a measure of intelligence.[7] The racist, of course, will use the failure rate of Negro examinees to "prove" what he has been saying all along: that Negroes, as a race, are innately inferior.

In truth, the quoted statistics, taken by themselves (as they are in the *Report*), prove absolutely nothing. The Kerner Commission, however, leaps eagerly to the gratuitous conclusion that the figures prove, incontrovertibly, that "segregation" is to blame for the failure of Negro candidates, and the low achievement of many Negro pupils:

> Several factors have converged to produce this critical situation. [First,] the vast majority of inner-city schools are rigidly segregated. . . . *Segregation* has operated to reduce the quality of educa-

tion provided in schools serving disadvantaged Negro neighborhoods. (p. 237, my emphasis)

In its later passages, the education section of the *Report* does a
truly notable job of confusing "segregation" based upon *race* (a
non-volitional attribute) with "segregation" by "*class*," i.e., socioeconomic level (a volitional attribute of a child's parents). In the
passage quoted above, however, the terms "segregation" and
"segregated schools" are clearly used in their commonly accepted
sense of "schools which contain pupils entirely or predominantly
of one race." By linking *racial* segregation of the schools to poor
scholastic achievement of some students who happen to be
Negroes, the Commission (no doubt unintentionally) lends cre-
dence to white racist dogmas of innate Negro inferiority:

> When disadvantaged children are *racially* isolated in the schools,
> they are deprived of one of the more significant ingredients of
> quality education: exposure to other children with strong educa-
> tional backgrounds. (p. 238)

The "disadvantaged" children here referred to are Negro children; *racial* isolation is the only variable mentioned. If racial
isolation, per se, deprives children of contact with children with
"strong educational backgrounds," then strong educational backgrounds (a factor dependent, in reality, upon the volitional value
structure of parents and children) are, by implication, a function
of race. Similarly, the Kerner Commission states that racial integration *in itself* does not wholly achieve quality education. Such
a statement implies that racial integration, as such, *does* affect the
level of learning to *some* degree.

Racism is a doctrine under which genetically determined differences are used as criteria for making distinctions among men in
situations where genetics are irrelevant, i.e., in issues involving
volitional activities or *volitionally acquired* attributes. The Kerner
Commission (at least by implication) repeatedly equates erudition
with "whiteness." The Commission proposes that Negro children
and white children be tossed together into a cement-mixer schoolhouse where, it is hoped, erudition-*qua*-whiteness will rub off.
These proposals are racism naked.

In accordance with their collectivist-racist bias, the Kerner Commission members categorically lump some twenty-odd million individuals into an inchoate mass, for which the Commission elects itself spokesman. "Negroes," it states, "perceive their capacity to shape their futures ('destiny control') on the basis of the numbers of whites in their schools." If some persons who are Negroes indeed do this, they are tragically in error—an error which the Kerner Commission, by pandering to it, sanctions and perpetuates.

EDUCATION BY OSMOSIS

Coupled with its doctrine of racial integration per se as a tool for achieving quality education, the Kerner Commission exhibits a nearly fanatical devotion to the doctrines of environmental determinism. Consequently, the *Report* attempts to discuss education while avoiding reference to the two genuinely critical factors in human learning: *intelligence* and *volition*. To the Commission, "background" is all.

> The *Coleman Report* and the *Report* of the Civil Rights Commission establish that the predominant socioeconomic *background* of the students in a school exerts a powerful impact upon achievement. Further, the *Coleman Report* found that "if a minority pupil from a home without much educational strength is put with schoolmates with strong educational *backgrounds*, his achievement is likely to increase." (p. 238, my emphasis)

Of course. If the "schoolmates with strong educational backgrounds" have themselves accepted education as a value; if they are intelligent; if they have attained a high level of educational achievement, then the stimulation of their example, of competition with keen minds, of the more challenging intellectual assignments possible in classes containing a high proportion of able children, would naturally excite any child placed in such a class to greater effort within his sphere of mental competence, provided that he, too, accepted learning as a value. The beneficial effects of such stimulation would seem likely to be greatest if there were no extreme disparity in intellectual capacity between the newcomer and the other children in the class.

But, if erudition and achievement can stimulate by propinquity, one might expect that the converse might also be true. Will not pupils with "strong education backgrounds" be stifled and stupefied in an atmosphere of plodding dullness? Might they not be discouraged into "nonachievement" if placed in classes predominantly composed of the "educationally deprived"? Sad to say, many a school child shortsightedly does only as much work as the minimum expected of him. If the intellectual level of the class is lowered, will the brighter child not be intellectually shortchanged and stunted to some degree?

Ah, no. "If a white pupil from a home that is strongly and effectively supportive of education is put in a school where most pupils do not come from such homes, his achievement will be little different than if he were in a school composed of others like himself." (Why is the child from a "strongly and effectively supportive" home gratuitously assumed to be white? Is one to conclude that a Negro child from such a home would perform differently? Or that there are no Negro homes "strongly and effectively supportive of education"? The *Report* gives no clue.)

Since the same child cannot be placed in both situations, what the above data actually mean is that *some* "minority pupils from homes without much educational strength" were placed in schools with classmates with "strong education backgrounds," and that the scholastic achievement of those particular pupils "improved" in an unspecified manner; that some "white pupils from homes supportive of education" were put into schools with the educationally "deprived," and that some were not, and that both sets of pupils reached approximately the same undefined level of achievement.

It is, of course, entirely possible that the beneficial effect of intellectual stimulation derived from association with better students will be greater, for the less apt or less "motivated" children, than the detrimental effect, upon bright children, of enforced intellectual starvation. However, the *Report* states that in schools where "ability grouping" is maintained, the transplanted products of the "ghetto" end up in classes with each other. Thus one suspects that the attempts to deprecate the debilitating effects of harnessing bright minds to the snailcrawl pace of the dull are actually elaborate rationalizations, designed to sugarcoat the schemes for forcibly stirring a sprinkling of the "educationally advantaged" in among the intellectually unwashed in the hope that erudition-by-osmosis will somehow be achieved. And erudition is tacitly equated with "background"—racial background at that.

One would, of course, be a fool to deny that the home background can make an immense difference to the scholastic achievement of a child, particularly in the early school years when the influence of the family is most strong. But the influence of "background" obtains only to the extent that a child accepts his parents' values and that he, *by his own volition*, absorbs and uses what his background—including his home, his neighborhood, the television shows he watches, the people he talks to: the total environment in which he moves—has to offer him. *Fundamentally*, it is *not* background which produces the scholastic achievement of any given individual. And it is not, ever, race.

Learning is a function of human intelligence, assimilating, and abstracting from, the components of the total environment at the direction of *human volition*: the *self*-motivation without which all exterior stimuli must fail.

But, in line with its credo that environment is all, and despite considerable evidence within the *Report* itself that, the longer "ghetto" children remain in the schools, the poorer their performance in relation to their potential becomes, the Kerner Commission typically recommends earlier and longer exposure to the school system under the guise of "enrichment" intended to counter the detrimental effects of the environment on the slum child's soma and the slum child's psyche.

"GIVE US THE CHILD UNTIL HE IS FIVE . . ."

Racial integration, according to Kerner, "provides benefits to the underprivileged, but it takes only a small step toward equality of educational opportunity." Actually, the Kerner Commission fails (understandably enough, on the basis of reality) to substantiate the claim to even that "small step." Nor does the *Coleman*

Report, as quoted by Kerner and crew, provide much proof of the supposed benefits of the *socioeconomic* integration which the courts are now rushing to implement. In the *Hobson* v. *Hansen* case (Washington, D. C.), Judge J. Skelly Wright ruled that "racially and socially homogeneous schools damage the minds and spirit of all children who attend them," and "block the attainment of the broader goals of democratic education, whether the segregation occurs by law or by fact."[8]

"Even if a school is [racially and socially] integrated," states the *Coleman Report*, "the heterogeneity of backgrounds with which children enter school is largely preserved in the heterogeneity of their performance when they finish." Education by racial rub-off and education by socioeconomic osmosis have somehow (surprise! surprise!) failed to materialize.

There is a plausible explanation for this, as there is a plausible explanation for the overall low scholastic performance of "ghetto" (slum) children *as a group*. It is an explanation which the Kerner Commission, consistently enough, refuses to recognize or pursue. To pursue it would be to run smack into the unpalatable truth that equality of education is, ultimately, unattainable, so long as inequality of intellect exists among men.

Slum areas, by definition, are slum areas precisely because the majority of the people who live there are poor, unskilled *and* dirty and sloppy. These attributes are frequently, although not necessarily, products of low intelligence. Judging from presently available evidence, intelligence (intellectual *capacity*, as distinguished from intellectual *achievement*) is hereditary. Brighter parents *as a group* tend to have brighter children. Less intelligent parents *as a group* tend to have less intelligent children. There is a significant correlation between intelligence of parents and their young. Although this correlation obviously cannot be used to judge the intelligence of any specific individual, it is nonetheless reasonable to assume that a substantial majority of children whose parents are more or less permanent slum dwellers might be children of lower than average intelligence. The less intelligent (or, at least, the less educated) also tend to have more children than better educated families do. The concentration of less able children in slum areas might be expected to remain relatively high, not only because of the larger family size prevalent among the less intelligent, but because those slum dwellers with ambition, ability, and related psychoepistemological traits are likely to remain in slum areas only temporarily. When they move up and on, the less able, and their children, are left behind.

"Intelligence" and "ability" are forbidden words, however. It is an article of the "liberal" faith that *all* children, if exposed to the "proper" background, will "achieve equally" in school. Clearly, it is environmental conditioning ("enrichment") which is required to fill in the gaps.

> In short, compensatory education is essential not only to improve the quality of education provided in segregated ghetto schools, but to make possible both meaningful integration and maximum achievement in integrated schools.
>
> Attainment of this goal will require adoption of a comprehensive approach designed to *reconstruct the ghetto child's social and intellectual environment*, compensate for disadvantages already suffered and provide necessary tools of essential literacy skills. (p. 244, my emphasis)
>
> Early childhood programs should involve parents and the home, as well as the child. This can be accomplished through community education classes, and use of community aides and mothers' assistants. To reduce the incidence of congenital abnormalities, these community-based programs should be tied in with prenatal training. (p. 247)

"Environmental reconstruction" ultimately means changing the value structure of a child's home, or counteracting it, and *negating the parents' right of choice in determining the content of their children's education* by, in effect, denying "ghetto" parents the right to raise their own children. Naturally, one does not put the proposition quite so bluntly; it must be prettied up a bit to con the peasants:

> Early childhood education is the very heart of the effort to reconstruct the environment which incapacitates disadvantaged children, even before they enter the school system. [Since children enter the school system only "slightly behind" the "advantaged," and leave it way behind, one might question whether it is the *environment* which "incapacitates" them!]

> We believe that the time has come to build on the success [sic] of Head Start and other preschool programs in order to bring the benefits of comprehensive early childhood education to all children from disadvantaged homes [to hell with any "benefits" for the "advantaged"!] and *to extend the reach to younger children*.
>
> Early childhood education programs should include provisions for medical care and food, so that the educational experience can have its intended impact. (p. 247, my emphasis)

In other words, children should be snatched from their parents at the earliest possible age (movements to make "early childhood education" compulsory are already afoot and gaining ground), classified, inoculated, fed a bureaucratically balanced diet, and brainwashed with whatever tripe the bureaucrats in their wisdom decide is necessary to "overcome the detrimental effect" of their parent's ideas—all in the name of "free" education.

Such tactics have already been applied in more enlightened countries than ours: "Give us the child until he is five," said the Nazis, "and he is ours." That, of course, was "indoctrination"; what the Kerner Commission proposes is "enrichment."

That's nice to know.

"Enrichment" is a mighty broad term. Some enrichers have interpreted it as including their teaching of "Black Power" slogans in Head Start classrooms festooned with pictures of Malcolm X. Other enrichers have taken a different tack: arranging "field trips" for disadvantaged tots. One such expedition explored the wonders of one of the more expensive luxury shopping centers in the East. (The press release extolling the trip neglected to state whether pocket money was provided.) Another sojourn was climaxed by a jet ride wangled out of an airline—surely an enriching experience, although one of which many a child of the despised and tax-bled middle class has yet to partake. The connection between such indubitably enjoyable excursions and Head Start's ostensible purpose of instilling "readiness" for the less obviously exciting mechanics of learning the three "R's" is, to say the least, somewhat obscure.

Moreover, the alleged success of Head Start is apparent primarily to those who are plumping for more and merrier Head Starts.

A 1969 study of Head Start conducted by Westinghouse Learning Corporation at the expense and behest of OEO made headlines when its less than eulogistic conclusions hit the newsrooms. The study was based upon the most extensive program of testing undertaken to date. Head-Starters and non-Head-Starters in the first, second, and third grades were tested for language development, learning "readiness," academic achievement, and a gamut of "personality" factors such as "positive self-concept," "desire for achievement in school," "attitudes toward school, home," etc. The test scores of Head-Starters and non-Head-Starters were then compared.

Whether or not the tests used were *in fact* valid measurements of "readiness" or "positive self-concept" is highly debatable. But the important point in relation to the present discussion is that, *by their own standards*, i. e., the tests, the Westinghouse testers found virtually no *meaningful* difference (or none at all, depending on which attribute was being measured) between Head Start children and their non–Head Start "peers." Whatever the kids were learning (and "common" sense whispers that they must have been learning *something*), it wasn't much help to them when they got into "real" school. The Summary of the Preliminary Draft of the *Westinghouse Report* states the conclusions as follows. (The painfully fractured English exposed here is typical of the whole Westinghouse draft. The draft, composed by whole flotillas of learned professors and educational "experts," offers ample evidence that education "deprivation" is not confined to the "ghettos." It's rife in universities, too.)[9]

> Summer [Head Start] programs [concludes the *Westinghouse Report*] appear to be ineffective in producing any gains in cognitive and affective development that persist into the elementary grades. . . .
>
> Head Start children, whether from summer or full-year programs, still appear to be in a disadvantaged position with respect to the national norms for the standardized tests of language development and scholastic *achievement* [i. e., tests of *knowledge acquired*]. . . .
>
> In sum, the Head Start children *could not be said to be appreciably difference* [sic] from their peers in the elementary grades who did not attend Head Start *in most aspects of cognitive and affective*

development measured in this study, with the exception of a slight, but nonetheless significant superiority [meaning, as one finds by reading further, a "statistically significant" superiority; meaning, according to the Summary's own definition, a superiority greater than *would be expected on the basis of chance*] of full-year Head Start children on the measures of cognitive development. (my emphasis)[10]

A more succinct summation of the Westinghouse findings was given by Dr. Verne S. Atwater, president of the Westinghouse Learning Corporation, and quoted by the *New York Times* of April 18, 1969. Said Dr. Atwater: "What we have been doing to date has simply not cut the mustard."

Naturally, this conclusion did not inhibit either Dr. Atwater or his colleagues from recommending that "large-scale efforts and substantial resources" (the "nation's" resources, of course) be allocated to "intervention programs" (note the terminology) for "poor young children," perhaps "extending downward toward infancy and upward into the primary grades" and including "training of parents to become more effective teachers of their children"; in other words, more Head Starts and more—lots more—money: *ours.*

Among the pro–Head-Starters, agonized yowls of indignation greeted the Westinghouse conclusions. In reading these protests, one gains the distinct impression that the protesters regard an OEO-financed study which reaches unfavorable (or at least less than laudatory) conclusions as dirty pool—not in the bond, and certainly not to be taken seriously by those who appropriate money for the Head Start fun and games. Dr. Martin Deutsch, director of the New York University Institute for Developmental Studies, begged the government (in somewhat unprofessorial language) not to "cop out." Dr. Deutsch buttressed his impassioned plea with the curiously revealing assertion that studies of his own, under way in Harlem, showed that "the concept of Head Start can be successful if carefully planned and carried out in ways somewhat different from the frantic efforts of the last few years."[11] The beleaguered taxpayers, who had just emptied their bank accounts into Internal Revenue and state coffers on the fifteenth of April, may have been less than charmed to read, on the eighteenth, that the scientific, sure-fire, and expensive enrichment programs they were picking up the tab for were now being characterized as "frantic efforts" by one of the programs' adherents while, in virtually the same breath, he pleaded for more of their money for more of the same.

Earlier, the Center for Urban Education had conducted a study of children in four Manhattan kindergartens. The conclusion? Head Start children "made out better than non–Head Starters only for the first few months. Then their initial advantages disappeared. . . . Head Start children adjusted more easily to school at first [not surprisingly—they had already been in school], but after some months others adjusted too, and caught up."[12]

Sargent Shriver, then czar of the OEO, had the predictable reaction. "The disappointment and discouragement of slum classrooms," wept Mr. Shriver, "caused many [Head Starters] to fall further behind than children who had not had the Head Start experience. The readiness and receptivity they had gained had been crushed by the broken promises of first grade."[13] (Organ tremolo . . . sobbing violins . . . up and out.) "Readiness" and "receptivity"—for *what*? Admittedly, it would be difficult to make the ABC's top an airplane ride.

When confronted with evidence of the failure of a program, the Kerner coterie has an invariable excuse—insufficient "funding"; and an invariable remedy—more of whatever flopped the first time. Thus Mr. Shriver suggested "a projection of Head Start into the primary grades which we might call Operation Keep Moving"; the Kerner Commission suggests the same thing; and a so-called "Follow Through" program, continuing through third grade, has actually been initiated, *post* Kerner and supposedly *propter* Kerner, by the bureaucratic environment-negaters. "Follow Through" uses children as guinea pigs (forcibly, since parents are compelled by law to send their children to school) to test "the benefits of curriculum change, lower pupil-teacher ratios, racial and socioeconomic mix, use of community aids, and community control."[14]

"Community control" has a nice, democratic ring to it. But "community control" by the residents of the "ghetto" means control of the curriculum by the very parents whose "home background" has such a supposedly baneful effect on the learning ability of their children. Ah, consistency. . . . One Preston Wilcox, erstwhile "militant" ("We've got to have more violence") and paid consultant of OEO, asserted in an interview with Shirley Scheibla of *Barron's* that "even though Negro parents may not be technically qualified to decide on school curricula and employment of teachers, they can learn, and, in a democracy, the parents should have the same opportunity to make mistakes as anybody else."[15]

Quite so. Were the schools privately owned and supported by tuition fees, "ghetto" parents—and all parents—would automatically exercise curriculum control. But that is not exactly what Mr. Wilcox or the Kerner Commission has in mind. "Ghetto" parents should not (horrors!) have the opportunity to *pay* for their mistakes—only to make them. Thus "centralized control over the raising of revenues" (translate: taxes) is a salient feature of the Kerner "community control" proposals.

As for "curriculum changes": the basic rationale for these experiments has been epitomized (rather more baldly than is usually the case) by author and education "expert" Paul Goodman in the *New York Review of Books.* "A normal child," quoth Goodman, will learn to read "spontaneously," unless "he is systematically interrupted and discouraged, for instance by trying to teach him." Let no one leap to the conclusion that such experts intend that there be no schools at all. Instead, we should have non-structured schools where, as in a recently initiated program in New York City, primary school children "select their own programs" in a completely non-graded system, without textbooks, regularly assigned teachers, or any overall educational plan or achievement standards whatsoever.

For all their lack of any tangible curriculum or focus, "enrichment" programs do not come cheaply. New York City's More Effective Schools program (MES) came to $994 per pupil per year —$470 more per pupil than the average cost then prevailing in the city's schools. After three years, a study by the Center for Urban Education culminated in the conclusion that MES was . . . well . . . a mess.[16] (The operative word was "ineffective.") A still more ambitious project in Ypsilanti, Michigan, combined "home visits, psychological consultation, medical services" and something called a task-orientated curriculum (Molotov cocktail construction? Police-car wrecking I and II?).[17] The cost was a whopping (especially for primary education) $1,500 per child—a sum which might leave many a middle-class taxpayer sorely in need of psychological consultation, not to speak of bankruptcy counselling, both of which he would, naturally, be expected to pay for himself.

No matter. The program was "promising," whatever that means, and the sky's the limit. Inner-city school budgets, testified Dr. Dan W. Dodson before the Kerner Commission, should be at least doubled. And who is to pay for the realization of Dr. Dodson's expensive dreams? "We recognize," states the Kerner Commission, "that the enrichment programs we recommend will be very costly." That is one prediction, at least, in which the Kerner Commission is sure to be proven accurate. "ESEA provides financial assistance for such programs, but amounts available do not match the need," the Commission moans plaintively. "To make a significant improvement in the quality of education provided in schools serving disadvantaged children ESEA funding should be substantially increased from its present level." ("Funding" and "be funded" are phrases which appear again and again in the *Report*. They sound so much more euphonious than "taxes" and "be taxed"; as "national resources" and "national wealth" roll more glibly around the tongue than "other people's money.")

"In addition," the Kerner Commission continues, "Title I should be modified to provide for greater concentration of aid to school districts having the greatest proportion of disadvantaged students. This can be accomplished by altering the formula governing eligibility *to exclude affluent school districts with less than the specified minimum numbers of poor students.*" (my italics) Translated, this means that the districts supplying the "aid" money shall be excluded from receiving "aid."

Court decisions have already been handed down which attempt to affirm the "constitutional right" of all children to attend schools which are both racially and socioeconomically "heterogeneous," and of the dull to be placed in classes with the bright. The *racial*-mixing mania led one ex-school superintendent to beg (presumably in jest) for a racial spectrometer to assist hardpressed school administrators in meeting their color quotas.[18] Now those administrators pursuing the chimera of "federal aid" (which much of the public persists in regarding as some kind of sourceless "free money"), and hoping for a temporary respite from "civil rights" suits, will have to meet, in addition to the color quota, a "poor quota." Isn't anyone disturbed about the amount of bureaucratic snooping which the implementation of enforced *socioeconomic* integration would entail? Perhaps not. A nation of organization men who, for the most part, are supinely accepting the prospect of a compulsory census of their income levels, toilet facilities, and marital histories, will presumably take it all in stride. But will the statistics shuffling and bus-schedule dovetailing leave school administrators any time to devote to such unimportant details as quality and content of instruction? Will the school-bus odysseys of the student pawns of this numbers game leave any time in the school day for learning? Oh, well. . . .

It is unlikely that "Follow Through" and its kindred programs, which are based on the same determinist premises, will be any more successful than Head Start at anything except throwing other people's money around and eliminating the poverty of a few erstwhile "militants" elevated into well-salaried opportunities for empire building. But why should the Kerner Commission be surprised? *According to the Commission's own premises, such programs cannot succeed.*

Negroes, after all, are innately inferior, permanently incapacitated by the inherited attitudes induced by the era of slavery. Hasn't the Commission devoted pages and pages to telling us so—implicitly and explicitly? Negro children are doomed at birth —fated by parentage and "background" to remain forever disadvantaged and unmotivated. The age of opportunity and the American Dream is past. Intelligence doesn't count—does not, indeed, exist. Environment is destiny, isn't it? If it is, then *no attempt* to negate its crushing and final predestination can succeed.

This is the inherent contradiction of the Kerner education proposals: that, while affirming a static universe where success or failure is preordained, the Commission—like the OEO and the whole national horde of social engineers—persists, in contradiction of its own premises, in promulgating "enrichment" programs: more and more and more of them.

"If school systems," said Sargent Shriver, "will pick up the challenge and keep moving one year at a time, the results will inevitably be a revolution in education systems from preschool through college."[19] Damn right. But what *kind* of revolution?

"Head Start" and "Follow Through" will be augmented by "Try Again" programs, succeeded in the fullness of time by "Last Chance." (Yes, Virginia, there *is* a program called "Last Chance." But it isn't a last chance—only the next-to-next-to-next-to-last.) When the kids come home from their round-the-world social studies cruises (travel is *so* enriching), they can still sign up for a "Stay in School" program for potential high school dropouts—for which President Johnson requested the piddling (to the Kerner Commission) appropriation of only 30 million dollars. Those who flub or miss that next-to-next-to-last chance can still try for "Upward Bound" (the program for college pre-dropouts); then for the Kerner Commission's proposed one-year college prep program, plus whatever "compensatory" programs-for-freshmen-illiterates the compliant colleges have meanwhile dreamed up.

The Fetish—and Contradiction—of "Relevance"

The advertised *raison d'être* of the Head Start and early childhood education programs is that the "ghetto" environment and the "disadvantaged" home are horribly deleterious to the young, and must be counteracted at all costs (to the productive). It is, therefore, surprising, at least to the naive, to find considerable space in the *Kerner Report* and the popular press devoted to bemoaning the lack of "relevance" of education to the "life styles" of the ghettos—the very life styles which are blamed for the poor achievement of ghetto children; the same life styles which education-by-racial-rub-off and education-by-socioeconomic-osmosis are intended to counteract.

Thus we find Harold B. Gores of the Ford Foundation blaming "the existence of two cultures in the cities" for the troubles of the schools. Many schools, according to Gores, are geared to "the wrong culture." "That culture," according to Gores, "is white, middle class, Anglo-Saxon, Protestant. The children attuned to it are success-oriented and have strong family ties."[20] If a success-oriented culture, inducing strong family ties, is the "wrong" culture, what culture, pray tell, might Mr. Gores consider "right"? The implication is plain as he continues:

In contrast, the Negro child in the ghetto doesn't know or appreciate the standards, values, or morals of the middle-class family. He may have no father. [One assumes that Mr. Gores is not suggesting that "ghetto children" were miraculously conceived, but is merely taking note of the evidence that "ghetto" fathers are often among the missing once conception has taken place.] His only close relative, his mother, may raise him to live for the pleasure of the moment. For such a child, there is no tomorrow to worry about or plan for.

Presumably Mr. Gores is suggesting that the idea that there is no tomorrow should be a vital part of the curriculum of "ghetto" children, lest attuning the curriculum to a different set of values seduce "ghetto" children into accepting an alien culture. It is her delusion that there is no tomorrow and that living for the pleasure of the moment is to her self-interest that probably landed, and certainly keeps, such a mother as Mr. Gores describes in the "ghetto." Mr. Gores' educational fantasies would seem a good bet for keeping her child there, too. Along these same lines of "thought" (to dignify the process beyond its deserts), the Kerner Commission deplores teachers who "are not in sympathy with the life-styles of their [ghetto] students." But didn't we hear the Commission insisting, elsewhere and at length, that exposure to advantaged life-styles and values is an important reason for socioeconomic integration? And isn't "relevant enrichment" a contradiction in terms?

"Since the needs and concerns of the ghetto community are seldom reflected in educational policy formulated on a citywide basis, the schools are often seen by ghetto youth as irrelevant," says the Kerner Commission. Are the residents of "ghetto" communities not human beings? Do they not need to earn, and are they not concerned with earning, their livelihoods, as all men must? Are not the basic fundamentals of literacy the primary, basic tool required by "ghetto" residents, if they are to work successfully? But naturally, if such experts on education as "ghetto youth" pronounce the schools irrelevant, we must hasten to adjust our curricula to their "demands." So speaks the learned Dr. Dodson:

> [The] divergence of goals (between the dominant class and ghetto youth) makes schools irrelevant for the youth of the slum. It removes knowledge as a tool for groups who are deviant to the ethos of the dominant society. It tends to destroy the sense of self-worth of minority group children. It breeds apathy, powerlessness, and low self-esteem. The majority of ghetto youth would prefer to forgo knowledge if it is at that cost. One cannot understand the alienation of modern ghetto youth except in the context of this conflict of goals.[21]

Suppose "ghetto youth" whose values are deviant to the ethos of the dominant society (modern philosophy teaches that there are no absolute standards of ethics—there is only the "ethos of society") demand classes in crapshooting, narcotics-smuggling, and ignition-wire jumping? Shall we provide them in the name of "relevance"?

Here we see the sick, sad end of educational pragmatism. There is tragic truth in the charge that education is irrelevant—and not merely in the "ghettos." Today's education is irrelevant to the needs and goals of man as a rational being for whom logical thought is the fundamental, irreplaceable tool of survival. But it is precisely the pragmatic educationists' preoccupation with spurious, concrete-bound, if-it's-not-in-today's-newspaper-it-doesn't-affect-me "relevance" which has brought about the miserable failure of the educational system. In their frantic flight from the rigors (and implications) of abstract thought, today's educators have retreated into a "life-adjustment" curriculum which, *because* of its obsession with folks-next-door-in-the-split-level-or-the-tenement immediacy, is outdated even as it is taught. It is useless in accomplishing what should be the primary goal of formal education: training the mind in the rigors of *purposeful* thought. Isabel Patterson has provided a cogent description of the products of the "life-adjustment," "group-think" educational process:

> Neither evidence nor logic penetrates the fog in which they have been reared. It is difficult to bring one to any conclusion, when detached from the group. They will say, "Well, I just don't think so," as if there could be no facts or connected mental processes, which should lead to one opinion rather than another, or distinguish a conviction from a taste. They have an impression that

"everything is different now," from anything that may have been in the past: though they have no idea how or why. Do not two and two make four? Does not a lever operate on exactly the same principle today as it did for Archimedes? They do not quite know. They may say, "Oh, I don't agree with you," but they can give no reason for dissent. They are "not quite convinced," but they can offer no argument in rebuttal. That is to say, when called upon to think, they cannot, because they have been trained to accept the class, the group, or the "social trend," as the sole authority.[22]

It is true enough that neither children nor adults will learn, in any but the most ephemeral pass-the-exam sense, that which they cannot themselves discern as useful to their personal goals. The most challenging task of an educator is the task of demonstrating the relationship between broad abstractions and specific concretes. This is the task on which modern education has defaulted. The *overall* results and implications of this default are beyond the scope of this particular book. But among the *specific* results are high school graduates unable to read; "business science" students expert in manipulation of the latest-model electric typewriter but innocent of even the rudiments of grammar or spelling; "domestic science" survivors able to make Jello and cream puffs, but unable to plan a meal; "vocational"-course veterans proficient in some obsolete and highly specialized industrial technique, but unable to use a ruler or read a blueprint; and the sort of belligerent educated barbarian who uses the freedom of speech which others died for to demand the destruction of the "educational establishment" while asking, "What in hell does the Mayflower mean to me?" These are the tragic end-products of a philosophy of education which denies the existence of both principles and mind.

"The quality of education offered by ghetto schools," says the *Kerner Report*, "is diminished by the use of curricula and materials poorly adapted to the life-experiences of the students. Few books used or courses offered reflect the harsh realities of life in the ghetto. ... This failure to include materials relevant to their own environment has made students skeptical of what they are being taught." Students today are well advised to be skeptical of what they are taught, but not for the reasons posited by the Kerner crew. Exposed here, in all its glory, is the futility, the self-defeating contradiction of the Kerner education program—a program which attempts to instill a new value system in children by making the content of their education "relevant" to the environment which (according to the Kerner thesis) produced the *old* value system which education is supposed to counteract.

One might suppose that "ghetto" children might already have a bellyful of harsh realities. Must they have drunks, muggers, overflowing garbage pails, disemboweled automobiles, and rats crawling through their textbooks, too? The memoirs and biographies of people who have surmounted slum childhoods give ample testimony to the power of "irrelevant" plays, books, and movies to kindle dreams; to bespeak the existence of a different world which one might aspire to reach:

> Very quickly, he became one of the regular denizens of the movie house. In the movies, he glimpsed the world outside and filled himself with its lore. "These films taught me about other people, how to dial a telephone, geography, names of places, things I never knew before. In a way, it was proof that there were other ways to live."[23]

"Life-adjustment" courses have already robbed "middle-class" children of reading texts which might fire their imaginations. Now "ghetto children" (for whom Dick, Jane, and Spot and the little split-level with the picket fence might at least be something new and different) are also to be denied even a glimpse of another kind of life. They must be taught to adapt to the dominant ethos of their slum society by means of "Dick and Jane in the Ghetto."

> Look. Look.
> See the boy.
> See the car. See the boy look at the car.
> See the boy. The boy is black. The boy is poor. The car is red. The car is new. See the boy want the car. Oh.
> See. See.
> See the boy take the car. See him go. See him go fast. Go. Go. Go.
> Look. Look. See the man. The man is old. See the car hit the old man. See the old man fall. Oh. Oh.
> See the cop. See him grab the boy.

Oh! Oh! Oh! Oh!
Is the boy bad?
No. No. The boy is not bad. The boy is black. The boy is poor.
The boy had no car. The boy wanted the car. It was new.
Look. Look. See the man. See the man in the black robe. The man
is a judge.
See. See. See the judge. See the judge pat the boy on the head.
See the judge give the boy a car.
The judge is a good judge.
Hooray! Hooray!

Thus might reading, "relevance," and indoctrination into the
ethos of the Kerner Commission and the corner bar proceed simultaneously. (In the light of today's educational atmosphere, it is
perhaps necessary to declare that the foregoing primer text is an
invention of the author and is not—at least in this exact form—
in use anywhere yet.)

Additional Kerner proposals for achieving "relevance" abound,
ad nauseam. Among them is a proposal for "teaching English as
a second language to children whose dialect already constitutes a
first language." Cynical survivors of public school language
courses might suggest that such a program would practically guarantee that "ghetto" children would never learn English at all.

But the ultimate in relevance has escaped the Kerner Commission; it remained for some club-wielding "ghetto youth" to suggest
it themselves. Demonstrating students at New Jersey's Rutgers
University (their forces augmented, in true community spirit, by
a number of non-students) recently demanded that "academic
credit be given for the black life experience." Herein obviously lies
the solution par excellence to the problem of "ghetto" education:
LEAP (Life Experience Award Program).

"Ghetto" children who, it is well known, are as hopelessly en-
trapped in their environment as flies in amber, could be awarded
college degrees at birth. Since a college diploma, per se, assures
high income and high status, the children of the disadvantaged
could thus leap the poverty gap in one fell swoop. Granted, such
a program wouldn't teach anyone to read, write, add, or subtract.
(The schools haven't been doing so well at it either.) Such irrelevant and unimportant skills could be picked up "spontaneously"

once children are freed from the "interference" of having anyone
try to teach them.

LEAP has one inestimable advantage. It would employ no
bureaucrats, no enrichment counsellors, no "community aides,"
no "mother-advisers," no computerized child-shuffling systems.
And thus LEAP would save the "non-deprived" one hell of a lot
of money, while freeing the "deprived" to pursue their chosen
goals.

Perhaps that is why LEAP cannot be found among the Kerner
proposals for educating the "disadvantaged."

THE INHERENT EVILS

The inadequacies and downright evils of the educational system
—in the "ghettos" as elsewhere—are real enough. The plight of
the Ocean Hill grandmother whose nine-year-old grandson can't
read . . . the bafflement and frustration of parents forced to submit
their children to the whims of an obdurate, patronizing, frequently
obtuse educational bureaucracy . . . the confusion of helpless children shuttled to and fro to appease some politically powerful
pressure group . . . the shocking spectacle of high school graduates
who are functionally illiterate: these and other symptoms of far
advanced pathology are the inevitable consequences of a school
system based upon an immoral premise and perpetuated by force.

Decades of political control of the schools have begotten a
generation of schooled illiterates. But their indoctrination in the
statist philosophies of their teachers has been so effective that they
have taken to the streets with bombs and brickbats to announce
their "grievances," to the alleviation of which by others their
mentors have taught them they have a "right." In this, at least, the
schools have been successful—as might have been expected.

If a supermarket sells rotten vegetables or shortweight meat, one
can transfer one's trade to another store, without paying to keep
the seller of shoddy goods in business. But parents who observe
at close range the failure of the schools to teach critical thought
or even simple literacy; parents who discover that their children
are being taught doctrines which they find immoral and repugnant
are rendered impotent, forced by threat of jail or fine to submit

their children to instruction they consider damaging, dangerous, or—at best—inept. A parent's right to determine the content of his child's education has been perverted into an adulterated privilege, for which he must pay the ransom of a double burden: the taxes which support the "public" schools plus the tuition fees of "private" education whose content is also dictated, in whole or in part, by the state. And this is called "free" education!

Twenty-five years ago, Isabel Patterson recognized the true nature of state-controlled education when she wrote:

> There can be no greater stretch of arbitrary power than is required to seize children from their parents, teach them whatever the authorities decree they shall be taught, and expropriate from the parents [and, she might have added, from those who have no children at all] the funds to pay for the procedure. . . . The intrinsic nature of the power authorized was so little realized that this was called "free education," the most absolute contradiction of facts by terminology of which the language is capable. Everything about such schools is compulsory, not free; and the true nature of the institution has developed so fully along its own lines with the passage of time that parents are now helpless when it is admitted by a school board that a small number of teachers are mentally unbalanced. The parents must still deliver their children into the power of those teachers, on penalty of a fine. . . .
>
> A tax-supported, compulsory educational system is the complete model of the totalitarian state. The extent of the power exercised, and its final implications, are not yet recognized in the United States, because parents are *allowed* to send their children to private schools, or to educate them at home—although they must still pay the school tax. But when that permission is granted, and the educational standard is prescribed, it is revocable; it is no longer a right, but a permission. In Russia, in [Nazi] Germany, it is no longer permitted.[25]

The "something for nothing" of "free public education" has been dearly bought. The present ills of American education are inherent in the system; in the immoral premise on which it was built—the premise that it is right to make others pay for one's children's education. That premise contains within it a corollary: he who pays the piper calls the tune. When parents implemented their "right" to make others pay for their children's schooling, they forfeited their control over the content of that schooling to everyone and to no one, which means, to the state which expropriates and then doles out the funds; the state which now has a force-supported monopoly on the formal education of every child in the nation.

There must be countless parents in the "ghettos" who earnestly value education; parents who do not picket or protest or hurl rocks at teachers; parents who writhe in inarticulate anguish as they watch their children being made voiceless pawns of the social planners whose frantic experiments with human guinea pigs fail and fail and fail. But those parents, who are genuinely concerned that Johnny can't read—the Ocean Hill grandmother among them —have yet to learn that the source of their plight is their own willingness to abdicate the responsibility of paying for the education of their own children in consonance with their own incomes, values, and goals. The answer to their problems is not the further extension of the arbitrary power of bureaucrats into every crevice and corner of their children's lives—and their own. The answer is an educational system freed of the rule of force and subjected to the disciplines of the market place; an educational system chosen and paid for, as food and all other needs of man are or should be paid for, by those who use them: an educational system of privately owned schools.

Were such a system instituted, those of the "deprived" who actually want schools "relevant" to squalor and fecklessness (if there be such people) could have them. Racists, black or white, who desire segregated schools in keeping with their irrational and vicious doctrines could have them. Parents who want their children subjected to the progressive "life-adjustment" inanities and experiments of the "experts" could have their wish. Those cop-outs and dropouts who prefer lounging on the streets to learning the 3R's could follow their whims—and bear the consequences of their choices, with no plunder-supported "Last Chance" programs to bail them out of illiteracy.

Under a system of privately owned schools, the "liberals" who want to enrich the lives of slum children by taking them on jet rides would be welcome to indulge their whims—*but at no one else's expense.* Were free enterprise and the profit motive introduced in education, those parents who want schools truly relevant to the nature of the human mind, of man and reality, would no longer be forced to beggar themselves in support of the dissemination of ideas which are destroying mind *and* man.

"Educational texts," wrote Isabel Patterson, "are necessarily selective, in subject matter, language, and point of view":

> Where teaching is conducted in private schools, there will be considerable variation in different schools; the parents must judge what they want their children taught, by the curriculum offered. Then each must strive for objective truth; and as there is no public authority to control opinion, adults must be supposed to exercise the final judgment on what they learned in school, after they have graduated. . . . But would not some children remain illiterate? They might, as some do now, and as they did in the past. The United States has had one president who did not learn to read until he was not only a grown man, but married and earning his own living. The truth is that in a free country, any person who remains illiterate might as well be left so, although simple literacy is . . . the elementary key to an indispensable part of education in civilization. But that further education in civilization *cannot be obtained at all* under full political control of the schools. It is possible only to a certain frame of mind in which knowledge is pursued voluntarily. . .[26]

The abolition of the state's force-supported monopoly of education; the return of the realm of education to private enterprise and the profit motive, are solutions which the Kerner Commission clearly never considered—could not even conceive of. (Its idea of "private enterprise participation" in education consists of "storefront schools and street academies" and "the use of businesses . . . as subcontractors," paid with government funds, to provide "competition" with the established public schools.) But in privately owned schools and the profit motive lies the only valid answer to the problem of educating "ghetto" children—and all children—in a manner relevant to their own and their parents' values, life styles, and goals. Education is an industry like any other, except that the quality of its product is of more crucial importance to human survival than that of almost any one could name. So long as the educational industry remains impervious to the supply-and-demand imperatives of the market place, it can continue with impunity to dispense both poison and pap.

Education, like any other product, will be suited to the varying requirements and tastes of its purchasers on the day when its producers are divested of their force-forged monopoly—when the educator, like the manufacturer, must submit his product to the uncoerced judgment of potential buyers, to succeed or fail in accordance with the stringent competition of a free market.

CHAPTER IX

Censorship by Intimidation

"We are deeply concerned," intones the Kerner Commission, "that millions of other Americans [than ourselves], who must rely on the media, likewise formed incorrect impressions and judgments about what went on in American cities last summer." (p. 202) The Commission's "concern" is touching—at least until one examines its concept of "incorrect" and "correct" judgments and impressions.

"We believe," the *Kerner Report* states, "that the media have thus far failed to report adequately on the causes and consequences of civil disorders and the underlying problems of race relations." (p. 201) True enough.

"Disorders are only one aspect of the dilemmas and difficulties of race relations in America. In defining, explaining, and reporting this broader, more complex, and ultimately far more fundamental subject, the communications media have, ironically, failed to communicate." (p. 210) Indeed. But *what* have the media failed to communicate? Thereby hangs a tale.

"Many of the inaccuracies of fact, tone, and mood [in the news reports of the riots] were due to the failure of reporters and editors to ask tough enough questions about official reports and to apply the most rigorous standards possible in evaluating and presenting the news." (p. 203)

One of the "official reports" about which reporters and editors would do well to ask a few tough questions—for the sake of their own hides—is the *Kerner Report* in general, its "recommendations" regarding news media in particular, and most especially its definitions of "adequacy," "accuracy," and "recommendations." So far the press has shown little inclination to do so. With a few exceptions, the news media greeted the *Report* with cries of joy and proceeded to swallow it whole.

"ANALYSIS" AND "ACCURACY"—OPERATIVE WORDS AND CONSPICUOUS ABSENCES

It may be recalled that the National Advisory Commission on Civil Disorders (the "Kerner Commission") was appointed by the President of the United States, and charged with the task of conducting an "untrammeled search" for "the truth, the whole truth" concerning the riots of the sixties. The untrammeled search was to include an investigation into what effect the mass media might have had on the riots. The Commission interpreted this mandate as meaning an exhaustive (or at least exhausting) survey of what the media *did* say about the riots, conducted on the basis of the Commission's opinions as to what the media *should* have said— the whole thing topped off with extensive "recommendations" as to what the media *should* say in the future, whom the media should hire to say it, and how the media might be induced to toe the line. The manner of investigation and the tone of the "recommendations" reveal more about the metaphysical and epistemological premises of the Commission, and its coercive political orientation, than about the "adequacy" of media reporting.

How did the Kerner Commission embark upon its untrammeled quest for truth; its rigorous, scientific, objective, painstaking evaluation of the accuracy (pardon—the "adequacy") of media coverage of riots and "race relations"? What nature of data did it gather in order to form its conclusions; what aspects of the data did it choose to emphasize in presenting its "recommendations"?

Well, it started by counting Negroes.

The vision of dedicated researchers attempting to ascertain truth by sitting in a projection room watching videotape clips and solemnly counting the Negroes and whites per frame smacks of parody. But this is what the Commission assigned its minions to do. They also counted "militants," "moderates," "Negro leaders," policemen, "public figures," minutes, seconds, and column inches.

> To obtain an objective source of data, the Commission arranged for a systematic, quantitative analysis of the content of newspapers, local television, and network coverage in 15 cities for a period of from 3 days before to 3 days after the disorders in each city. . . .
> Within each city, for the period specified, the study was comprehensive. Every daily newspaper and all network and local television news films were analyzed, and scripts and logs were examined. In all, 955 network and local television sequences and 3,779 newspaper articles dealing with riot and race relations news were analyzed. Each separate analysis was coded and the cards cross-tabulated by computer. . . . The material was measured to determine the amount of space devoted to news of riot activity; the nature of the display compared with other news coverage; and the types of stories, articles, and television programming presented. We sought specific statistical information on such matters as the amount of space or time devoted to different kinds of riot stories, the *types and identities* of persons most often depicted or interviewed, the frequency with which race relations were mentioned in riot stories or identified as the cause of riot activity, (p. 204, my italics)

When all the punch cards had been punched, shuffled, reshuffled, sorted, tabulated, matched, cross-matched, spat out by the marvels of modern science, and perused by the members of the Commission, what gems of wisdom were mined from the mountain of paper? That television coverage was more "calm" and "factual" than "emotional" and "rumor-laden" on the basis of the unspecified classifying criteria of the researchers who viewed it. That "newspaper coverage of civil disturbances in the summer of

1967 was more calm, factual, and restrained than outwardly [??] emotional or inflammatory." And that television coverage "tended to give the impression that the riots were confrontations between Negroes and whites." The basis for this last, momentous conclusion was that not enough Negroes were shown on television:

> Television newscasts during the periods of actual disorder in 1967 tended to emphasize law enforcement activities, thereby overshadowing underlying grievances and tensions. This conclusion is based on the *relatively* [??] *high frequency with which television showed and described law enforcement agents*, police, National Guardsmen, and army troops performing control functions.
>
> Television coverage tended to give the impression that the riots were confrontations between Negroes and whites rather than responses by Negroes to underlying slum problems. The control agents were predominantly white. The ratio of white male adults to Negro male adults shown on television was high (1:2) considering that the riots took place in predominantly Negro neighborhoods.*(*The white male adult category in this computation does not include law enforcement agents or public officials.) And some interviews with whites involved landlords or proprietors who lost property or suffered business losses because of the disturbances and thus held strongly antagonistic attitudes.
>
> The content analysis shows that by far the most frequent "actor" appearances on television were Negro male adults, white male adults, law enforcement officers, and public officials. We cannot tell from a content analysis whether there was any preconceived editorial policy of portraying the riots as racial confrontations requiring the intervention of law enforcement agents. *But the content analysis does present a visual three-way alignment of Negroes, white bystanders, and public officials or enforcement agents. This alignment tended to create an impression that the riots were predominantly racial confrontations* involving clashes between black and white citizens. (pp. 204–5, my emphasis)

What comes out of a computer is determined by what goes in. Thus does technology serve absurdity.

It is strange to find the Kerner Commission taking the press to task for presenting the riots as a black-white confrontation. Elsewhere in the *Report* the Commission had stressed the idea that the primary focus of looting and arson (correction—"disorder") had been on "symbols of the white power structure." The primary theme of the *Kerner Report*, and of the reams and reams of copy concerning the riots which preceded and followed it, has been the litany of a developing black/white schism in America. The *Report* itself (in other portions) refers to the riots of the sixties as "race riots."

But this contradiction is of less importance here than the *basis* for the Commission's assessments and complaints: numbers— visual image counts. Are we to suppose that television viewers all turned the sound off and reached their "attitudes" and "responses" and "impressions" regarding the focus and causes of the riots purely on the basis of the facial pigmentation of those whose images flickered across the screen? Does the number of times policemen were shown prove in itself that "law enforcement" was the primary emphasis? Didn't the ubiquitous commentators and electronic entrails-readers *say* anything? What did they say about the actions of policemen? Of rioters?

What of the "Negro male adults" and "white male adults" shown? What were they doing? What views did they express when interviewed? Did they condone rioting or oppose it? Did they speak for themselves or purport to speak for a group? If the latter, what manner of group was it? How large? How influential? How representative of the views of the individuals for whom the spokesmen were claiming to speak? Should "fairness," "accuracy," and "adequacy" be guaranteed by requiring that reporters, before televising events, acquire a census tabulation of the area involved, and that sequences then be scrupulously filmed or edited to insure that each split-second image contains the requisite ratio of Negroes to whites to Orientals to Polynesians to American Indians? (Naturally, the "whites" would have to be shown in the proper ethnic proportions: so many Germans, so many Puerto Ricans, so many Irishmen, so many Italians.) What would all this have to do with the facts of the events being televised?

But at least the *criteria* for determining the black-white ratio can be deduced with relative ease. (Since the Kerner criteria for determining "types and identities" and attributes such as "calm" or "emotional" are nowhere stated, deduction and inference are the sole means by which a reader can arrive at the standards of classification.) Any person who looked "black" was presumably counted as a Negro; any person who appeared "white" must have been counted as "white." The method may be fraught with many pitfalls, but at least it's relatively clear-cut. The criteria for designating "Negro leaders," "moderates," and "militants" are deduced with more difficulty.

> The Commission made a special effort to analyze television coverage of Negro leaders. To do this, Negro leaders were divided into three categories: (a) celebrities or public figures, who did not claim any organizational following (e.g., social scientist Dr. Kenneth B. Clark, comedian Dick Gregory); (b) "moderate" Negro leaders, who *claim* a political or organizational following; and (c) "militant" Negro leaders who *claim* a political or organizational following. During the riot periods surveyed, Negro leaders appeared infrequently on network news broadcasts and were about equally divided among celebrity or public figures, moderate leaders, and militant leaders. On local television, Negro leaders appeared more often. Of the three categories, "moderate" Negro leaders were shown on local stations more than twice as often as Negro leaders identified primarily as celebrities or public figures and three times more frequently than militant leaders. (p. 205, my emphasis)

Isn't a "leader" without a following a contradiction in terms? The *actual* classifications number, not three, but two: (1) "Negro public figures," and (2) "Negro leaders," with the latter being subcategorized as "moderate" and "militant."

Lest I be accused of intractability, I shall oblige the Kerner Commission by applying both the "compassion" and the "skepticism" they so ardently desire to *their* official report. I shall forgo any detailed analysis of their assignment of "public figure" status, compassionately confining myself to a single (skeptical) question: What percentage of the "Negro public" (as distinguished from the "liberal," "intellectual" in-group) had ever heard of Dr. Clark?

In any event, the category, "Negro leader," and its subcategories offer even more fertile fields for speculation than does category (1). The term "Negro leader" is in itself of considerable significance. Unlike such designations as "Catholic leader," or "socialist leader" or "conservative leader"—all of which imply leadership of groups of individuals who have an identifiable, however loosely defined, set of principles and values in common—the term "Negro leader" implies leadership of a group of individuals who have nothing in common except "Negroness," i.e., skin color and other non-volitional physiological attributes. Such a concept is inherently racist, as it presupposes that genetic attributes connote commonly held values and goals among the individuals who possess those attributes. (See Chapter IV.)

From the above-quoted passage, one infers also that a "Negro leader," as defined by the Kerner Commission, has two distinguishing characteristics: (1) he is a Negro; and (2) he *claims* a political or organizational following, presumably of Negroes. By such criteria, a "Negro leader" need not *have* a political or organizational following of any significant size; he may speak for a minuscule number—or even none—of the more than 20 million individuals in the United States besides himself who happen to be "black." His *claim* is sufficient to get him television time before an audience of thousands or millions—and a courteous hearing from prestigious national commissions—while he presents his "demands." An American Negro Air Force colonel, David James, Jr., succinctly described the "leader"-manufacturing process. In an AP dispatch from Vietnam (August 10, 1967), Col. James was quoted as follows: "Some nut stands on the street corner saying, 'Let's burn this city down,' and everyone walks past him. Then a reporter hears him and writes a story about him. The next day, there are television people and newspaper and radio reporters at the corner, and several hundred people gather around. The guy says, 'Let's burn this city down,' and suddenly he's a leader." One is reminded of the remark, variously attributed, that Mr. Stokely Carmichael, the much-publicized advocate of armed revolution, has a following of "five Negroes and five hundred white newsmen." (Naturally the Kerner Commission did *not* reproach the networks for giving approximately equal time to "moderate" and "militant" leaders, although it is generally known that the "followings" of the former are vastly greater in size than those of the latter.)

The Kerner Commission reports no attempt to verify the "claims" of "Negro leaders" to be known as such, even by the Commission's (and the news media's) vague standards. The self-appointed "leaders" were simply classified as "moderate" or "militant." The criteria for these classifications must also be inferred from the *Report* as a whole, e.g., a "militant Negro leader" advocates razing the facilities of production and murdering the productive; a "moderate" Negro leader merely advocates confiscating the facilities of, and seizing the fruits of, production, thereby eating the productive alive. (See Chapter II, "The Foregone Conclusion.")

"Negro leaders" quoted as such elsewhere in the *Report* and in the news media, are unanimous in their view that "grievances" constitute a moral justification for violating the rights of others. They differ only as to whether such violations should be direct (looting, beating, burning) or indirect (governmental extortion). A subcategory of the latter group condemns the policies of the former, not on moral grounds, but on the grounds that rioting is an "impractical" means of acquiring *legal* looting tools, since it tends to incite "backlash" and "retaliation" from the victims. The thrust of the Kerner complaints regarding riot coverage and "race relations coverage" as a whole is that such "Negro leaders"—and their viewpoints—were given *insufficient* attention by the press in general and television ("the universal appliance in the ghetto") in particular. This complaint may come as a surprise to those television viewers who do not share the Kerner *weltanschauung*.

Besides counting Negroes and policemen, the Commission "analyzed" 955 television riot and "racial" sequences (the term "racial sequences" is not defined) to determine, by means of standards which the Commission did not choose to name, whether each sequence was "emotional," "calm," or "normal." (Evidently it is not normal to be calm.) The diligent researchers succeeded in classifying 837 of the sequences (the remaining 118 evidently had them stumped); 494 sequences were classified as "calm"; 262 were labeled "emotional"; and 81, "normal"—perhaps calmly emotional or emotionally calm?

Continuing its tireless search for truth, the Commission also directed its field survey teams to question government officials, law enforcement agents, media personnel, and "ordinary" citizens about their "*attitudes and reactions*" to reporting of the riots, and "conducted special interviews with ghetto residents about their *response* to the coverage." (my emphasis)

"All of these *data, impressions and attitudes*," states the Commission (my emphasis), "provide the foundation for our conclusions."

An "attitude" is a "manner, disposition, feeling, position, etc., with regard to a person or thing; tendency or orientation, esp[ecially] of the mind."[1] An "impression" is "the first and immediate effect upon the mind in outward or inward perception; sensation," or "a notion, remembrance, belief, etc., often of a vague or indistinct nature."[2] A "reaction" is "an action in response to some influence, event, etc."[3]

"Our conclusions," states the Commission, "are based upon subjective as well as objective factors; interviews as well as statistics; isolated examples as well as general trends."

The objective is that which exists in reality, independent of the wishes, emotions, attitudes, notions, remembrances, or beliefs of the beholder; to be objective is to be "free from personal feelings, or prejudice; based on facts, unbiased."[4] The objective factors—data—which the Commission chose to stress in forming its conclusions consisted of statistics which may have been accurate enough in themselves, but irrelevant (e.g., the Negro-white tabulation; the policeman count); plus statistics compiled from a painstaking tabulation of snippets of information classified on the basis of unspecified and very possibly completely subjective criteria ("calm," "normal," "moderate," "militant")—as though the exhaustive arrangement and rearrangement of numbers with no identifiable referents in reality would, in some miraculous fashion, result in a determination of truth.

Thus the "objective factors" referred to are, in actuality, mere bones tossed out to divert those few among the brainwashed masses who might still feebly protest that an untrammeled search for the "whole truth" should concern itself with *facts—relevant* facts. The statistics are an intricate smokescreen. Objectivity, truth, and judgment are factors conspicuous by their absence. The operative words are "attitudes," "impressions," "subjective factors"—*feelings*. What is of prime importance in this enlightened epoch is not what happened, nor even what people *thought* happened, but what they *felt*.

What, then, did the Kerner Commission and its "ghetto" informants *feel* about press coverage of the riots of the sixties, and to what "recommendations" did its feelings impel the Commission?

EPITAPH FOR JOURNALISM

The standard of journalism which held that *facts* belong on the news pages and opinions, wishes, and feelings, on the editorial pages, has been dying a lingering death over the last few decades —a victim of modern philosophy. When the victim finally expires completely and is laid to rest, the Kerner Commission's summary regarding news media will make a splendidly suitable epitaph:

> Along with the country as a whole, the press has too long basked in a *white world*, looking out of it, if at all, with *white men's eyes and a white perspective*. That is no longer good enough. The *painful* process of readjustment that is *required* of American news media *must* begin now. They *must* make a reality of [*racial*] integration —both in their product and personnel. They *must* insist on the highest standards of accuracy—not only reporting single events with care and *skepticism*, but placing each event into *meaningful perspective*. They must report the travail of our cities with *compassion* and in depth.
>
> In all this, the Commission asks for fair and courageous journalism—*commitment* and coverage that are worthy of one of the crucial domestic stories in America's history. (p. 213, my emphasis)

In analyzing this summation, it is important to bear in mind that the Commission makes no distinction between reporting and editorializing; between news description, news analysis, and news commentary. (Neither, of course, does today's press.)

"Commitment"—to what? "Compassion"—toward whom? If a "white perspective" is not "meaningful," just what sort of perspective *is*? A "black" perspective? Who but a racist would speak in such terms? Is "accuracy" to result from "skepticism"? "Must"? A strong term for those only empowered to "recommend."

What terms are shockingly absent from that astounding summation? "Facts" and "objectivity."

Facts are statements of that which exists. Journalism involves ascertaining facts about events; sorting disparate facts into logical order; extracting the relevant and important from the insignificant; recording the resultant account of an event in a form in which it can be disseminated. Television and radio journalism differ from newspaper journalism in that the spoken word and/or visual images are employed in place of the written word. Journalism differs from biography, history, and other non-fiction writing in that it usually deals with *immediately* current events ("news"), which are described to a wider audience than most other non-fiction reaches. Because of the importance of speed and the relatively limited space available for devotion to a given subject (in the case of television and radio, "space" is time), journalism most often confines itself to the highlights of a given event. This is especially true of television and radio. This space/time limitation necessarily means that journalists must be extremely selective in what they choose to report; objectivity is of crucial importance; emphasis on irrelevant details may create an entirely false picture of the event.

"[Press] objectivity," Lanny Friedlander has written,[5] "is the concept of justice applied to the field of journalism. Justice requires that each man be treated precisely as he deserves, with no exceptions. Objectivity requires that each word, fact, opinion, and syllogism be handled with [an equally] high level of precision." Press objectivity necessarily requires that *fact* be strictly differentiated from opinion or speculation.

> Objectivity is the method by which the journalist (or any man) identifies attributes of reality. It is the recognition that emotions are not means of cognition, that existence exists, independent of man's perception of it, and that there is but one means of perceiving and understanding it: a process of rational thought. . . .
>
> The same rules that apply to writing about physics also apply to the study of human events. . . . The journalist is required, as is the scientist, to record what happens, not what is desired to happen. If a journalist wishes to analyze an event, he must adhere to the same strict rules of evidence as must the scientist. He must present undoctored facts, and only relevant facts.[6]

"Compassion," "commitment," and "skepticism" are *feelings*. They are emotions and attitudes. What place have they in reporting or analyzing the news? To *approach* events with "compassion" and "commitment" and "skepticism" is to commit the double treason of making an a priori appraisal based upon emotion rather than reality. But of course, to the men of the Kerner Commission (and most of their Pavlovian puppets of the press), facts and reality do not exist; the *objective* reporting of events independently of one's "feelings" about them is not even considered. To men such as the men of the Kerner Commission, the world is composed of warring factions blindly driven by feelings, notions, beliefs, attitudes, and impressions, any or all of which are at once valid and invalid, since none can be assessed on the basis of its relationship to objective reality. "Adequate" press coverage of any given event means—in the Kerner lexicon—getting one's own gang into the newsrooms, where they can proceed to display "compassion," "commitment," and "skepticism" in accordance with their whim-determined values.

What values the Kerner Commission intends to have conveyed may be ascertained from the *Report* as a whole. (See Chapters II and III.) The Commission excoriates the news media for "emphasizing law enforcement activities" and "overshadowing the underlying grievances and tensions"; for giving the impression that "police and press work together and toward the same ends," and for obtaining too much of their information from police sources; for presenting interviews with those who lost property or suffered business losses because of the "disturbances" and "thus held antagonistic attitudes" toward the rioters. In short, the Commission and its "ghetto" informants feel that the "burning sense of grievance" of the arsonists and looters and their intellectual eggers-on received too little attention; that the suffering of the victims, the destruction of stores and homes and the savings of lifetimes, and the activities of law enforcement personnel who were trying to protect the rights of the victims, received too much.

How, then, does the Commission propose to make sure that its particular attitudes and impressions are presented "adequately" to the public?

BURIED BLACKJACKS AND DANGEROUS DIALECTIC

The Commission proposes that the news media should recruit Negroes because they are Negroes, in order that the "special viewpoint" which Negroes, *qua* Negroes, are presumed to have will be conveyed in news reports.

> The journalistic profession has been shockingly backward in *seeking out*, hiring, training, and promoting Negroes. Fewer than 5 percent of the people employed by the news business in editorial jobs in the United States today are Negroes. ...
>
> News organizations must employ enough Negroes in positions of significant responsibility to establish an effective link to *Negro actions and ideas* and to meet legitimate employment expectations. Tokenism—the hiring of one Negro reporter, or even two or three —is no longer enough. Negro reporters are essential, but so are Negro editors, writers, and commentators. ... Editorial decisions about which stories to cover and which to use are made by editors. ... We urge the news media to do everything possible to train and promote their Negro reporters to positions where those who are qualified can contribute to and have an effect on policy decisions. (p. 211, my emphasis)

It is vital to note that what is being "urged" here is *not* non-prejudicial, unbiased hiring practices based upon objectively delineated job qualifications. As a matter of fact, the Commission itself admits that qualified journalists who are Negroes are not, at present, to be found.

> It is not enough, though, as many editors have pointed out to the Commission, to search for Negro journalists. Journalism is not very popular as a career for aspiring young Negroes. The starting pay is comparatively low and it is a business which has, until recently, discouraged and rejected them. The recruitment of Negro reporters must extend beyond established journalists, or those who have already formed ambitions along these lines. It must become a commitment to *seek out* young Negro men and women, inspire them to become—and then train them as—journalists. ... For if the media are to comprehend and then to project the Negro community, they must have the help of Negroes. If the media are to report with wisdom, understanding, and sympathy on the problems of the cities and the problems of the black man ... they must employ, promote and listen to Negro journalists. (p. 212, my emphasis)

What is being asked here is blatant racism—recruitment of, and preferential treatment for, members of a given race *because* they are members of a given race; tactics based upon the corollary assumption that it is the race of an editor which will make him determine "which stories to cover and which to use"—the assumption that questions of newsworthiness, relevance, importance, and accuracy of news items cannot and will not be resolved on the basis of objective criteria; the assumption that men are incapable of abstraction and deduction; that men of different races are innately inclined to different decisions based on a "perspective" decreed by the pigmentation of their skin.

> The scarcity of Negroes in responsible news jobs intensifies the difficulties of communicating the reality of the contemporary American city to white newspaper and television audiences. The special viewpoint of the Negro who has lived through these problems and bears their marks upon him is, as we have seen, notably absent from what is, on the whole, a white press. . . . [A] change in the reality of employment and advancement opportunities for Negroes in journalism [requires] an aggressive placement program, *seeking out newspapers, television and radio stations that discriminate, whether consciously or unconsciously, and mobilizing the pressures, public, private, and legal, necessary to break the pattern.* (p. 213, my emphasis)

Persuasion, in other words, just might not do the job. The governmental blackjack is required: "public" and "legal" pressures mean *coercion—force*—applied to make men hire employees on racial grounds. Legally sanctioned force is to be used against legally disarmed victims—victims who will be required to "prove" that they have not "discriminated" either "consciously or unconsciously." And, since it is logically impossible to prove a negative, the victims of "public, private and legal" pressures must inevitably be compelled to meet whatever racist quotas of "special viewpoint" journalists the Commission and its bully-boys decree. (In June of 1969, the Supreme Court ruled that a quota system—one "black" teacher to five "white" teachers—must be instituted by Montgomery County, Alabama, schools, thus establishing a legal precedent for enforced racial quotas. Quotas, the Court ruled, are necessary to "expedite, by means of specific *commands*, the day when a completely unified, unitary, non-discriminatory [!!] school system becomes a reality instead of a hope." The ruling was unanimous.)[7] (my emphasis)

The primary instrument for imposition of pressures is to be an "Institute of Urban Communications."

The Commission is aware that in this area, as in all other aspects of race relations, the problems are great and it is much easier to state them than to solve them. Various pressures—competitive, financial, advertising—may impede progress toward more balanced in-depth coverage and toward hiring and training of more Negro personnel. Most newspapers and local television and radio stations do not have the resources or the time to keep abreast of all the technical advances, academic theories, and government programs [even the government can't keep track of all the government programs] affecting the cities and the lives of their black inhabitants.

The Commission believes that some of these problems could be resolved if there were a central organization to develop, gather, and distribute talent, resources, and information and to keep the work of the press in this field under review. For this reason, the Commission proposes the establishment of an Institute of Urban Communications on a private, non-profit basis. The Institute would have neither governmental ties nor governmental authority [neither does the Ford Foundation—officially]. Its board would consist in substantial part of professional journalists [Walter Lippmann, James Reston, and Chet Huntley would seem good choices], and, for the rest, of distinguished public figures [like Dr. Kenneth Clark or Dr. Dodson—but it'll be hard to find a replacement equal to the late Martin Luther King]. . . . Funding would be sought initially from private foundations. Ultimately, it may be hoped, financial support would be forthcoming from within the profession. [The same profession which does not have the "resources" to do the job on its own.] (p. 212, my emphasis)

The "initial" tasks of the Institute would include "training and education for journalists in the field of urban affairs"; recruitment, training, and placement—"*aggressive*" placement—of "Negro journalists"; "police-press relations" (see below); and "review of media performance on riots and racial issues."

The Institute is supposed to "review press and television coverage" (presumably counting Negroes all the while) and "publicly award praise or blame."

The Commission recognizes that government restraints or guidelines in this field are both unworkable and imcompatible with our

Constitution and traditions. Internal guidelines or voluntary advance arrangements may be useful, but they tend to be rather
general, and the standards they prescribe are neither self-applying
nor self-enforcing. (p. 213)

If voluntary standards and guidelines established by the news
media themselves are "general" and not "self-enforcing," why
should "voluntary" codes imposed by the Institute fare better?
What is the alternative to voluntary codes? Does the Commission
hope that no one will recognize the alternative if it scrupulously
refrains from naming it out loud?

> We believe it would be healthy for reporters and editors who
> work in this sensitive field to know that others will be viewing their
> work and will hold them *publicly accountable* for lapses from ac-
> cepted standards of good journalism. (p. 213, my emphasis)

"Accepted" and "accountable"? By and to whom? Anyone who
communicates with others, whether by means of the spoken or the
written word, is constantly accountable to them and to himself for
the accuracy and precision of his statements. Each individual
hearing or reading the words of another must assess the statements
of others for himself, on the basis of his perception of the facts of
reality. But it is not *that* sort of accounting—nor is reality the sort
of standard—which the Commission has in mind. It was George
Orwell in his prophetic book, *1984*, who coined the phrase for
what the Commission *does* have in mind: "*Big Brother is watching
you!*"

The Commission also makes recommendations for riot coverage
as such. These ought to have been headed: "How to Stage the
Show." Among these recommendations are: a "moratorium" on
news for either a specified or an "open-ended" period after "disturbances" break out (such moratorium to be "basically" voluntary); and the installation of official information centers in city
halls, staffed by official information officers (did someone whisper
"propaganda centers"? Shhh!). The most noteworthy significance
of these suggestions for riot showmanship (other than their censorship implications) is their assumption that riots are now a fact of

life. They may be expected to continue over a time span long enough to justify investment in special "official" facilities (including videotaping studios) for riot coverage. But that's another story.

Dangerous Dialectic

To "recommend" means: "(1) to present as worthy of confidence, acceptance, use, etc.; commend, mention favorably. (2) to represent or urge as advisable or expedient. (3) to advise, as an alternative; suggest ... as appropriate, beneficial, or the like."[8] Recommendations are *suggestions*; they are *proposals*; they are *not* orders. Whence, then, come all the "musts" in the Kerner text and summation? Whence the talk of "painful readjustments" which "must" be begun *now*? Are these mere figures of speech?

Just how does the Kerner Commission propose to enforce its so-called recommendations and those of its proposed Institute? What weapons does it possess—but choose not to mention—by which it may enforce compliance with its "standards" of "adequacy"?

The Commission, obviously possessed of finely tuned antennae for sensing emanations from the political wavelengths, appears well aware that the American public and the press remain extraordinarily sensitive about anything which smacks of government censorship (except in the case of sexual "obscenity," where "conservatives," particularly, tend to fall headlong into an abyss carved out by their philosophical contradictions). Although a years-long campaign has been going on (spearheaded by the FCC, the FTC, and the likes of *Consumer Reports*) to pervert the meaning of the term and thereby bring censorship in the back door, the Commission still finds it expedient to tread softly. Its blackjack is screened behind a fog of words; obeisance is duly made to the national delusion of a "free press." The Commission finds it prudent to forgo advocating *open* governmental coercion of the news media; to employ, instead, a more dangerous (precisely because it is hidden) variant: closed-doors, indirect, "guideline" censorship dictated by "private" pressure groups and pull; implemented through legal pressure and intimidation. One doesn't *call* it censorship (even indirect censorship), of course. That wouldn't be prudent either.

Thus the Kerner section on news media opens with a ritual incantation:

> Freedom of the press is not the issue. A free press is indispensable to the preservation of the other freedoms this Nation cherishes. The recommendations in this chapter have thus been developed under the strong conviction that only a press unhindered by government can contribute to freedom. (p. 201)

But freedom of the press *is* the issue. Having uttered the obligatory lip service to the rights of life, liberty, and property (from which the rights of free speech and free press derive), the Kerner Commission feels free to proceed in its attempts to negate these rights; first, by defending them on irrelevant or specious grounds; then, by perverting rights into privileges granted by permission.

The arguments against overt censorship which the Kerner Commission (in passing) advances are logically indefensible; therefore they serve, not to affirm, but to undercut that which they purport to defend. These arguments, the "argument from practicality" and the "argument from tradition," imply that, if someone *were* able to "envision a system of governmental restraints" which would eliminate effects the Commission doesn't like, the only barrier to imposing such restraints would be *tradition*.

> The Commission believes that none of [the] private or official reactions ["conditioned" by news reports] was decisive in determining the course of the disorders. Even if they had been more significant than we think, however, we cannot envision a system of governmental restraints that *could successfully eliminate* these effects. And an effort to formulate and impose such restraints would be inconsistent with fundamental *traditions* in our society. (p. 203, my emphasis)

As to the "argument from practicality": Nazi Germany did, and Soviet Russia does, pretty well at envisioning and implementing "effective" strictures on "undesirable" reporting in the name of the "public good."

As to the "argument from tradition": if only tradition precludes governmental "restraints," freedom of the press is not a matter of moral principle, of rights. It is merely a matter of custom; of doing things the way they have always been done, for no better reason than that they have always been done that way. Such an argument implies that men may speak and write as they choose, and use the press facilities they own as they choose, not because it is their inherent right to do so, but because it is "traditional." For good or ill, "traditions" fall by the wayside constantly. If only custom prohibited the establishment of censorship, there would be no logical ground to oppose it.

But another of the Commission's arguments is still more revealing of the Commission's implicit intent. That argument may be characterized briefly as "the argument from we-can't-get-away-with-it-openly-*yet*":

> Pressure from the Federal government for action along the lines proposed ["moratoriums" and "police-press guidelines"] would be *suspect*, probably, by both press and local officials. But the Institute could undertake the task of *stimulating community action* in line with the Commission's recommendations *without arousing local hostility and suspicion.* (p. 213, my emphasis)

Government pressure is not *wrong*. It's just "suspect." The Institute of Urban Affairs (did someone mention the Trojan Horse?) is an elaborately designed mechanism for "stimulating community action," i.e., for sneaking the legal-blackjack wielders inside the local barricades before the citizenry wake up enough to realize what hit them.

Then comes the *coup de grâce*:

> A society that values and relies on a free press as intensely as ours does is *entitled to demand in return* responsibility from the press and conscientious attention by the press to its own deficiencies. . . . (p. 203, my emphasis)

> It is *unacceptable* that the press, itself the *special beneficiary* of fundamental constitutional protections, should lag so far behind

other fields in giving effect to the *fundamental human right* to equality of [employment] opportunity. (p. 213, my emphasis)

"Unacceptable"? To *whom*? "Demand in return"? For *what*? What the first statement above amounts to is an unspeakable perversion: "In return for the right to say what you wish, we are entitled to demand that you say what we want you to." The second statement implies that Constitutional protection of men's inherent right to freedom of expression is a special "beneficence," in return for which the donors (the "public"—meaning their elected and self-appointed spokesmen) are entitled to "demand" that the recipients provide jobs for the "public's" chosen protégés as a "fundamental human right." A "fundamental human right" to a job is a contradiction in terms. The implementation of such a "right" requires that the *employer* be denied *his* right to choose his employees. (See Chapter III: "The Immoral Premises.")

The right of free speech—a derivative of the rights of liberty and property, both ultimately deriving from the primary right to life— is inherent in the nature of man. The "right" to a job, or to the use of press facilities which others must provide, is *not.* The basic, crucial innovation of the American Constitution and Declaration of Independence was precisely their recognition that rights are *not* a gift; not a matter of governmental or "public" or "society's" beneficence; that government's proper function was *not* to pose as grantor of rights which men innately possess (thereby gaining the philosophical weapon with which to abrogate rights), but to protect innate rights from violation by force and its variant, fraud. A right and a permission are not the same thing. The Kerner Commission's attempted perversion of rights into privileges (and its converse: the perversion of "grievances and demands" into "rights") has been the statists' principal tool for enslavement throughout recorded time. This time, it is the press which the statists seek to enslave by indirection.

It is vital to remember, in this connection, that censorship, by definition, is a *governmental* activity. Censorship is *legal* suppression of ideas by force; *legal* coercive dictation of the content of any or all means of communication; *legal* confiscation of "unacceptable" communications. It is only government which can

legally use force (or the threat of force) to intimidate reporters, editors, publishers, commentators; it is only government
which can *legally* seize and burn books or imprison writers; it
is only government which can *legally* use coercion to control the
content of news dispatches, books, or radio and television programs.

A television station owner, a program sponsor, a book or newspaper publisher, is *not* exercising censorship if he excludes certain
ideas from the publications or the broadcasts he pays for. An
advertiser who refuses to advertise in publications he finds offen-
sive—or which are working to destroy him—is *not* exercising
censorship. No forcible suppression of ideas is involved in such
exclusions. "Codes" and "guidelines" evolved by the owners of
press facilities (or their freely chosen employees or agents) are *not*
censorship. Whether the decisions or codes are arbitrary, capricious, irrational—or entirely just—on the basis of objective reality,
or in anyone's opinion, is irrelevant. The right to decide what shall
or shall not be said by means of the facilities one owns is part of
the right of use and disposal of one's property; of the right to
engage in any action which does not violate the rights of other
men. (Fraud, slander, and libel—which *do* violate the rights of
other men, and for which legal recourse does and should exist—
are not at issue here.) A "free press" is not a press everyone may
make free of. It is not a press whose facilities are available, regardless of the desires of the owners, to anyone who wishes access to
them—with or without payment. A free press is a press free of
legalized coercion; a system of communications in which the right
of men to express their ideas at their own expense is protected, not
inhibited, by law. A free system of communications is a system in
which anyone may use whatever facilities he owns to express and
disseminate his ideas without fear of *governmental* reprisals.

The Buried Blackjack

The *press* in the United States is still *relatively* free, although
obscenity statutes and various laws regulating advertising have
provided an entering wedge for governmental interference with
freedom of expression—and the anti-trust laws have also been

utilized for this purpose to an increasing extent in recent years.

But radio and television are not free, and have not been—practically since the inception of commercial broadcasting. Radio and television stations operate by permission: by license from the Federal Communications Commission.

> The Act of 1927 [which established the Federal Radio Commission, later the Federal Communications Commission] did not confine the government to the role of a traffic policeman of the air who protects the rights of broadcasters from technical interference (which is all that was needed and all that a government should properly do). It established service to the "public interest, convenience, or necessity" as the criterion by which the Federal Radio Commission was to judge applicants for broadcasting licenses and accept or reject them. Since there is no such thing as the "public interest" (other than the sum of the individual interests of individual citizens), since that collectivist catch phrase has never been and never can be defined, it amounted to a blank check on totalitarian power over the broadcasting industry, granted to whatever bureaucrats happened to be appointed to the Commission.[9]

Thus it has been decreed that it is in the "public interest" for Austin, Texas (whose television station happened to be owned by the family of Lyndon Johnson) to have only one television channel. It is in the "public interest" that a company wishing to sell "pay-television" broadcasts of motion pictures, concerts, and sports events be driven to near-bankruptcy, kept dangling for years, and finally prevented from doing business after public-spirited petitions from disinterested theater owners and "free" television station owners deluged the FCC. It is in the "public interest" that a radio station "owned" by a conservative group be hounded, forced into expensive lawsuits, and repeatedly threatened with license revocation at the behest of "liberals" who disagree with it; that the station be permitted, finally, to keep its license at the price of granting "equal time" to those whose views its "owners" oppose. It is in the "public interest" that advertisers of a product the bureaucrats disapprove of be forced to pay for declarations of the harmfulness of their product, and be threatened with a government ban on all advertising of their wares.

In a free market, the individual members of the public *do* control which publications and ideas will be successfully disseminated and which shall wither for lack of support. Such control is not exercised through force, but through the mechanism of the free market. In a free market the public—that is, individual men —decides what it will read, watch, listen to, buy (either directly or through purchase of advertised goods), ignore, or wrap the garbage in. But such voluntary control is unsatisfactory to the Kerner Commission and its fellow apostles of ideas-by-force. The free market provides no guarantee that the public will buy the Commission's "perspective." In fact, indications are that much of the public won't.

> To the editors who say "we have run thousands of inches on the ghetto which nobody reads," and to television executives who bemoan scores of under-watched [!!!] documentaries, we say, "find more ways of telling this story, for it is a story you, as journalists *must* tell—honestly, realistically, and imaginatively." [That is, with a "black perspective."] It is the responsibility of the news media to tell the story of race relations in America, and with notable exceptions, the media have not yet turned to the task with the wisdom, sensitivity, and expertise it demands. (p. 211, my emphasis.)

In other words: "Boys, it's up to you to sell our pitch; to ram it down the public's throat; whether you go broke doing it or not; whether anyone listens or not. We'll help you make sure there's nothing else to listen to." *This* is the Kerner conception of a "free press"!

It is true that millions of Americans formed incorrect impressions and judgments about what went on in American cities in the "long, hot summers" of the sixties. It is true that "inaccuracies of fact, tone, and mood" are rampant in the press. It is true that press objectivity has been abandoned, officially, *on principle*, by the leading players in the nation's "symphony of tape players all playing the same tape."[10] It is true that editors and reporters have not applied rigorous standards in evaluating and presenting the news. It is true that in "defining, explaining, and reporting" riots and race relations in the United States, "the communications media have, ironically, failed to communicate"—*objectively.*

The Kerner Commission's blackjack-backed "recommendations" are designed to ensure that the news media never will.

CHAPTER X

Of Heroes . . . and Villains . . . and Victims: The Commission and the "Cops"

On Sunday evening, the sixteenth of July, 1967, during one of the "disorders" investigated by the Kerner Commission, Patrolman John Gleason of the Plainfield, New Jersey, Police Department stood guard—with two reserve officers—at an intersection on the fringes of the "ghetto."

That Sunday evening Patrolman Gleason entered the "ghetto" to arrest one Bobby Williams (Negro, 22) who had been spotted pursuing two (white) youths out of the "ghetto," and, presumably, had ignored an order to halt.

In the course of his pursuit of Williams, Patrolman Gleason penetrated some blocks into the "ghetto," alone and on foot. "Ghetto" residents who were "milling about" expressed (in the words of the *Report*) a "kind of shock and amazement" that a policeman should dare venture unaccompanied "so deep" into their jungle.

Patrolman Gleason, a policeman of many years' service, the son of a police lieutenant, entered the "ghetto" a living, breathing human being who was trying to do his job.

Some time later, the mangled, mutilated, blood-drenched corpse which had been Patrolman Gleason was removed from the pavement where he met his death.

During what the Kerner Commission terms a "confrontation" with his quarry—a "confrontation" in which, "some" witnesses said, Williams brandished a hammer; and, "some" witnesses said, he did not—Patrolman Gleason shot and wounded his assailant.

For his "crime," Gleason paid with his life.

On the pavements of Plainfield, New Jersey, in the failing light of a Sunday evening in a "long, hot summer," Patrolman Gleason was tripped, then beaten, kicked, and stomped to death by the self-appointed avengers of the assailant he had wounded. Of the many spectators, some, it is said, tried to intervene; but, says the *Report*, they were "brushed aside."

The sole comment of the Kerner Commission on the "incident" of the brutal murder of Patrolman Gleason is to quote the statement of a witness that "under the circumstances and in the atmosphere that prevailed at that moment, any police officer, black or white, would have been killed."

No doubt it is of great comfort to Patrolman Gleason's widow and children in their grief to learn that his murderers were not motivated by racism.

It is not with the fate of Patrolman John Gleason, or Detective Fred Toto of Newark (referred to, in the *Report*, merely as "a white detective" who was shot) or men like them that the *Kerner Report* is concerned. Nor is it the opinions of officials like Mayor Thomas Whelan of Jersey City that the *Report*'s authors have chosen to present. Addressing the (1967) annual convention of the New Jersey State P.B.A., Mayor Whelan said this of the deaths of the two policemen:

> ... These men have been called victims of the long, hot summer of 1967. But they were not victims. They were human sacrifices— offered upon the altar of the philosophy that says: don't get anybody mad; don't hurt anybody's feelings; and, for heaven's sake, don't expect anybody to obey the law.

They were sacrificed by that philosophy that says every day is
open season—not only on policemen—but on all of organized society.

Mayor Whelan also testified before the Kerner Commission. If
he expressed similar sentiments to them, the Commission chose
not to include them in its *Report.* That is not surprising. The
Kerner Report is a 250,000-word tract extolling the philosophy
which Mayor Whelan deplored.

It is not only fiction which has heroes and villains. "Non-fiction" like the *Kerner Report* has them, too. And, as in writing
officially identified as fiction, the answer to the question of who
shall be presented as hero and who as villain is determined by the
value premises of the writer. Whether the resulting characteriza-
tions are accepted as the author intends is determined by the value
premises of the reader.

The preceding chapters of this book demonstrate plainly where
the value premises of the Kerner Commission lie. Because of those
value premises, the Kerner accounts of the riots themselves read
like bated-breath cops-'n'-robbers or soap-opera sagas instead of
the detailed, definitive, dispassionate, objective description of
events which the *Report* pretends to be. The Kerner narratives,
however, differ from the cops-'n'-robbers thrillers of an earlier,
less enlightened day: the Kerner tales are in tune with their times.
Today it is the "cops" who are treated as villains and the "robbers"
who are treated as their victims. It is those who appease and
applaud the robber-"victims" who are the heroes of the *Kerner
Report.*

OF "VICTIMS"

For every action of the rioters, excuses are found. The rioters,
after all, had "grievances" aplenty—ample excuse, in some eyes,
for setting whole cities ablaze. In Atlanta, for example:

["Ghetto" residents] were bitter about their inability to get the
city government to correct conditions and make improvements.
Garbage sometimes was not picked up for 2 weeks in succession.

Overflowing garbage cans, littered streets, and cluttered empty lots were breeding grounds for rats. Inadequate storm drains led to flooded streets. Although residents had obtained title to several empty lots for use as playgrounds, the city failed to provide the equipment and men necessary to convert them.

The area lacked a swimming pool. A nearby park was inaccessible because of the lack of a road. (p. 29)

In Newark, in the beginning of July, 1967:

... there were 24,000 unemployed Negroes within the city limits. Their ranks were swelled by an estimated 20,000 teenagers, many of whom, with school out and the summer recreation program curtailed due to lack of funds, had no place to go. (p. 32)

In Cincinnati:

In the 90-degree temperature of Monday, June 12, as throughout the summer, Negro youngsters roamed the streets. The two swimming pools available to them could accommodate only a handful. (p. 26)

In the process of roaming the streets, one Cincinnati Negro youngster whiled away the sweltering minutes by making a head-count of truckdrivers. Armed with the information that only 1 in 50-odd drivers was a Negro (the 2 percent figure is, says the Kerner Commission, "remarkably accurate"), he began to redress the injustice by organizing rock-throwing and strong-arming crews to prevent deliveries by white drivers.

Late in the afternoon, the youths began to interfere with deliveries being made by white drivers. Dr. Bruce Green, president of the local NAACP chapter, ... asked his colleague, Dr. Robert Reid, ... to go and try to calm the youngsters. ...

They were drawing up plans for a meeting with merchants ... when word came of an altercation at a nearby drugstore. ... The owner of the store was complaining [a sorehead, obviously] to the police that earlier the youths had been interfering with his business; he declared that he wasn't going to stand for it. [How unreasonable—a racist attitude, without a doubt.]

Dr. Reid was attempting to mediate when a police sergeant arrived and asked the officers what was going on. One allegedly replied that they had been called in because "young nigger punks were disrupting deliveries to the stores."

A dispute arose between Dr. Reid and the sergeant as to whether the officer had said "nigger." After further discussion, the sergeant told the kids to "break it up!" (p. 26)

At a rally protesting this and similar incidents of police "brutality," a (Negro) speaker "incensed" the youthful victims of the drugstore encounter by attempting to defend the police. (Freedom of speech doesn't apply to Uncle Toms.) As the meeting broke up, brickbats began flying. Thus began the Cincinnati riots: 63 persons were injured; 12 were hospitalized; 40 fires were started "but only 11 resulted in loss of more than $1,000" each.

In New Brunswick, "dissatisfaction in the Negro community revolved around several issues," to wit:

The closing of a local teenage coffeehouse by the police department, the lack of a swimming pool and other recreation facilities, and the release of a white couple on very low bond after they had been arrested for allegedly shooting at three Negro teenagers. (p. 46)

In Plainfield, New Jersey, where Patrolman Gleason was murdered, the "grievances" of the "ghetto" were manifold. There weren't enough swimming pools there, either.

In the summer of 1966 trouble was narrowly averted over the issue of a swimming pool for Negro youngsters. In the summer of 1967, instead of having built the pool, the city began busing the children to the county pool a half-hour's ride distant. The fare was 25 cents per person, and the children had to provide their own lunch, a considerable strain on a frequent basis for a poor family with several children. [When the kids were home they didn't eat?]

The bus operated only on 3 days in midweek. On weekends the county pool was too crowded to accommodate children from the Plainfield ghetto. (pp. 41-42)

Before examining further "grievances" of the exploited and deprived, perhaps we should pause for a moment of silence while we shed a sympathetic tear or two for all those poor ghetto children who could only go swimming three times a week—at 25¢ a throw, at that—and had to sweat every weekend all summer; and for all the work-wracked mothers who were brutally forced to pack dozens and dozens and dozens of peanut butter sandwiches because there was no free lunch at the pool. In the light of the ghastly deprivations which the "Profiles of Disorder" disclose, the Kerner Commission was clearly remiss in not issuing a tear vial with each copy of its *Report.*

The toil-worn mothers and (when present) fathers and their parched, pool-less offspring had, moreover, crosses to bear far heavier even than four sweaty swimless days a week. The city administration of Plainfield—and even some of their soul brothers —were cruelly unsympathetic to their plight.

> As in Englewood, there was a division between the Negro middle class, which lived in the East side "gilded ghetto" [!!!] and the unskilled, unemployed and underemployed poor on the West side.
>
> Geared to the needs of a suburban middle class, the part-time and fragmented city government . . . was unprepared to cope with the problems of a growing disadvantaged population. . . . Accustomed to viewing politics as a gentlemen's pastime, city officials were startled and upset by the intensity with which demands issued from the ghetto. (p. 41)

Thus the city's common council had "not responded" to a list of 19 "demands and complaints" tacked to the door of city hall by the NAACP. Presumably this was because only two out of eleven council members (18 per cent) were Negroes—12 per cent less than the percentage of Negroes in the population. Besides, the council Negroes were "middle-class" Negroes from the "gilded ghetto" and therefore didn't count. The "poverty area" was forced to rely on representation by two white women—one appointed by the council to replace a Negro who cravenly moved away. The schools, of course, were lousy, by virtue of the fact that they had "created *de facto* segregation within a supposedly integrated school system" by means of a "track system" separating abler children from the less able, i.e., the educationally deprived.

Most of the youngsters from white middle-class districts were in the higher track, most from Negro poverty areas in the lower. [Where the "gilded ghetto" progeny were placed is not revealed.] Relations were strained between some white teachers and Negro pupils. Two-thirds of the school dropouts were estimated to be Negro. (p. 42.)

The preceding litanies of grievance are, it might be noted, part and parcel of the Kerner "Profiles of Disorders"—the overtures, one might say, whose themes recur throughout the riot operas proper.

Most grievous of all the grievances, however, in Plainfield as everywhere, were grievances against the police.

... And Villains

"Deep hostility" to police is identified by the Kerner Commission as a "primary cause" of all the disorders surveyed.

In Newark, Detroit, Watts, and Harlem—in practically every city that has experienced racial disruption since the summer of 1964, abrasive relationships between police and Negroes and other minority groups have been a major source of grievance, tension and, ultimately, disorder. (p. 157)

Three northern New Jersey communities—Jersey City, Paterson, and Elizabeth—had had disorders in previous years, the first two in 1964, Elizabeth in both 1964 and 1965. In general, these seem to have developed from resentment against the police. The most serious outbreak had occurred in Jersey City after police had arrested a woman and a rumor circulated that the woman had been beaten. (p. 38)

Had the woman been beaten? The *Report* does not say.

In Newark, New Jersey, the so-called "precipitating incident" was the arrest (and rumored beating) of a (Negro) cabdriver, one John Smith, whom the Kerner Commission describes as "an unlikely candidate to set a riot in motion."

Forty years old, a Georgian by birth, he had attended college [a scholar!] for a year before entering the Army in 1950. In 1953 he had been honorably discharged with the rank of corporal [a defender of the nation!]. A chess-playing trumpet player [an egghead!], he had worked as a musician and a factory hand before, in 1963, becoming a cabdriver.

As a cabdriver, he appeared [only appeared, mind you!] to be a hazard. Within a relatively short period of time he had eight or nine accidents. His license was revoked [a victim deprived of his livelihood]. When, with a woman passenger in his cab, he was stopped by police, he was in violation of that revocation. (pp. 32–33).

The *Report* states that, when stopped, Smith had, "according to police reports" been "tailgating a police car." After all that biographical data, who needs details of the arrest? A police report on the arrest states:

Early in the evening of July 12th Smith was traveling west on 15th Avenue in the predominantly Negro Central Ward of Newark. In front of him was a patrol car of the Newark Police Department with two officers riding inside. Smith apparently was driving in a highly erratic manner, alternatively [sic] accelerating and braking and blinking his high beams. After tailgating the patrol car for about a block, Smith suddenly shot by it at the intersection of 15th Avenue and South Seventh Street, and sped down the wrong side of the street for about another block. The patrol car pursued the cab.[1]

The police report also states that:

Smith's cab was overtaken and stopped at South Ninth Street. He was asked for his license and registration. (In truth, Smith's license was at the time revoked and he had had eight or nine accidents.) He responded immediately with curses and verbal abuses to the patrolmen. The patrolmen then advised him that he was under arrest, whereupon Smith threw open his car door so as to strike one of the police officers in the chest, leaped from his car and assaulted the officer. The other patrolman came to his aid and Smith was subdued and placed in the patrol car. En route to the precinct house Smith again assaulted the policeman, again without provocation, and had to be forcibly restrained. Both officers were injured.[2]

Some months later, a jury convicted Smith of assaulting the police officers. Neither the assault on the officers, the injuries of the officers, nor the events of the actual arrest are disclosed by the Kerner version; Smith's trumpet and chess-playing activities and academic background are certainly more relevant than such picayune details as the circumstances of his arrest. Immediately after the passage cited above, the Kerner version continues:

> From the high-rise towers of the Reverend William P. Hayes housing project ["inadequate" housing] the residents can look down on the orange-red brick facade [local color] of the Fourth Precinct Police Station and observe every movement [reconnoiter the enemy's camp]. Shortly after 9:30 P.M., people saw Smith, *who either refused or was unable to walk*, being dragged out of a police car and into the front door of the station. (p. 33, my emphasis)

Did Smith refuse, or was he unable to walk? Apparently the Commission, which interviewed hundreds of witnesses and took 1,500 depositions ("confidential" depositions now safely stashed away in the National Archives), was unable to reach a conclusion.

A police report on the same sequence of events states:

> Shortly after 9:30 P.M., the trio arrived at the Fourth Precinct Police Station. [No local color—no wonder this report got so little press coverage.] Smith refused to leave the patrol car and had to be partially dragged, partially carried, into the precinct.[3]

A jury (stacked, no doubt, with "law-and-order" backlashers) concluded that the police version was true.

"Within a few minutes," the *Kerner Report* continues, "at least two civil rights leaders received calls from a hysterical woman declaring a cabdriver was being beaten by the police:

> ... A crowd formed on the grounds of the housing project across the narrow [all "ghetto" streets are narrow and "inadequate"] street from the station. As more and more people arrived, the description of the beating purportedly administered to Smith became more and more exaggerated. The descriptions were *supported by* other complaints of police malpractice that, over the years, had been submitted for investigation—but had never been heard of again. (p. 33, my emphasis)

What had been the actual outcome of investigations of the complaints which "supported" the beating charge? Were the complaints found groundless? Or were they quashed? If the Commission attempted to find out, it kept the information to itself.

Thus began the Newark riot. Twenty-three persons were killed; 13 "serious" fires and 250 alarms were reported; ten million dollars' worth of damage was done.

In Jersey City, too, "police brutality" was rife:

> The police department, like Newark's, one of the largest in the Nation for a city of its size, has a reputation for toughness. A successful white executive recalled that *in his childhood*: "We were accustomed to the special service division of the police department. If we were caught hanging around we were picked up by the police, taken to a nearby precinct, and beaten with a rubber hose." (p. 39, emphasis mine)

The hasty reader may miss the information that the alleged beatings took place many years prior to the riots of the sixties. Yet this is a serious charge. Are such practices still prevalent? The Commission offers no recent examples—or indeed any except this one man's "reminiscence." And, oh yes—the Jersey City Police Department had only 35 Negroes on an 825-man force.

Although "insufficient police protection" is cited elsewhere in the *Report* as a persistent "ghetto grievance," and we are expected to believe that people commit murder and mayhem because they want more policemen around, in Elizabeth, New Jersey, the "ghetto" was aggrieved because police (after the Newark riots) increased their patrols.

> ... the very presence of so many officers contributed to rising tensions. Residents of the 12-block by three-block ghetto, jammed between the New Jersey Turnpike and the waterfront, expressed the opinion that: "We are being punished but we haven't done anything."
>
> "The community," another said later, "felt it was in a concentration camp." (p. 39)

The sheer presence of increased patrols is evidently construed as a "punishment." The mayor of Elizabeth, moreover, was as "repressive" as his concentration-camp police:

> Early in the evening, the mayor agreed to meet with a delegation of 13 community leaders. When they entered his office, the chief of police [i.e., an agent of the enemy] was already present. The mayor read him an order that, if he were faced with sniping or flagrant looting, his men were to: "Shoot to kill. ... Force will be met with superior force." An officer's deviation from this order, the mayor said, would be considered dereliction of duty.
>
> Some members of the delegation believed the mayor had staged the reading of this order for their benefit [Shucks, now. How come they got *that* idea?] and were not pleased by his action. [The mayor, apparently, didn't ask for their list of "demands." That's not the sort of meeting that "community leaders" expect.] They proposed a "peacekeeper task force." The mayor agreed to let them try. (p. 40)

The "disorders" in Elizabeth after that were relatively minor. The Commission credits the "peacekeeper task force" for this happy turn of events: "As the peacekeepers began to make their influence felt, the police withdrew from the area. There was no further trouble." Perhaps the "peacekeepers" kept the peace by informing their friends that, if they made further trouble, they'd be clobbered? Such a speculation would be out of keeping with the Commission's philosophy. "Repressive police tactics" are, after all, a primary cause of disorder.

So, also, were police guilty in Plainfield, where Patrolman Gleason met his death:

> Relations between the police and the Negro community, tenuous at best, had been further troubled the week prior to the Newark outbreak. After being handcuffed during a routine arrest in a housing project, a woman had fallen down a flight of stairs. The officer said she had slipped. Negro residents claimed he had pushed her. (p. 42)

In the week prior to the "spontaneous" Plainfield disorder, "militants" circulated photographs showing bruises supposedly inflicted on this woman by the police. In a subsequent court hearing, testimony disclosed that the bruises had been artistically applied by the lady's husband, with the aid of lipstick and shoe polish.[4] This information, however, the Kerner Commission chose to omit.

The official "precipitating incident" of the first phase of the Plainfield disorders was allegedly the refusal of an off-duty policeman "moonlighting" as a diner guard to take one Negro youth to the hospital and arrest another after a scuffle. The policeman is described by the Kerner Commission as "number two" on the Negro community's "color-blind" " '10-most-wanted' list of unpopular police officers." (Two officers on the list were Negroes.)

> The youngsters were incensed. They believed that, had the two participants in the incident been white, the older youth would have been arrested, the younger [who had lain "bleeding on the pavement"] taken to a hospital immediately. (p. 43)

Instead, the officer had allegedly told the injured youth to "go home and wash up."

> On the way [back] to the housing project where most of them lived, the youths ... smashed three or four windows. An observer interpreted their behavior as a reaction to the incident at the diner, in effect challenging the police officer: "If you won't do anything about that, then let's see you do something about this!" (p. 43)

A number of the youngsters, their passions apparently progressing from incensed to incendiary, repaired to the rear of a service station where, according to police records, they started making Molotov cocktails. (The *Report* does not mention this.)

During the next two nights, rioting intensified. Bottles and bricks were thrown, and "a white fireman" was burned by a Molotov cocktail. Windows were smashed and stores were looted, as the youngsters expressed their burning desire to improve community conditions.

> As window smashing continued, liquor stores and taverns were especially hard hit. Some of the youths believed that there was an excess concentration of bars in the Negro section, and that these were an unhealthy influence in the community. (p. 43)

A heavy rain quenched the reformers' ardor; and things quieted down to mere sporadic rock-throwing until the next day. Having drawn up a formal "petition of grievances," a couple of hundred aggrieved deprived "piled into a caravan of cars" and headed for a county park several blocks away to stage a war dance; i.e., a "protest meeting." Dispersed by the unsympathetic park police (the protesters had no meeting permit), the caravan returned to Plainfield, "horns blowing and yelling."

Police were ordered out again. It was at this point that Patrolman Gleason committed his dastardly crime of entering the "ghetto," which the police had been ordered to isolate, and shooting his attacker. It was the death of Patrolman Gleason—or, more precisely, the "ghetto" residents' fears of "reprisals" from Gleason's fellow officers—which fanned the flames of disorder anew and caused (according to the Kerner interpretation) the most bloody phase of the Plainfield "disturbance."

> After [a score of youths] had beaten Gleason to death[5] ... fear swept over the ghetto. Many residents—both lawless and law-abiding,—were convinced, on the basis of what had occurred in Newark, that law enforcement officers, bent on vengeance, would come into the ghetto shooting. (p. 45)

What had "occurred in Newark"? Had a "brutal" policeman been killed, and had police, seeking vengeance, shot up everyone in sight? The Kerner account of the Newark disturbances contains no parallel situation.

The Plainfield drama continues:

> People began actively to prepare to defend themselves. There was no lack of weapons. Forty-six carbines were stolen from a nearby arms manufacturing plant and passed out in the street by a young Negro, a former newspaper boy. (p. 45)

Such was the terror of police vindictiveness in Plainfield that an innocent lad—a former newspaperboy, mind you—was metamorphosed on the instant into a trigger-happy thief. "Most of the weapons fell into the hands of youths, who began firing them wildly. A fire station was peppered with shots."

"Peppered" sounds so aimless, so youthful and so prankish. The account given at a United States Senate hearing had a slightly more ominous ring:

> The central fire headquarters ... then came under automatic weapons fire. This very effectively kept all fire apparatus locked up in the building. ... When we went up there to relieve those firemen, who were under heavy automatic weapons fire without any guns at all, we came under very heavy fire. This was no sniping. This was a land action. This was war.
>
> The firemen were in there unprotected. Their windows were all shot out. The fire equipment was being punctured by these bullets, and we later learned through our intelligence that two squads of five men each equipped with carbines had walked down Fourth Street, split, and deliberately laid siege to the fire station, and at the same time someone else several blocks away had pulled the fire box so continuously it ran the spring down. Now there is no other conclusion to draw than [that] this squad of men were trying to bring the firemen out of the firehouse to assassinate them.[6]

The New Jersey P.B.A. investigation report states:

> As a result of this action against the fire department, and others assaulted by the rioters when fire apparatus was responding to alarms, six pieces of fire apparatus were damaged and fire headquarters badly shot up.[7]

These accounts, however, are from law enforcement sources and indubitably prejudiced. An armored personnel carrier was required to relieve the firemen only because the police were panicky cowards scared of a few little boys. The Kerner Commission, after all, has stated that "reports of sniper fire were greatly exaggerated." Word from on high has been given—and only paranoids would voice doubts.

In the case of the Plainfield fire station, the only account the

Commission cared to give was that the "fire station had been besieged for 5 hours. During this period, only one fire had been reported in the city." In other words: No harm done. The kids got a little target practice, and the firemen had no place to go anyway. The remainder of riot activity is dismissed with few words: *"Reports of* sniper firing, wild shooting, and general chaos continued into the early morning hours." (my emphasis) Chaos didn't continue—only reports did? Were too much space devoted to describing the activities of the rioters, too little space might have remained for detailing their grievances.

The mayhem in Plainfield, we are expected to believe, was primarily caused by "ghetto" fears of police reprisals against lawless and law-abiding alike. What specific grounds (other than "what happened in Newark") did residents have for such fears? The Commission cites none. Was the belief that police would come in shooting—if, indeed, most residents held such a belief—then groundless? The Commission implies not. Does "fear" of "reprisals" (augmented, we must remember, by the underlying grievances of two-track schools and three-day pools) justify stealing carbines for "self-defense"; laying siege to fire stations; searing firemen with gas-bombs; slashing fire hose; smashing every window in sight and whaling the broken glass at policemen? The Kerner Commission says nothing to counter its implication that such acts were understandable expressions of "grievance."

While all this was going on in Plainfield: while fire engines were being punctured by rifle fire and wildly shooting ex-newsboys roamed the streets, where were the police? "Law enforcement officers," says the Kerner Commission, "continued their cordon about the area, but made no attempt to enter it except, occasionally, to rescue someone." The reader might consider such behavior on the part of police irresponsible. He would be right. The containment tactic was ordered, not by the Plainfield police—who, indeed, protested it—but at the behest of the State "Community Relations" Commissioner, Paul Yvlisaker, who believed that "ghetto residents" (some 14,000 of them) should police themselves, because the sight of police officers would inflame them.[8]

Which "ghetto residents" were likely to be "inflamed" at the sight of policemen? With all hell breaking loose around them; with "youths" firing wildly in the streets; with stores being looted and firebombs thrown, one might think that law-abiding men and women would more likely be "inflamed" at the absence of police than at their presence. But such would be mere layman's conjecture, unsupported by sociological expertise. Besides, it is unlikely that law-abiding "ghetto" residents were consulted in the matter; during a riot prudent residents were unlikely to be out on the street making "demands."

> At a meeting in the early afternoon it was agreed [by everyone, ostensibly, but the Plainfield Police Department] that to inject police into the ghetto would be to risk bloodshed [whose?]; that, instead, law enforcement personnel should continue their cordon.
>
> All during the day various meetings took place between government officials and Negro representatives [representing *which* Negroes?]. Police were anxious to recover the carbines that had been stolen. . . . Negroes wanted assurances against retaliation. . . .
>
> At 8 P.M., [state officials], accompanied by the mayor, went to the housing project [where Gleason had been murdered] and spoke to several hundred Negroes [the cream of the community, beyond a doubt]. . . . There were demands that officials give concrete evidence that they were prepared to deal with Negro grievances [the non-sociological term for this is "extortion"]. . . .
>
> At 9:15 P.M., L. C. [a Plainfield "Human Relations Commission" official and—although the *Report* glosses it over—a former Black Muslim] rushed in claiming that—as a result of the failure to resolve any of the outstanding problems [officials had not commenced, forthwith, to dig a swimming pool], and reports that people who had been arrested by the police were being beaten—violence was about to explode anew. (p. 45)

Whose reports of beatings? Were the reports true? Were the shoe-polish-and-lipstick boys at it again? The Commission does not say. In return for a promise to "try" to cool down the impending "violence" and to "try to induce" the carbine-stealers to return their hardware, L. C. "demanded" that those who had been arrested during the riot be released. ("L. C." evidently had a pretty good idea where the carbines might be—but asking him to disclose such privileged information would be unconstitutional and anti-Negro.) "At 4 o'clock Tuesday morning, a dozen prisoners were released from jail. Plainfield police officers considered this a 'sell-out' " (p. 45)

How unsporting of the police. Police resentment of community relations expert Yvlisaker, who engineered the "deal," was plainly paranoid. Release of legally arrested prisoners when their buddies threaten "violence" is demonstrably practical police procedure, is it not?

Were the carbines returned forthwith? No.

> When, by noon on Wednesday, the stolen carbines had not been returned, the governor decided to authorize a mass search. At 2 P.M., a convoy of state police and National Guard troops prepared to enter the area. In order to direct the search as to likely locations, a handful of Plainfield police officers were spotted throughout the 28 vehicles of the convoy.
>
> As the convoy prepared to depart, the state community affairs commissioner [Yvlisaker is never mentioned by name in the *Report*] . . . ordered their removal from the vehicles. The basis for his order was that their participation might ignite a clash between them and the Negro citizens. (p. 45)

A massive house-to-house search, without warrants, would seem a serious violation of rights and of constitutional strictures against search and seizure. A search for 46 carbines concealed somewhere amidst a population of 14,000, conducted by personnel unfamiliar with the neighborhood, would appear a futile endeavor to boot. The *Report* voices no objections on such grounds—from "community relations" man Yvlisaker or from the Commission.

In place of the local police officers who would be most likely to know (and point out) possible places of concealment, the convoy was staffed (at guess whose suggestion?) with "community liaison aides," i.e., "ghetto" dwellers with prison records.[9] *Their* presence, presumably, would ignite no clashes. "According to witnesses and newspaper accounts, some men in the search force left apartments in shambles." (p. 45) The 46 carbines—it seems superfluous to say—were not recovered.

Yvlisaker's tender concern for the tensions of the rioters cut little ice with the local police:

For the Plainfield police, the removal of the officers from the convoy had been a humiliating experience. A half hour after the conclusion of the search, in a meeting charged with emotion, the entire department threatened to resign unless the state community affairs commissioner left the city. He acceded to the demand. (p. 45)

Another humanitarian crucified by small-minded and repressive reactionaries! After Yvlisaker's departure, Plainfield calmed down. (The police report states that numerous "ghetto" luminaries promptly departed for Detroit, which blew up shortly thereafter. The *Kerner Report* omits this information: the riots were spontaneous expressions of grievance, remember?) The *Report*, which ends with Yvlisaker's crucifixion, does not state how or why the Plainfield disorders subsided.

Community Relations Director Yvlisaker and two Plainfield "Human Relations" Commissioners are listed among witnesses at the Kerner Hearings. Plainfield Mayor Hetfield and Police Captain Campbell are not. When the New Jersey State P.B.A. held its own riot hearings, Director Yvlisaker was asked to testify. He refused.

... AND MURDERERS

In account after account of the "disorders," law enforcement officers come off worst. The benefit of the doubt, it seems, is a benefit due looters only. When police aren't beating boys with rubber hoses, they are stripping female prisoners and "fondling" them, while brother officers take pictures. When police in Newark forcibly dispersed rock- and firebomb-throwing mobs, the actions are described as "police-Negro clashes." Is one to assume that only the pigmentation of the besieging mobs led the police to "attack" them? Presumably, if the mob had been white, police would have plied them with ice cream cones. In Tampa, 200 "protesters" were met by 300 officers—three against two, more proof that fuzz don't fight fair. The casual reader of the riot profiles is left with the impression that most of the damage and virtually all the injuries were inflicted by the police. The travails of innocent bystanders allegedly shot by the police receive lengthy and loving accounts.

> [In Atlanta], as two police officers chased several boys down the street [harassment!], a cherry bomb or incendiary device [the Commission couldn't possibly have ascertained which] exploded at the officers' feet. In response [overreaction], several shots were fired from a group of police consisting mostly of Negro officers [traitors to their race]. The discharge from a shotgun struck in the midst of several persons sitting on the front porch of a house [in the middle of a riot?]. A 46-year-old man was killed; a 9-year-old boy was critically injured.... H. "Rap" Brown, who had returned to the city that afternoon, [attempted without success] to initiate a demonstration against *the shooting of the Negroes on the porch.* (p. 30, my emphasis)

Were "the Negroes on the porch" gunned down in cold blood and on purpose? After using all that type and space to identify people as "black" and "white" (and chess-playing), had the Commission too little printing budget left to afford the adjective "accidental"?

> [In Newark] about 60 persons had been on the street watching the looting. As the police arrived, three of the looters cut directly in front of the group of spectators. The police fired at the looters. Bullets plowed into the spectators. (p. 36)

Every spectator sport has its hazards. Ball-game fans run the risk of being beaned by fouls. Auto-race devotees are sometimes struck by runaway race cars. And aficionados of the new American summer sport of looting take the risk of being hit by stray bullets (in cities where police are so Neanderthal as to shoot). If that occurs, it is the fault of the police who opened fire; of the mayors who ordered them to; of "society" in general; but not of the looters—or of the fools who are watching the fun.

> At 8 P.M., Mrs. L. M. bundled her husband, her husband's brother, and her four sons into the family car to drive to a restaurant for dinner. [In the middle of a riot, who wants to cook?] On the return trip her husband, who was driving, panicked as he approached a National Guard roadblock. He slowed the car, then

> quickly swerved around. A shot rang out. When the family reached
> home, everyone began piling out of the car. Ten-year-old Eddie
> failed to move. Shot through the head, he was dead. (p. 36)

Very dramatic. Even the reader who does not react with instant
rage at the National Guard will be moved at the death of Eddie
M.—as anyone with a scintilla of compassion would be. Readers
possessed of "common" sense will also feel regret that the boy,
through no fault of his own, had a fool for a father and a mother
none too bright. If cars swerve and head away from roadblocks,
in the middle of riots, are law enforcement officers totally wrong
to fire at them? *Who* fired the "shot" that "rang out" and killed
Eddie M.? What proof does the Commission offer to back up its
implication that the Guard killed the boy? None.

> During the course of three nights, according to dozens of eye-
> witness reports, law enforcement officers shot into and smashed
> windows of businesses that contained signs indicating they were
> Negro-owned.
> At 11 P.M., on Sunday, July 16, Mrs. Lucile Pugh looked out of
> the window to see if the streets were clear. She then asked her
> 11-year-old son, Michael, to take the garbage out. As he reached
> the street and was illuminated by a street light, a shot rang out. He
> died. (p. 38)

What is the impression given by this apparent *non sequitur? Is*
it a *non sequitur?* The account of Michael Pugh's death is
preceded and followed by stories of police brutality. Was Michael
Pugh gunned down by police for the innocent act of emptying the
garbage? From the Kerner account, who can tell?

> Bullets continued to spatter against the walls of the buildings.
> Finally, as the firing died down, Morris—whose [73-year-old] step-
> father died that evening [after being shot by police]—yelled to a
> sergeant that innocent people were being shot.
> "Tell the black bastards to stop shooting at us," the sergeant,
> according to Morris [an Urban League director], replied.
> "They don't have guns; no one is shooting at you," Morris said.
> "You shut up, there's a sniper on the roof," the sergeant yelled.
> A short time later, . . . in the same vicinity, a police detective was

killed by a small caliber bullet. The origin of the shot could not be
determined. Later during the riot, a fireman was killed by a .30
caliber bullet. Snipers were *blamed for* the deaths of both. (p. 36,
my emphasis)

The obvious inference here is that the cops had rocks in their
heads and snipers on the brain—and were surly, profane racists to
boot. Were any of the police using .30 caliber weapons? The *Report* does not say. Is there any reason why the deaths of "a detective" and "a fireman" should *not* have been "blamed" on snipers?
The *Report* adduces none. The deaths of "a" fireman and "a"
policeman, of course, do not warrant more than a passing mention,
undignified by the use of names or the description of mourners.
(The detective was Fred Toto; he was shot and killed in daylight.
The fireman was Newark Fire Captain Michael Moran, who was
shot on the night of July 15, while fighting a fire.)[10]
Only those shot—or allegedly shot—by law enforcement officers or subsidiary villains (shopkeepers) receive rhapsodic re-
quiems.

An hour before midnight [in Detroit], a 45-year-old white man,
Walter Grzanka, together with three white companions, went into
the street. Shortly thereafter, a market was broken into. Inside the
show window, a Negro man began filling bags with groceries and
handing them to confederates outside the store. Grzanka twice
went over to the store, accepted bags [interracial cooperation!], and
placed them down behind his companions across the street. On the
third occasion he entered the market. When he emerged, the market owner, driving by in his car, shot and killed him.
In Grzanka's pockets, police found seven cigars, four packages
of pipe tobacco, and nine pairs of shoelaces. (p. 53)

Imagine that capitalist exploiter killing a man for such piddling
thefts!
The Kerner account of the riots in Newark closes with the
following vignette:

By Monday afternoon, July 17, state police and National Guard
forces were withdrawn. That evening, a Catholic priest saw two
Negro men walking down the street. They were carrying a case of

soda and two bags of groceries. An unmarked car with five police officers pulled up beside them. Two white [and therefore racist] officers got out of the car. Accusing the men of looting, the officers made them put the groceries on the sidewalk, then kicked the bags open, scattering their contents all over the street.

Telling the men, "Get out of here," the officers drove off. The Catholic priest went across the street to help gather the groceries. One of the men turned to him: "I've just been back from Vietnam 2 days," he said, "and this is what I get. I feel like going home and getting a rifle and shooting the cops."

Of the 250 fire alarms, many had been false, and 13 were considered by the city to have been "serious." Of the $10,251,000 damage total, four-fifths was due to stock loss. Damage to buildings and fixtures was less than $2 million.

Twenty-three persons were killed—a white detective, a white fireman, and 21 Negroes. One was 73-year-old Isaac Harrison. Six were women. Two were children. (p. 38)

Thus does the Kerner Commission choose to conclude its tale (correction: unbiased account) of the Newark riots. (The tale of Michael Pugh immediately precedes the above quotation.) What is the overwhelming impression left with the reader? That law enforcement forces lost only two men, while dispatching 21 Negroes, mostly women, children, and grandfathers. That fires were mostly not "serious" (a term left undefined). That "stock loss" is somehow less serious than damage to buildings and fixtures—and that $2 million damage to the latter can be described as "only." (Granted, it's a small amount compared with what the Commission wants to give the rioters to soothe their grievances.)

Granted that police behavior such as the closing anecdote describes is despicable. If the policemen had reason to suspect the men of looting, the proper procedure would have been to take them into custody. It is interesting to note, though, that even *this* spine-chilling drama of police brutality contains no conclusive evidence that the persecuted men had actually *bought* the groceries they were "carrying." The reader is merely led to assume that they had.

Yes, there are policemen who are overbearing, even brutal, in fact as well as by "10-most-wanted-in-the-ghetto" reputation. Yes, there are policemen who are unintelligent. Yes, there are policemen who are racists. Yes, much of the tactical conduct during the riots (especially by Guard units, who are soldiers, not policemen) appears inappropriate to the obtaining conditions. (The wholesale use of long-range rifles or machine guns in close city quarters seems, for example, unwise.) But the Kerner narratives of the riots are slanted so as to make it appear that brutal, stupid, cowardly, rude, and racist police acts were the *norm.*

Even when, elsewhere in the *Report,* statistics are quoted in ostensible defense of the police, it is done in such a way as to cast doubt:

> The true extent of excessive and unjustified use of force is difficult to determine. One survey done for the Crime Commission suggests that *when police-citizen contacts are systematically observed* [but not when they are not so observed?], the vast majority are handled without antagonism or incident. Of 5,339 police-citizen contacts observed in slum precincts in three large cities, in the opinion of the observer only 20—about three-tenths of 1 percent—involved excessive or unnecessary force. And although *almost all those subjected to such force were poor* [this was in *slum* districts, remember], more than half were white. Verbal discourtesy was more common—15 percent of all such contacts began with a "brusque or nasty command" on the part of the officer. Again, however, the objects of such commands were more likely to be white than Negro. (p. 159, my emphasis)

But, the Commission hastens to say, "such 'observer' surveys may not fully reflect the normal pattern of police conduct." Objective investigators who state that policemen are not likely to be bright, and cite as evidence a 1916 test of *30 candidates* which concluded that they had "markedly inferior" I.Q.'s; authorities who quote reams of data showing that policemen score high on the "F-Scale" (Fascism Scale) of thoroughly discredited (elsewhere) "personality tests"; the experts who indulge in pages of speculation about possible Freudian-homosexual motivations of policemen based on "low" rankings on a "masculinity scale" (only "editors, clergymen, and artists" ranked more feminine),[11] may suddenly turn cagey when faced with a study of over 5,000 incidents which indicates that police are not as "brutal" as "ghetto" dwellers are encouraged to think.

The use of dramatic anecdotes such as those from which a small sampling is quoted above may be justified on the grounds that such stories lend "human interest" to what might otherwise be a dull, "factual" account. But why are nearly all the anecdotes concerned with police "brutality" and none concerned with police bravery? Did *no* law enforcement officers behave with intelligence, valor, or compassion? Did no policeman or fireman rescue a riot victim? In Newark, for instance, police made 150,000 arrests between 1960 and 1967. There were only 67 complaints of excessive force during that period—but there were 1,000 assaults upon policemen, resulting in 500 police injuries.[12] More than one out of ten policemen was physically assaulted in 1966; the percentage grows yearly.[13] Was there no space for this information among the rubber-hose reminiscences?

During the Newark riots over 1,000 persons were injured; ten million dollars' worth of property was destroyed. Did the victims of looting and arson have no tales to tell? Amongst the endlessly repetitive laments for innocent bystanders shot by the cops, is there no place for the tragic stories of shopkeepers ruined by arson and plunder; of people left homeless by the blocks-wide arson in Detroit? Well, there was room for one:

> A Negro plainclothes officer was standing at an intersection when a man threw a Molotov cocktail into a business establishment at the corner. In the heat of the afternoon, fanned by the 20 to 25 m.p.h. winds of both Sunday and Monday, the fire reached the home next door within minutes. As residents uselessly sprayed the flames with garden hoses, the fire jumped from roof to roof of adjacent two-and-three-story buildings. Within the hour, the entire block was in flames. The ninth house in the burning row belonged to the arsonist who had thrown the Molotov cocktail. (p.51)

Shall we all cry?

The Commission never misses a chance to point out how many "Negroes" were killed by "police officers":

> Of the 43 persons who were killed during the [Detroit] riot, 33 were Negro and 10 were white. Seventeen were looters, of whom two were white. Fifteen citizens (of whom four were white), one white National Guardsman, one white fireman, and one Negro

private guard died as a result of gunshot wounds. Most of these deaths appear to have been accidental, but criminal homicide is suspected in some. ... Action by police officers accounted for 20 and, very likely, 21 of the deaths; action by National Guard for seven; and, very likely, nine; action by the Army [who were ordered to keep guns unloaded] for one. ... Rioters were responsible for two, and perhaps three of the deaths. ... (p. 60)

But the Commission makes every attempt to minimize the damage and loss caused by the rioters:

[Detroit] damage estimates, originally set as high as $500 million, were quickly scaled down. The city assessor's office placed the loss —excluding business stock, private furnishings, and the buildings of churches and charitable institutions—at approximately $22 million. Insurance payments, according to the State Insurance Bureau, will come to about $32 million, representing an estimated 65 to 75 percent of the total loss. (p. 61)

Elsewhere the Commission emphasizes that most "ghetto" property is un- or under-insured. At that point, of course, the Commission has other axes (notably coercive insurance "pool" plans) to grind. Business stock, private furnishings, and church and charitable property don't count. They don't cost anyone money, after all. If we exclude a few more categories, we ought to be able to "scale down" the damage to nil—especially after the gutted buildings and rubble-strewn lots, still wasteland years after the "disorders," are forgotten by all but their bankrupted owners. The rest of us can keep our minds on police "brutality," where they belong.

... AND HEROES

Let it not be supposed, however, that the Kerner sagas lack heroes. Reactionary minds may not appreciate their brand of heroism, but the Commission does. There were, for instance, potential rioters who remained true-blue to their principles:

In the midst of chaos, there were some unexpected individual responses.

Twenty-four-year-old E. G., a Negro born in Savannah, Ga., had come to Detroit in 1965 to attend Wayne State University. [Educational deprivation!] Rebellion had been building in him for a long time because, "You just had to bow down to the white man. . . . When the insurance man would come by he would always call out to my mother by her first name and we were expected to smile and greet him happily. . . . Man, I know he would never have thought of me or my father going to his home and calling his wife by her first name. [Has the reader ever met an insurance man who doesn't call everybody by his first name? It's a "conditioned reflex"—like saying "God forbid!" after suggesting one might "pass away."] Then once I saw a white man slapping a young pregnant Negro woman on the street with such force that she just spun around and fell. I'll never forget that."

When a friend called to tell him about the riot on 12th Street, E. G. went there expecting a "true revolt," but was disappointed as soon as he saw looting begin. "I wanted to see the people really rise up in revolt. When I saw the first person coming out of the store with things in his arms, I really got sick to my stomach and wanted to go home. Rebellion against the white suppressors [insurance men and such] is one thing, but one measly pair of shoes or some food completely ruins the whole concept."

E. G. was standing in a crowd, watching firemen work, when Fire Chief Alvin Wall called for help from the spectators. E. G. responded. His reasoning was: "No matter what color someone is, whether they are green or pink or blue, I'd help them if they were in trouble. [Insurance men excepted, of course.] That's all there is to it."

He worked with the firemen for 4 days, the only Negro in an all-white crew. (pp. 52–53)

It is such inspiring examples of virtue and idealism among the "deprived" which restore one's dwindling optimism regarding the future of our Republic.

Nor was E. G. the only hero among the oppressed. There were, for example, the unnamed young worthies who caused the "deprived" residents of Elizabeth, New Jersey (whom police patrol reinforcements had given a "punished," "concentration-camp" feeling—see p. 39 of the *Kerner Report*), temporarily to forget their crushing "grievances." The youths provided comic relief.

Workers from the anti-poverty agency and the Human Relations Commission began circulating through the area, attempting to get the kids off the street. . . . Based on what had happened [in Newark] they feared that, if the disturbance were not curbed, it would turn into a bloodbath. The peacemakers were making little headway when a chicken fluttered out of the shattered window of a poultry market. One youth tried to throw gasoline on it and set it afire. [Ah, the innocent pastimes of youth!] As the gasoline sloshed onto the pavement, the chicken leaped. The flames merely singed its feathers. [You can't win 'em all.] A gangling 6-foot youth attempted to stomp the chicken. [Native resourcefulness.] The bird, which had appeared dead, reacted violently. As it fluttered and darted out of his way, the youth screamed, slipped, and tumbled against the tree.

The stark comedy [that's what the men said—comedy!] reduced the tension. People laughed. Soon some began to drift home. (p. 40)

If that's all it takes to relieve tension, a new riot-stopping technique is ready to hand. No doubt the poultry dealers of the nation (in return for a small subsidy—chicken prices are down again) can be induced to volunteer their wares. The pullet population, by nature inarticulate, is in a poor position to object to making the supreme sacrifice in the name of community stability. Live-bird barbecues and chicken-stomping contests can be set up in the midst of "disorders." So long as the stompers are black and the pullets white, the animal lovers may keep mum.

Unfortunately, after the inmates of Elizabeth returned to their camp barracks, the weight of their grievances flopped back upon their poor, stooped shoulders, and rioting broke out anew. The mayor then announced that looters and snipers would be shot (see above), but it is not the mayor who is credited with the peace which subsequently ensued. The Kerner hero of the concentration camp was Muslim "militant" Hesham Jaaber.

Although Jaaber believed that certain people were sucking the life blood out of the community—"count the number of taverns and bars in the Elizabeth port area and compare them with the number of recreation facilities" [Supply and demand? No, bloodsucking.]— he had witnessed the carnage in Newark and believed it could serve no purpose to have a riot. Two dozen of his followers, in red fezzes, took to the streets to urge order. He himself traveled about in a car with a bullhorn. . . . There was no further trouble. (p. 40)

How can a Neanderthal mayor compete with charisma like that?

Even city officials—"progressive" ones—may get an occasional kindly nod. Newark police commissioner Dominick Spina fares reasonably well. After all, Spina is more of a "new breed" official. He held "open house" to hear "grievances"—although nobody came. He organized police-precinct councils; cajoled each precinct into sponsoring an Explorer Scout Troop; made "human relations" training mandatory for his policemen; let Citizen Observers ride in police cars—or would have: after a few weeks none showed up. When looting broke out, he decided "to use only a minimum number of police, without helmets or nightsticks . . . to avoid irritating or inflaming people."[14] The city administration of Newark, as forward-looking as any, denied police requests for riot equipment; it was their "constant hope" that "these things would not occur." They chose not to conduct riot training, so as "not to incense Negroes."[15] In the weeks prior to the Newark riots, "militants" were permitted to disrupt school and planning board meetings and shout threats of bloodshed ("Nagasaki and Hiroshima will look like Sunday school pictures compared to what Newark is going to look like when we get done with Newark") at war-on-poverty meetings, unopposed. One "Colonel Hassan," described by the Kerner Commission as "a one-man-show," was left to roll merrily on his way, calling for armed revolt, disrupting meetings, tearing transcripts out of stenotype machines (*Kerner Report*) and smashing the machines (Senate Hearings) without fear of police "repression." Unofficial, verbal orders were given, "no arrest regardless of what happens, no arrest. Don't antagonize them."[16] That's show biz!

It was in Newark, Detroit, and Plainfield—where the greatest propitiation and the most listening to "grievances" occurred; where the mayor reacted to rioting by promising appointment of a Negro police captain (Newark); where policemen were ordered not to shoot looters or stop them (Detroit) and "ghetto" residents were left to police themselves (Plainfield)—that the greatest damage occurred. It was where police made advance preparations (Englewood) and mayors announced firm policies (Jersey City, Elizabeth) that little damage resulted.

During the four days of the Newark riot, when Jersey City [where the litany of "grievances," from lack of swimming pools to piled-up garbage to rubber-hose-wielding police, was the same as anywhere else] was flooded with tales of all description, Mayor Whelan [see above] announced that if there were any disturbances he would "meet force with force." The ghetto area was saturated with police officers.

On Monday and Tuesday, July 17 and 18, when crowds gathered and a few rocks were thrown, mass arrests were made. Only one store was broken into, and pilferage was limited to items such as candy and chewing gum. (p. 39)

Such "repressive" tactics merit little rhapsody. Mayor Whelan is not hero material in Kerner terms.

For New Brunswick (New Jersey) Mayor Patricia Sheehan, however, the Commission pulls out all the stops.

By Monday, according to Mayor Patricia Sheehan, the town was "haunted by what happened in Newark and Plainfield." James E. Amos, the associate director of the anti-poverty program in Middlesex County, said there was a "tenseness in the air" that "got thicker and thicker." (p. 46)

With such atmosphere rife in town, one might think that the Mayor might evince concern over the preparedness of the police, especially in light of their lack of equipment. "We had no equipment to use," a police lieutenant testified at the P.B.A. hearings. "We had to go home and get our own weapons. ... We had to use our own personal ammunition and our own personal guns. ... even today [after the "long, hot summer"] we still don't even have any riot equipment, except that we were donated I believe 18 shotguns."

After the first night of "disturbances," which the *Kerner Report* describes as "random vandalism" and the Mayor as "like Halloween—a gigantic night of mischief," the Mayor does not appear to have worried about equipping the police for more to come. The lady had more modern methods on her mind. She arranged a meeting with "deprived" youngsters, that they might better air their woes.

Although initially hostile, the 35 teenagers who made up the group "poured out their souls to the mayor." The mayor and city commissioners agreed to the drawing up of a statement by the negro youths attacking discrimination, inferior educational and employment opportunities, police harassment, and poor housing.

Four of the young people began broadcasting over the radio station, urging their "soul brothers and sisters" to "cool it, because you will only get hurt and the mayor has talked with us and is going to do something for us." Other youths circulated through the streets with the same message. (p. 46)

In the face of such crucial government needs as public housing, schools, and (oh, yes—see above) swimming pools, the police department's equipment understandably would have to wait. Despite the efforts of the Mayor and her youthful emissaries, a new "confrontation" developed that night. When police turned out to enforce a curfew announced by the Mayor, "a crowd" became "angry at the massive show of force by police in [borrowed] riot dress."

"If you don't get the cops out of here," one man warned, "we are all going to get our guns." Asked to return to their homes, the people replied, "we will go home when you get the police out of the area." (p. 46)

Meekly the people's savior complied, and the police—over the protests of the chief—left. "Elements" of "the crowd" then "appeared" at the police station.

Mayor Sheehan went out onto the steps of the station. Using a bullhorn, she talked to the people and asked [asked!] that she be given [!] an opportunity to correct conditions. The crowd was boisterous. Some persons challenged the mayor. But finally, the opinion, "She's new! Give her a chance!" prevailed.

A demand was issued by the people in the crowd that all persons arrested the previous night be released. Told this had already been done, the people were suspicious. They asked to be allowed to inspect the jail cells.

It was agreed to permit representatives of the people to look in the cells to satisfy themselves that everyone had been released.

The crowd dispersed. (pp. 46-47)

Before "dispersing," the crowd issued an ultimatum: Better housing within about a month—or they'd be back with another riot. On their way to the police station, the "crowd" who "appeared" there showed their gratitude for police withdrawal by smashing car windshields and overturning trash cans all the way. During the "gigantic night of mischief " like "Halloween," stores had been looted, fires started, Molotov cocktails thrown; damage to the tune of $89,000 was inflicted. Neither this nor the lack of police equipment is mentioned in the *Kerner Report.* That would spoil the story.

"The New Brunswick riot," the *Report* concludes, "had failed to materialize."

CHAPTER XI

Carte Blanche for Chaos

The Kerner Commission does not intend to suggest, its *Report* states, "that the majority of the rioters, who shared the disadvantaged conditions" and the "intense and pervasive grievances" upon which the Commission blamed the riots, "necessarily articulated in their own minds the connection between that background and their actions."

The rioters had no *need* to articulate the alleged connection. The men of the Kerner Commission, and the Commission's intellectual kin, have been articulating it for them throughout all the long years which have culminated in, and produced, the Age of the Rioter.

"You are right!" cries the Kerner Commission to men who, claiming to be "deprived," use force to take what is not theirs; who destroy what they have not produced; who hate what they refuse to understand. "You are right to burn, to beat, to loot, to dispossess. You are right even to kill. You are right to raze and to pillage and to plunder. You are right to flout any laws you care not to obey. You are right to demand tribute from those who produce, for they are guilty—guilty by virtue of their production, guilty of having what you have not." The rioters are right, says the Kerner Commission; right, said Lyndon Johnson and Hubert Humphrey; right, nod the pundits of the press; right, echoes Richard Nixon. They are right to demand "a piece of the action; a share of the wealth."

To the savage mentality of the rioters and their apologists, a "piece of the action" means, not participation in the act of producing, but participation in consuming the "national affluence" which other men have produced. In the statist, determinist societies which are such men's spiritual homes, wealth is a static quantity —a carcass brought down and devoured by ravening predators. Each chunk torn off by one is consumed at the expense of his neighbor, and he who devours the largest portion has seized it from the jaws of another with an equal claim. If a man produces no wealth, or little, it is, says the Commission, the fault of those who *do* produce; thus, says the Commission, the poor are not poor, but "deprived."

"You are right," cry the Lindsays and the Kerners to Negroes who hate white men. "You are right to hate; you are right to attack, to rob, to seek laws expropriating from all whose skins are white. You are right to rampage and to riot, for we have wronged you. We are guilty, guilty, guilty, all of us, every one, for the sins of any white man anywhere. We are guilty of the sins of white men who died years before our birth, who enslaved ancestors who died years before *your* birth. We are guilty of the acts of those we have never met, never seen; we are guilty of wrongs we have never committed, guilty because our skins are white."

It is white racism, claims the Commission, which is destroying the nation. The riots of the late 1960's, in which most of the supposed "have-nots" who participated were individuals who happened to be Negroes, were, the Commission declares, expressions of hatred for white men, all white men; hatred induced by the injustices, recent and ancient, which some white men have perpetrated against some Negroes. The stores ransacked and destroyed, the homes burned, the policemen stoned, the firemen ambushed, were targets, claims the Commission, because they were symbols of the "white power structure" which keeps Negroes in thrall and in despair; which has deprived the "deprived" of "their share of the nation's resources."

The Commission ignores the implications of sentences in its own *Report* which contravene its predetermined theme and accusations.

Although the "typical rioter" described by the Commission was "somewhat better educated" than his non-rioting neighbors, he was "more likely" than they to be working as an unskilled, frequently laid-off laborer. The rioter, the Commission states, "feels strongly that he deserves a better job, and that he is barred from achieving it, not because of lack of training, ability, or ambition, but because of discrimination by employers." His "feeling," of course, is treated by the Commission as fact. *Why* the rioter's neighbors, Negroes "somewhat less educated than he," were "somewhat more likely" to have better jobs, is a question the Commission, like the rioter, feels it best to leave unexplored.

The rioter, says the Commission, "takes great pride in his race" and is "extremely hostile to whites." It is whites, says the Commission, whose discrimination has barred the rioter from the better job he feels he deserves. It is white racism, says the Commission, which must be blamed for the rioter's "grievances." Yet the rioter, says the Commission, "*is almost equally hostile to middle-class Negroes.*" (my emphasis) The Commission does not care to state why.

The "typical rioter," in a word, is hostile to those who produce, who achieve. His lust for destruction finds focus on those who, by their achievements, negate the "feeling" of victimization by which he excuses his own non-production and salves his pseudo-self-esteem. "Middle-class Negroes"—those who have worked their way out of the "ghetto" to which he claims he is "confined"—are living proof that the "confinement" he complains of is imposed by his own defaults, his own inadequacies. And thus he says of those individuals whose race is Negro and who have produced what he has not: "Negroes who make a lot of money think they are better than other Negroes; Negroes who make a lot of money are just as bad as whites." And the smokescreen produced by the heat of his hatred and envy helps him hide from himself the fact that those who choose to think, who choose to produce, *at whatever level their abilities permit, are* better than those who choose to do neither.

But, says the Kerner Commission, the "feeling" of the rioter is right. If the non-productive are poor, the productive are guilty of "depriving" them. If any Negro does not achieve affluence or status, it is the fault of all white men, who discriminate against him. If the streets of slums are dirty, it is due, not to those who fling their refuse on the pavements, but to "society." And if the residents of such slums are Negroes, says Kenneth Clark, the filth on the streets is the fault of *white* "society."

This is the theme of the *Kerner Report:* the theme of collective guilt and collective "rights"; the theme that the sins of some are cause for the guilt of all; that those who "have not" have been deprived by those who "have"; that those men who are "white" are guilty, by virtue of their race, for any injustices suffered by men who happen to be "black"; that those who produce are guilty, by virtue of their production, for any "grievances" felt by those who have not produced.

The theme of the *Kerner Report,* and of the laws it has spawned, is that "grievances," real or imagined, are just cause for arson and pillage; that the productive citizens of a nation are guilty—to the extent of their productivity—for every slight, every "need," every "deprivation" suffered by the non-productive and the anti-productive.

The purpose of the *Kerner Report* and of those who are implementing the payment of its blackmail claims is to reduce the entire population of a nation to the state of galley slaves lashed by guilt —and the lash is wielded by the Kerner Commission and men like them in a frantic effort to forget their *own* guilt. For it is *they* who are the racists. It is they who cannot see or write of a man without referring to his color. It is they, and their soul brothers in government, in teaching, and in the press, who describe all actions and ideas in terms of the race of the actors and thinkers. It is they who never forget the color of their own skin; they who never face and deal with a man as a man: not as a "black" man or as a "white" man, but *as a man.* It is the Lindsays and the Kerners and the Wilkinses and the Finches who wield the lash to hide from themselves their guilty knowledge that it is they, and not the producers they accuse of "depriving" the "deprived," who are the parasites. It is they who gain glory by distributing wealth that is not theirs;

it is they who gain their "status" through their concern for the "disadvantaged"; they who trade in human misery; they whose lives and position depend upon it. It is they who need the "needy" as the source of their counterfeit pride.

It is white men, says the Commission, who are guilty of causing the misery of Negroes. It is the "affluent," says the Commission, who are guilty of causing the misery of the "deprived."

Words like those of the Kerner Commission serve as self-fulfilling prophecies. If human beings who happen to be Negro and human beings who happen to be white now hurl ugly racist imprecations at each other across a deepening schism—who is to blame? If those whose production is greater and those whose production is less now regard each other as threats, what is the cause? If men who happen to be Negroes see white skin per se as the focus of hatred and the cause of all their troubles; if the man in the slum sees the man in the suburb per se as his enemy—who has been telling them to? If men "polarize" into groups on racist and economic grounds; if the nation descends into a total war of race against race, *who sowed the seeds of destruction?*

Should it come as a surprise that the "have-nots" believe what they have been told for years—and proceed to act accordingly? If men are told that initiatory force "in a good cause" is justified; if men are constantly bombarded with the theory that plunder is a legitimate reaction to "deprivation"; and that destruction is a legitimate response to discrimination, why should those who propound the theory, day and night, by every means of communication available to them, be surprised to be taken at their word— *overtly?*

It is futile for the men of the Kerner Commission to advance proposals for the containment of riots; it is sheer hypocrisy for them to utter occasional disclaimers denying that they sanction violence; it is sheer evasion for them to protest that what they propose is not blackmail. It *is.* And if they do not know it, the rioters do.

No amount of pious ritual incantations in support of a civilized order, no halfhearted, lukewarm, self-disqualifying statements of sympathy for police who risk their lives to protect the decent and the innocent, can successfully counteract the fact that the Kerner accounts of the riots are, *at base, in principle,* sanctions of initiatory force. It is forcible expropriation, indirect and direct, which is sanctioned implicitly by the *Report*'s premises and implemented explicitly through its proposals.

"Not even the most professional and devoted law enforcement agency alone can quell civil disorder any more than it can prevent civil disorder," the Commission itself states. "A thin blue line is too thin. Maintaining civil peace is the responsibility of the entire community, particularly public officials." We now live in a society where the majority of individuals have come to sanction and even to applaud initiatory force on the part of favored groups of individuals whose ends are claimed to justify their means. We live in a society where the majority of intellectual leaders and public officials equate *retaliatory* force with *initiatory* force. We live in a society where initiatory force (physical assault, forcible occupation of buildings, destruction of property) wielded by "demonstrators" and rioting "deprived" is not distinguished from the retaliatory force wielded by a policeman who evicts a "demonstrator" and quells a riot. And worse, we live in a society where many excuse the first and condemn the second. In a society where initiatory force is excused, even hailed, as "legitimate dissent" or "expression of pervasive grievances," while retaliatory force is damned as "police brutality," the "thin blue line" is, in effect, disarmed.

When force displaces rational persuasion; when the jungle law of club and fang is promulgated, implicitly or explicitly, by public officials themselves; when a desire for law and order is equated with and damned as racism and repression; when excuse after excuse, apologia after apologia, is proffered to explain criminal behavior, while the actions of those who enforce the law are hampered and denigrated; when the enforcers themselves are indiscriminately scorned and reviled; *no* proposals of tools or tactics for "keeping order" can, if implemented, succeed for long.

"We happen to think that protection of life, particularly innocent life, is more important than protecting property or anything else," said John V. Lindsay, Mayor of New York City and Vice Chairman of the Kerner Commission, in response to the order of Mayor Daley of Chicago that looters who refuse to halt be fired upon. "We are not going to turn disorder into chaos through the unprincipled use of armed force. In short, we are not going to shoot children in New York." Nothing, neither the protection of the property of the innocent, nor "anything else," in the Commission's view, is worth injuring "children" engaged in looting. Nothing, least of all property, is worth offending those who might be aroused by the injury of looters into perpetrating further destruction.

A policy of shooting at rioters, said then Attorney General Ramsey Clark, would "tend toward a very dangerous escalation of the very problem we are trying to solve." The policy of using deadly retaliatory force could, he said, "easily drive a larger portion of the black community to terrorist and guerrilla tactics." There is a name for the policy described by Messrs. Clark and Lindsay. It is an ugly name—and the Kerner Commission avoids using it, as though, by refusing to name it, one could change the policy's nature. The name of such a policy is "appeasement." It was tried by the government of another country in recent history, when a small gang of racist thugs used destruction and terror to cow a government into granting them power. The government was the Weimar Republic. The country was Germany.

By sanctioning initiatory force on the one hand; by refraining from retaliatory force on the other, lest the initiators of force be enraged into further violence, the would-be keepers of the "public peace" destroy their own philosophical base. They rob themselves of the armor of moral rectitude; they concede the enemy's premises. It is through these concessions that the enemy will win. Any temporary "peace" bought with appeasement and tribute becomes no peace at all. It is merely a tenuous truce bought by blood sacrifice, by enslaving the innocent and the productive to the service of evil and of "need."

When an entire nation is told that "grievances" justify riots; that an explosion in the cities can be prevented only by larger and larger blackmail payments to those poised to throw the bombs; when people are told that the purpose of government is *not* protecting the life, liberty, and property of innocent citizens, but is granting the would-be bombers *legal* means for their acts of plunder, lest open looting cause them to be hurt; when the people of a nation believe this, and the productive fail to protest such injustice, that nation has become a jungle. Hand-to-hand savagery of all against all has been staved off merely for the duration of the booty-bought cannibal feast.

In *this*, the philosophical climate of a nation, lies the answer to the "disorders" which are rending the nation asunder.

The *Kerner Report*, which attempts to explain those "disorders" on the basis of the philosophical premises that needs confer rights and that government should be an instrument of legal plunder, is a frantic, last-ditch attempt to evade and obscure the Commission members' knowledge that it is they—and their soul brothers in politics, in the press, in the once-safe, smug sanctums of universities (which that same philosophy is now turning into battlegrounds)—whose policies brought the riots into being.

In the guise of an official document, the *Report* voices the demands of a drunken bum on a street corner, drowning his mind in mooched alcohol and ranting that the world owes him a living—and the demands of a hold-up man who makes the identical claim and seeks to enforce it at gunpoint.

The *Report* claims to defend human rights—by obliterating the very concept of rights. The *Report* treats men's "needs" as rights to what other men produce; thus the *Report* and the programs based upon it abrogate every man's right to keep what he has produced for himself.

The *Report* inveighs against racism—and proposes to institutionalize it, by law.

The *Report* deplores violence—and declares that looters must be *given* what they were stealing, and more—more, and more, and still more.

The *Report* gives lip service to law—and terms enforcement of the law "brutality," reserving sympathetic hearing for men who incite mobs to pillage and arson; who claim that a thief who shoots a policeman is acting in "self-defense."

The *Report* speaks of freedom for all men—and advances proposals for government manipulation of the thoughts and the actions even of infants.

The *Report* prates of justice—and proposes that the victims of riots be forced to pay for shoes, swimming pools, schools, status, rat traps, and garbage pails for those who have dispossessed them.

The *Report* lauds the freedom of the press—and presents schemes for censorship by pull and by pressure.

The *Report* speaks of incentives to production—and proposes to kill all incentive by making incompetence the coin of the realm.

The *Report* bewails the plight of the unemployed—and proposes still more laws to make employing them uneconomic.

The *Report* hails individualism, self-determination, and productivity—and seeks the further enslavement of the "haves" to any whim of the "have-nots."

The *Report* praises the "free enterprise" system—and proposes the final destruction of the remnants of capitalism and the abundance which only capitalism can produce, by means of a fascist system of nominal private ownership castrated by statist controls.

No American who values the remnants of his liberty can afford to ignore the direct impact of this peculiar document upon *him*. The *Report* is not the puling of some street ruffian or anonymous unwashed bum, though it shares his premises and his outlook. The *Report* is the ruffians' *official* mouthpiece and marching order. The *Report* was produced, and is being implemented, by the intellectual and political "elite" of our nation. It is our leaders who are now invoking their power to back the demands of rampaging rioters with the "enforcement arsenal" of *law*.

As the proposals of the *Kerner Report*, one by one, become law, it is the productive, the innocent, the decent citizens of the nation who are paying their enormous costs in matter and in spirit. Each citizen of the nation, *because and to the extent of* his productiveness, his intelligence, his integrity, his love for his work, his eagerness to assume responsibility for his own life, and his compassion for undeserved human suffering—his virtue, his ability—is being made, at the *Report*'s decree, a slave shackled to the claims of need and of evil. As the mobs take to the streets, the campuses, the factories, to wreak havoc in answer to the sanction officially given them, it is the victims of that havoc whose lives will be mortgaged to pay for the plunder.

—Be it the shopkeeper who stares blankly at the smoking ruins of a business which had been the sum of all the effort of all his days;

—Be it the aging widow who must trudge 20 blocks to buy food, because the shop she had dealt with has closed its doors forever, its interior ransacked, its records burned;

—Be it the young couple struggling to earn their living, who can find no apartment within their means to live in, because mortgage funds, backed by their taxes, have vanished into reeking high-rises whose "deprived" residents urinate in the hallways;

—Be it the factory worker who has painfully accumulated good references and good skills, only to see a promised job vanish into the hands of some slouching lout whose claim for preference is his refusal to hold any job is all his 20-odd years:

Each, with his hours and his effort, *which are his life itself,* will pay the cost of the Kerner Commission's blackmail payments; will pay for every cent of tribute buying tenuous peace from looting mobs, for every building which crumbles at their displeasure, for every ounce of looted merchandise.

Gutted stores, razed buildings, stolen goods, expropriated alms and the taxes which pay for them—these are the costs which are tangible and seen; these are the costs most will know they are paying. There are others: losses in matter and in spirit, which will not be seen, because they will never be. The architect who envisions a skyscraper soaring above the earth, but will never see it rise; the would-be industrialist whose products might have lightened men's labor, lengthened men's lives, given men joy; those whose enterprises will die stillborn, because men who might have financed their ventures saw their capital vanish into taxes; those whose vision enabled them to see what had not been seen, to create what had never been created; those who are the makers of wealth, but who give up and give in when productivity is penalized and incompetence enshrined—they, and all who would have used and enjoyed the products of their creation (even as the "deprived" in the "ghettos" of today use multihued clothing and television sets and transistor radios and refrigerators they take for granted) will suffer the loss of what might have been, had the "mainspring of human progress" and the right to enjoy the fruits of one's labor not been destroyed. Such was the fate of those living in the static societies from which the "American Dream" promised escape; the static, statist societies into whose likeness the Kerner Commission seeks to distort what is left of that dream.

The ideas in the *Kerner Report* are not new. They are the stale sediment of all the statist swill poured out over the centuries by dictators and demagogues and their intellectual henchmen; from the Caesars through Bismarck through Roosevelt through Johnson through Finch; from Plato through Hegel through Galbraith through Kenneth B. Clark. It is the disease of statism which has tarnished the glory of the American Dream. It is statism which the original government of America recognized and repudiated as the evil it is. It is statism which has now seeped up from the intellectual sewers of the ages and threatens to engulf America. It is statism which is the political expression of the idea that men have the "right" to force others to serve their needs. The mobs in our streets are the logical product of that doctrine.

The *Kerner Report* is not an explanation of the violence that is rocking the nation. It is an attempt to exonerate those who perpetrate that violence. The *Report* is not a reasoned proposal for the prevention of pillage. It is an open invitation for more of the same. That invitation will be accepted.

The "long, hot summers" which the *Report* pretends to explain are, in fact, the savage offspring of the ideas propounded by the *Kerner Report* itself. The "long, hot summers," and springs and autumns and winters, of violence will continue; the streets of our cities will see neither peace, nor freedom, nor prosperity, until the ideas which spawn and support street violence are understood and totally repudiated.

The value—the *only* value—of the *Kerner Report* lies in its suitability as a laboratory specimen whose meticulous dissection may assist in that understanding and hasten that repudiation. The *Kerner Report* is worthless, except as a typically noisome bit of flotsam cast up by the sewer-tide of statism in which the United States is drowning.

Sewage has its uses.

The *Kerner Report* will have played a part in ending the violence in our streets, on the day when the majority of Americans recognize and repudiate the philosophy the *Report* epitomizes for what it is: a blank check for need, drawn against ability; a blank check for evil, drawn against innocence.

The American Dream will live again as the shining vision it once had been on the day when the productive, the able, the virtuous of America stop payment on the *carte blanche* for chaos drawn against their lives.

Lillian R. Boehme
April, 1968–July, 1969

Supplementary Reading

The following list is not a "bibliography" in the conventional sense. It is not my intention to list exhaustively (and exhaustingly) every book, magazine article, and newspaper story read in the course of writing *Carte Blanche for Chaos*. Rather, I wish to give the reader a list of sources in which he may substantiate, or further pursue, points made or ideas alluded to in this book. A number of the books listed below are of tremendously broad scope. These are listed because, in whole or in part, they helped to provide the philosophical and politico-economic foundation upon which this book was based. Others provide historical or sociological background material; still others pertain to specific proposals for interventionist measures discussed in one or another chapter of *Carte Blanche*; several are books with whose theses I totally or partially disagree. All have value in furnishing further understanding of the politico-economic philosophies which form a *Carte Blanche for Chaos*.

Lillian R. Boehme

Anderson, Martin. *The Federal Bulldozer*. Cambridge, Mass.: M.I.T. Press, 1964. McGraw-Hill Paperback Edition, New York: McGraw-Hill Book Company, 1967.

Ballvé, Faustino. *Essentials of Economics: A Brief Survey of Principles and Policies*. Translated from the Spanish and edited by Arthur Goddard. Princeton: D. Van Nostrand Co., Inc., 1963.

Bastiat, Frédéric. *Economic Sophisms*. Translated from the French and edited by Arthur Goddard. Princeton: D. Van Nostrand Co., Inc., 1964.

———. *Selected Essays on Political Economy*. Translated from the French by Seymour Cain. Princeton: D. Van Nostrand Co., Inc., 1964.

Brink, William and Harris, Louis. *The Negro Revolution in America*. New York: Simon and Schuster, Inc., 1964.

Chamberlain, John. *The Enterprising Americans—A Business History of the United States*. New York: Harper and Row, Publishers, 1963. Harper Colophon (paper) Edition, 1963.

———. *The Roots of Capitalism*. Revised Edition. Princeton: D. Van Nostrand Co., Inc., 1959, 1965.

Clark, Kenneth B. *Dark Ghetto: Dilemmas of Social Power*. New York: Harper and Row, Publishers, 1965. Harper Torchbooks (paper) Edition, 1967.

Cooley, Oscar W. *Paying Men Not to Work*. Caldwell, Idaho: The Caxton Printers, Ltd., 1964.

Department of Philosophy, University of Colorado. *Readings on Fascism and National Socialism*. Chicago: The Swallow Press, Inc. (paper). No date.

Ewers, Carolyn H. *Sidney Poitier: The Long Journey*. New York: New American Library, Inc., Signet Books (paper), 1969.

Fairchild, Fred Rogers and Shelly, Thomas J. *Understanding Our Free Economy*. Fourth Edition. Princeton: D. Van Nostrand Co., Inc., 1965.

Foley, Eugene P. *The Achieving Ghetto*. Washington, D.C.: The National Press, Inc., 1968.

Friendly, Fred W. *Due to Circumstances Beyond Our Control*. New York: Random House, Inc., 1967. Vintage Books (paper) Edition, New York: Random House, Inc., 1968.

Furnas, J. C. *Goodbye to Uncle Tom: An analysis of the myths pertaining to the American Negro, from their origins to the misconceptions of today*. New York: William Sloane Associates, 1956.

Galbraith, John Kenneth. *The Affluent Society*. Boston: Houghton Mifflin Co., 1958. Mentor Books (paper) Edition, New York: New

American Library of World Literature, Inc., 1958 (?).

Greenspan, Alan. "Antitrust," based on a paper given at the Antitrust Seminar of the National Association of Business Economists, Cleveland, September 25, 1961, in *Capitalism: The Unknown Ideal.* New York: New American Library, Inc., 1966.

————. "The Assault on Integrity." *The Objectivist Newsletter,* August, 1963.

————. "Gold and Economic Freedom," in *Capitalism: The Unknown Ideal.* New York: New American Library, Inc., 1966.

Griffin, John Howard. *Black Like Me.* Boston: Houghton Mifflin Company, 1961. Signet (paper) Edition, New York: New American Library, Inc., 1961.

Harrington, Michael. *The Other America: Poverty in the United States.* New York: The Macmillan Co., 1963. Penguin Books (paper) Edition, Baltimore, Md.: Penguin Books, Inc., 1964.

Hazlitt, Henry. *Economics in One Lesson.* New York: Harper and Row, 1946.

Hessen, Robert. "The Effects of the Industrial Revolution on Women and Children." *The Objectivist Newsletter,* April, November, 1962.

Hoffman, Banesh. *The Tyranny of Testing.* New York: The Crowell-Collier Press, 1962.

Irion, H. Gifford, Hearing Examiner, Federal Communications Commission. Initial Decision, Findings, and Conclusion, in re Applications of Brandywine–Main Line Radio, Inc. for Renewal of Licenses of Stations WXUR and WXUR, FM, Media, Pennsylvania, Docket No. 17141, issued December 10, 1968, released December 13, 1968.

Jacobs, Jane. *The Death and Life of Great American Cities.* New York: Random House, Inc., 1961. Vintage Books (paper) Edition, New York: Random House, Inc. (no date).

Klein, Herbert T. *The Police: Damned if They Do—Damned if They Don't.* New York: Crown Publishers, Inc., 1968.

Koerner, James D. *The Miseducation of American Teachers.* Boston: Houghton Mifflin Co., 1965.

Lyons, Eugene. *David Sarnoff.* New York: Harper and Row, 1966. Pyramid (paper) Edition, New York: Pyramid Publications, Inc., 1967, pp. 1–73, 191–273.

————. *Herbert Hoover.* Garden City, New York: Doubleday and Co., Inc., 1964. Chapter XIV, pp. 159–73.

Moynihan, Daniel Patrick. "The Negro Family: The Case for National Action," in Rainwater, Lee and William L. Yancey, *The Moynihan Report and the Politics of Controversy.* Cambridge, Mass.: The M.I.T. Press, 1967.

National Advisory Commission on Civil Disorders. *Report of the National Advisory Commission on Civil Disorders, March 1, 1968.* Washington, D.C.: U.S. Government Printing Office, 1968.

Neiderhoffer, Arthur. *Behind the Shield: The Police in Urban Society.* Garden City, New York: Doubleday and Co., Inc., 1967. Anchor Books (paper) Edition, 1969.

Patterson, Isabel. *The God of the Machine.* Caldwell, Idaho: The Caxton Printers, Ltd., 1946, reissued 1964.

President's Commission on Law Enforcement and Administration of Justice. *The Challenge of Crime in a Free Society.* New York: Avon Books, 1968.

Rand, Ayn. "The Objectivist Ethics," "Man's Rights," "Collectivized 'Rights' ," "The Nature of Government," in *The Virtue of Selfishness.* New York: New American Library, Inc., 1964.

———. "The Property Status of the Airwaves," in *Capitalism: The Unknown Ideal.* New York: New American Library, Inc., 1966.

Rickenbacker, Edward V. *Rickenbacker: An Autobiography.* Englewood Cliffs, N. J.: Prentice-Hall, Inc., 1967.

Riot Study Commission of the New Jersey State Patrolmen's Benevolent Association, Inc. *The Road to Anarchy.* Maplewood, N.J.: New Jersey State P.B.A., 1968.

Scheibla, Shirley. *Poverty Is Where the Money Is.* New Rochelle, New York: Arlington House, 1968.

Shirer, William L. *The Rise and Fall of the Third Reich.* New York: Simon and Schuster, 1959.

Smith, Adam. *An Inquiry into the Causes of the Wealth of Nations.* Volumes I and II. Edited by Edwin Cannan. New Rochelle, New York: Arlington House, 1966.

United States Commission on Civil Rights. *Freedom to Be Free, Century of Emancipation 1863–1963.* Washington, D.C.: U.S. Government Printing Office, 1963.

Urban America, Inc. and The Urban Coalition. *One Year Later: An Assessment of the Nation's Response to the Crisis Described by the National Advisory Commission on Civil Disorders.* Washington, D.C., 1969.

Walker, Daniel. *Rights in Conflict. Report to the National Commission on the Causes and Prevention of Violence.* Introduction by Max Frankel. New York: E. P. Dutton and Co., 1968. Bantam Books (paper) Edition, New York: Bantam Books, Inc., 1968.

Weaver, Henry Grady. *The Mainspring of Human Progress.* Revised Edition. Irvington-on-Hudson, New York: Foundation for Economic Education, Inc., 1953.

Westinghouse Learning Corporation and Ohio University. *The Impact of Head Start.* (Preliminary Draft.) New York: Westinghouse Learning Corporation, April, 1969. (Xerox copy.)

Wortham, Anne. ". . . Because I Am an Individualist." *The Libertarian,* October, 1967. *The Freeman,* November, 1967.

―――. "Individualism vs. Racism." *The Freeman,* January, 1966.

Notes

CHAPTER II

The Foregone Conclusion

1. Remarks of President Lyndon Johnson to a group of leaders of senior citizens' organizations in the Fish Room of the White House, January 15, 1964.

2. Hubert H. Humphrey, Vice President of the United States, addressing the National Association of County Officials, New Orleans, July 18, 1966, as quoted in *U. S. News and World Report*, August 14, 1967, p. 10.

3. Remarks of the President upon issuing an Executive Order establishing a National Advisory Commission on Civil Disorders, July 29, 1967.

4. The remaining members of the Commission were Representatives James C. Corman and William M. McCulloch; Katherine Graham Peden, Kentucky Commissioner of Commerce and radio station owner (see Chapter IX); and Herbert Jenkins, Chief of Police, Atlanta, Georgia.

5. Frédéric Bastiat, "The Law," *Selected Essays on Political Economy* (Princeton, New Jersey: D. Van Nostrand Company, Inc.), 1964.

6. *Webster's New Collegiate Dictionary*, Second Edition. See also Lillian R. Boehme, "Defining Our Terms: Capitalism," *The Libertarian*, II:2, December, 1966.

7. *Woodbury* (New Jersey) *Daily Times*, May 31, 1968, p. 1.

8. Michael Harrington, *The Other America: Poverty in the United States* (New York: The Macmillan Company, Inc.), 1963.

9. "A Nation within a Nation," *Time*, May 17, 1968, p. 24.

10. *Time*, May 17, 1968, p. 24.

11. Nathan Ausubel, *Pictorial History of the Jewish People* (New York, 1953), p. 101.

12. *The New York Times*, May 5, 1968.

CHAPTER III

The Immoral Premises

1. Ayn Rand, "Man's Rights," *The Virtue of Selfishness* (New York: The New American Library, Inc.), 1964. For a fuller discussion of the question of rights, the reader is referred to this, and its companion article, "Collectivized 'Rights'," in the same book.

CHAPTER IV

Racism Institutionalized

1. For examples, see William Brink and Louis Harris, *The Negro Revolution in America* (New York: Simon and Schuster), 1964, p. 33; and Kenneth B. Clark, *Dark Ghetto: Dilemmas of Social Power* (New York: Harper and Row), 1965, the entire book.

2. Julius Duscha, "Postscript to the Story of Seventh Street," *The New York Times Sunday Magazine*, June 2, 1968, p. 45.

CHAPTER V

A Fallacy Compounded

1. Frédéric Bastiat, "The State," *Selected Essays on Political Economy* (Princeton: D. Van Nostrand Company, Inc.), 1964, p. 142.

2. Kenneth B. Clark, *Dark Ghetto: Dilemmas of Social Power* (New York: Harper and Row), 1965, Harper Torchbooks (paper) Edition, 1967, pp. 55-56.

3. "Changing America—What 1970 Census Will Show," *U.S. News and World Report*, June 2, 1969, pp. 68-71.

4. *Ibid.*

5. Herman P. Miller, Special Assistant to the Census Bureau, as quoted by Shirley Scheibla, *Poverty Is Where the Money Is* (New Rochelle, New York: Arlington House), 1968, p. 21; also "A Nation within a Nation, *Time*, May 17, 1968, p. 24.

6. Michael Harrington, *The Other America: Poverty in the United States* (New York: The Macmillan Company), 1962, Penguin Books (paper) Edition, 1963, p. 68.

7. Bastiat, "The State," *loc. cit.*

8. Scheibla, *op. cit.*, citing *House Education and Labor Committee Report on Economic Opportunity Act Amendments of 1966*, p. 95; statement by Senator Strom Thurmond, May 23, 1966; *Republican Poverty Memo*, May 13, 1966; and *Congressional Record*, April 26, 1966, p. 8691.

9. Richard Severo, "HarYou Aide Held in $466,150 Fraud," *The New York Times*, March 13, 1969.

10. Yale Brozen, "The Untruth of the Obvious," *The Freeman*, XVIII:6, June, 1968, p. 329.

11. David E. Kaun, Stanford University Ph.D. thesis, 1964, Dissertation Abstracts, XXV:2, p. 881, cited by James E. Blair, "Regarding the Minimum Wage," *The Freeman*, XV:7, July, 1965, p. 19.

12. *Monthly Labor Review*, March, 1960, pp. 238-42, cited by Blair, "Regarding the Minimum Wage."

13. Blair, "Regarding the Minimum Wage," pp. 20-21.

14. For one illustration, see the childhood of Eddie Rickenbacker as recounted in Edward V. Rickenbacker, *Rickenbacker: An Autobiography* (Englewood Cliffs, New Jersey: Prentice-Hall, Inc.), 1967; see also Lillian R. Boehme, "Of Penguins, Thermometers, and Environmental Determinism," *The Libertarian*, IV:6, April, 1969, which deals with this problem in some detail.

15. Jane Jacobs, *The Death and Life of Great American Cities* (New York: Random House, Inc.), 1961, Vintage Books (paper) Edition, pp. 203-04.

16. Martin Anderson, *The Federal Bulldozer* (Cambridge, Mass.: M.I.T. Press), 1964, McGraw-Hill Paperback Edition, 1967, pp. 196-210.

17. " 'Substandard' Label Put on 421,000 Housing Units," *The Woodbury* (New Jersey) *Daily Times*, September 18, 1968.

18. Anderson, *The Federal Bulldozer*.

19. Anderson, *The Federal Bulldozer*, Introduction to the Paperback Edition, 1967, p. ix.

20. Jacobs, *The Death and Life of Great American Cities*, p. 312.

21. Jacobs, pp. 5-6.

22. "Inside Story: How HUD Tried to Suppress the Douglas Report," *House and Home*, September, 1969, p. 12 [no author given].

23. Seth S. King, "$140 Million Back Realty Taxes Are Owed to City, a Record," *The New York Times*, March 12, 1969.

24. Jacobs, *The Death and Life of Great American Cities*, p. 315.

25. Anderson, *The Federal Bulldozer*, p. 227.

26. *Reason*, I:7, January, 1969, p. 4.

27. "Rent Controls Are Closer than You Think," *House and Home*, July, 1969, XXXVI:1, p. 8.

28. Jacobs, *The Death and Life of Great American Cities*, p. 334 (footnote).

CHAPTER VI

The Obscene Currency: Incompetence

1. "Target: Negro Jobs," *Newsweek*, July 1, 1968, pp. 21-30.

2. "Training the Unemployables," *U. S. News and World Report*, July 1, 1968, pp. 54-57.

3. *Ibid.*

4. *Newsweek, loc. cit.*

5. National Alliance of Businessmen (N.A.B.), "Jobs—Employer's Digest" (Washington, D.C.: National Alliance of Businessmen), pamphlet, probably 1968, p. 5.

6. James A. Norton, President, Greater Cleveland Associated Foundation, in a speech presented at the 17th Semi-Annual Meeting, Manufacturing Chemists Association, New York City, November 21, 1967 (mimeographed publicity copy of speech).

7. *Newsweek*, loc. cit.

8. *Ibid.*

9. N.A.B., "Jobs–Employer's Digest," *loc. cit.*

10. "Business and the Urban Crisis," A McGraw-Hill Special Report (New York: McGraw-Hill Publishing Company, Inc.), 1968 (pamphlet), p. C3. This pamphlet was distributed to all readers of McGraw-Hill's forty-four business periodicals.

11. Henry J. Taylor, "Inheritance," syndicated column, November 26, 1968.

12. "A Hard-Sell Push for Hard-Core Selling," *Business Week*, September 27, 1969, p. 36.

13. "Business and the Urban Crisis," *op. cit.*, p. C5.

14. *Ibid.*, p. C9.

15. "On Hiring the Hard-Core Jobless" (Interview), *U. S. News and World Report*, October 14, 1968, pp. 82-86.

16. "Business and the Urban Crisis," *op. cit.*, p. C8.

17. N.A.B., "Jobs–Employer's Digest," *op. cit.*

18. *Newsweek, loc. cit.*

19. *Ibid.*

20. *Ibid.*

21. "Official of one large American Company" as quoted in "Washington Whispers," *U. S. News and World Report*, February 17, 1969, p. 27.

CHAPTER VII

The Disqualifying Adjective

1. The Urban Coalition and Urban America, Inc., *One Year Later: An Assessment of the Nation's Response to the Crisis Described by the National Advisory Commission on Civil Disorders* (Washington, D.C.: The

Urban Coalition and Urban America, Inc.), 1969.

2. Richard M. Nixon, "Bridges to Human Dignity, The Programs," N.B.C. Radio Network, May 2, 1968, as reprinted in *Nixon Speaks Out* (New York: Nixon-Agnew Campaign Committee), 1968, p. 68.

3. Richard M. Nixon, "Bridges to Human Dignity, The Concept," C.B.S. Radio Network, April 25, 1968, as reprinted in *Ibid.*, p. 65.

4. See William H. Whyte Jr., *The Organization Man* (New York: Simon and Schuster), 1956, Anchor Books (paper) Edition, 1967, Chapter 11, p. 155 *et seqq.*

5. Floyd B. McKissick, "What Is American Business Doing about Black People," *Newsletter on Black Capitalism*, I:2, May, 1969.

6. *One Year Later*, p. 13. Subsequent statements attributed to the Urban Coalition are from *One Year Later* unless otherwise noted.

7. Allan T. Demaree, "Business Picks Up the Urban Challenge," *Fortune*, April, 1969, p. 103.

8. *Newsletter On Black Capitalism, loc. cit.*

9. See Lillian R. Boehme, "Interring the American Dream," *The Libertarian*, IV:9, July, 1969, for a discussion of the "public/private" sector thesis and its recent variant, the "public/private/independent" sector argument.

10. Demaree, *op. cit.*

CHAPTER VIII

The Inherent Contradiction

1. Urban America, Inc. and The Urban Coalition, *One Year Later: An Assessment of the Nation's Response to the Crisis Described by the National Advisory Commission on Civil Disorders* (Washington, D.C.: Urban America, Inc. and The Urban Coalition), 1969.

2. Edmund Contoski, *The Manifesto of Individualism* (New York: The Exposition Press, Inc.), 1968, pp. 57–58.

3. Kenneth B. Clark, *Dark Ghetto* (New York: Harper and Row Publishers, Inc.), 1965; Harper Torchbooks (paper) Edition, 1967, p. 120. Data are drawn from standard tests given third, sixth, and eighth grades in all New York City public schools.

4. *Ibid.*, p. 124.

5. See Martin L. Gross, *The Brain Watchers*, particularly Chapter Ten, "Once Upon a Mind" (New York: Random House, Inc.), 1962, Signet Books (paper) Edition, 1963, pp. 196–200. Also Banesh Hoffman, *The Tyranny of Testing* (New York: The Crowell-Collier Publishing Company), 1962, Collier Books (paper) Edition, 1964, pp. 105–13; and William H. Whyte, Jr., *The Organization Man* (Simon and Schuster, 1956), Anchor Books (paper) Edition (Doubleday and Company), 1957, Part IV, p. 189 *et seqq.*

6. Daniel P. Moynihan, *The Negro Family: The Case for National Action* (generally known as "The Moynihan Report"), issued by the Office of Policy Planning and Research, U.S. Department of Labor, March 1965, as reprinted in Lee Rainwater and William L. Yancey, *The Moynihan Report and the Politics of Controversy* (Cambridge, Mass.: The M.I.T. Press), 1967, pp. 82–83.

7. Hoffman, *op. cit.* (See note 5, above.)

8. "When Courts Try to Run the Public Schools," *U.S. News and World Report*, April 21, 1969, p. 95.

9. See Lillian R. Boehme, "The Non-Education of American Teachers" and "The Murder of the Mind: An Indictment," *The Libertarian*, III: 1, November, 1967.

10. Westinghouse Learning Corporation and Ohio University, *The Impact of Head Start: An Evaluation of the Effects of Head Start Experience on Children's Cognitive and Affective Development*, Preliminary Draft (typescript), (New York: Westinghouse Learning Corporation), April, 1969, pp. 0-4 and 0-5.

11. *The New York Times,* April 18, 1969.

12. Shirley Scheibla, *Poverty Is Where the Money Is* (New Rochelle, N. Y.: Arlington House, Inc.), 1968, pp. 182–184.

13. As quoted in *ibid,* p. 183.

14. *One Year Later,* p. 31. (See Note 1, above.)

15. As quoted in Scheibla, *op. cit.,* pp. 217–18.

16. *One Year Later,* p. 31. Also "Business and the Urban Crisis, A McGraw-Hill Special Report" (pamphlet) (New York: McGraw-Hill Publishing Co., Inc.), 1968, p. 15.

17. "Business and the Urban Crisis," p. 15.

18. Dr. Carl F. Hansen, in "When Courts Try to Run the Public Schools," *U.S. News and World Report,* April 21, 1969, pp. 94–96.

19. As quoted in Scheibla, *op. cit.*

20. As quoted in "Business and the Urban Crisis," p. 15.

21. Dan W. Dodson Ph.D., Director, Center for Human Relations and Community Studies, New York University, in testimony before the Kerner Commission.

22. Isabel Patterson, *The God of the Machine* (Caldwell, Idaho: The Caxton Printers), 1943; reissued 1964, p. 267.

23. Carolyn H. Ewers, *Sidney Poitier: The Long Journey* (New York: New American Library), 1969 (paper), pp. 18–19.

24. Patterson, *op. cit.,* p. 269.

25. *Ibid.,* p. 272.

26. *Ibid.,* pp. 271, 273.

CHAPTER IX

Censorship by Intimidation

1. *Random House Dictionary of the English Language*, Unabridged Edition, 1966.

2. *Ibid.*

3. *Ibid.*

4. *Ibid.*

5. Lanny Friedlander, "Obituary for Objectivity: A Report on the American Press (Part I)," *Reason*, I:10, April, 1969.

6. *Ibid.*

7. "The Supreme Court: Firm Against Evasion," *Time*, June 13, 1969.

8. *Random House Dictionary of the English Language*, Unabridged Edition, 1966.

9. Ayn Rand, "The Property Status of the Airwaves," in Ayn Rand, Nathaniel Branden, and others, *Capitalism: The Unknown Ideal* (New York: New American Library, Inc.), 1966.

10. Friedlander, *op. cit.*

CHAPTER X

Of Heroes ... and Villains ... and Victims

1. *The Road to Anarchy*, Report of the Findings of the Riot Study Commission of the New Jersey State Patrolmen's Benevolent Association (Maplewood, New Jersey: N.J.S.P.B.A.), 1968, pp. 65–66.

2. *Loc. cit.*

3. *Loc. cit.*

4. *Op. cit.*, p. 6.

5. As of this writing, eleven "youths" are under indictment for murder and awaiting trial in Union County, New Jersey, in connection with Patrolman Gleason's death.

6. Lt. Daniel S. Hennessey, Plainfield, New Jersey, Police Department, in testimony at the United States Senate Anti-Riot Bill Hearings (proceedings, p. 195).

7. *The Road to Anarchy*, p. 63.

8. *Ibid.*, pp. 136-37; also *Kerner Report*, p. 45.

9. *The Road to Anarchy, loc. cit.*

10. *Ibid.*, p. 69.

11. Arthur Neiderhoffer, *Behind the Shield: the Police in Urban Society* (Garden City, New York: Doubleday and Company), 1967, Anchor Books (paper) Edition, 1969, pp. 6, 126–34.

12. *The Road to Anarchy*, p. 41.

13. J. Edgar Hoover, "Violence in American Society—A Problem of Critical Concern," *George Washington Law Review* 407, 413 (1967), as reprinted in *Congressional Record*, February 12, 1968, p. E703. The rate of assaults has been increasing markedly each year.

14. *The Road to Anarchy*, pp. 17 and 67.

15. *Ibid.*, p. 17.

16. United States Senate Anti-Riot Bill Hearings (proceedings, pp. 368–69).